Advance Praise for *FORGOTTEN HURRICANE*

"2005 was a record-breaking year for hurricanes—and for the political blame game left amidst all the devastation and heartache. Stitched into the fabric of crippling disaster is a resiliency that defines ordinary survivors who first responded to evacuees from one storm before fleeing another not one month later. *FORGOTTEN HURRICANE: Conversations With My Neighbors* is the healing medicine of dialogue that gives Rita her proper respect. Joyce King is a native Texan with deep Louisiana roots and she has survived hurricanes since childhood. King's tender journey to make certain Rita will not be forgotten is provocative and inspirational. Ms. King's down-to-earth recount of events brings back my memories of the aftermath of Andrew in South Florida, but probably all of us can relate to surviving 'our' storm."

—Jerry D. Jarrell, former director, National Hurricane Center, Miami

"Texas born and Louisiana bred, Joyce King's heart and pen, straddle both states. Perhaps that's why even as Hurrican Katrina continues to eclipse Hurricane Rita in the media and in the nation's memory, King swims determinedly against that tide. *FORGOTTEN HURRICANE* is testimony of her strong, sure stroke. King winds her way to New Orleans just in time to face mixed emotions around the French Quarter Festival. En route, she retraces Rita's devastation and its extraordinary impact, then and now, on the lives of ordinary people. The resulting first-person accounts are compelling, enraging, redeeming. Lacing her own hurricane size loss on the journey to the larger narrative, King ropes you to the spot where she is: deep in the hearts of her subjects. Her familiarity with hurricanes—she lists them like old friends—enables King to tune into her beleaguered neighbors' voices. How else to explain her perfectly pitched humor and irony under such traumatic circumstances? *FORGOTTEN HURRICANE* wraps with startling poignancy. In the end, Rita won't be forgotten anymore."

—Bernestine Singley, former Texas and Massachusetts Assistant Attorney General, is author of the award-winning anthology, *When Race Becomes Real: Black and White Writers Confront Their Personal Histories*

"The storyteller returns to the complex, steamy, soul-bearing, bi-racial culture of her girlhood, where, in the wake of one of the ugliest racial hate crimes in recent American history, Joyce King had witnessed a beautiful awakening, a redemption. This redemption is again reflected in Jasper's quiet, stoic, heroic response to the devastating hurricane that came a hundred miles inland to toss the entire community into another tragedy."

—Albert Arthur Allison, author of *To Defy the Monster*

Praise for *HATE CRIME*

"A heartbreaking story of stupid hatred and the endless ramifications of one cruel and vicious act. This book mocks fatuous notions of closure. Joyce King eloquently demands that we subsume bigotry with respect and love. Her argument is angry, righteous, and tender."

—JAMES ELLROY, author of *My Dark Places* and *L. A. Confidential*

"*HATE CRIME* is a gripping account of an unimaginably brutal murder. It is also a lesson in how to look racism straight in the eye and not blink."

—*O Magazine (Oprah)*

"A Southern story of unbelievable cruelty and a passionate pursuit for justice. An important chapter in the American struggle for civil rights."

—MORRIS DEES, chief trial counsel, Southern Poverty Law Center

"A riveting journey behind the scenes of one of the most shocking crimes in modern history. King goes beyond the sound bites to craft a provocative book filled with revelations on race and the criminal justice system. This story will give you hope even as it breaks your heart, will make you think about how far America still has to go in the struggle for racial equality."

—TAVIS SMILEY, author of *The Covenant with Black America*

"In her book, she achieves a remarkable balance of candor, clarity and feeling. A southern black woman, King knows the territory." **—*Los Angeles Times***

"King's book is about moving on. She narrated the story in the first person, making it difficult for the reader to hold any personal demons at arm's length. By confronting her own fears—because fears are the glue for stereotypes—she helps readers confront their own." **—*Eclipse Magazine***

"King makes us look at the outrage and agony in this important book, hoping it will help us to understand." **—*Hope Magazine***

"The book, published by Pantheon Books, is more than just a factual account of the crime and trials, which ended with white supremacists Bill King and Russell Brewer being sent to death row and Shawn Berry receiving a life prison term. With Byrd's hideous death as the backdrop, King takes readers through her own anguish as a black woman entering a part of Texas that holds unpleasant memories from her childhood." **—*The Associated Press***

"Racial-issues author not afraid of 'wrong' side…"
—*headline from The Dallas Morning News*

"Achieves its greatest possible goal: setting the event in history as a disturbing record of continued American racism." **—*San Francisco Chronicle***

"Ms. King's perspective and personal reflections as a black Southern woman are what make her tale worth reading." **—*The Dallas Morning News***

"This book is a study of racist psychology that reads like a novel."
—*Psychology Today*

"Fascinating…" **—*Houston Chronicle***

Heather! You are the best at what you Do! Good Luck on the move!

FORGOTTEN HURRICANE

Thank you for everything!

CONVERSATIONS
With My Neighbors

Joyce King

Crown Me Publishers

Dec 2006

This is a work of non-fiction. All its characters are real, as are their names, the cities, towns and parishes where they reside, the intimate details of their personal lives. All quotes are factual. They are not from memory, but from hours of recorded conversations I was privileged to have. Hurricane volunteers, first responders and survivors in this work strengthened my thesis of our ordinary and eternal bond.

For further information, please contact:

crownmepublishers.com

　　Or

write to the author at

jfkjoyceking.com

The front cover photo was courtesy of Julie Burleigh and is of a home in Creole, Louisiana.

Photo of President Bush with Jefferson County Sheriff Mitch Woods Courtesy of The Beaumont Enterprise—Scott Eslinger/Photographer

Book design by:

ARBOR BOOKS, INC.
19 Spear Road, Ste 202
Ramsey, NJ 07446
www.arborbooks.com

Printed in the United States

FORGOTTEN HURRICANE
Joyce King

1. Title 2. Author 3. U.S. HistoryNatural Disasters/Hurricane Rita

Library of Congress Control Number: 2006907010
ISBN: 0-9788344-0-2

For George Mitchell Woods
A Safe Harbor in the Storm

Jefferson County Sheriff Mitch Woods and President George W. Bush

TABLE OF CONTENTS

ONE

"Joyce, I'm so glad to hear your voice," Angel started, "I was just thinking about what you might be doing and wishing you could see all that's happened."

Angel San Juan, a reporter for the CBS television affiliate in Beaumont, Texas, was my lifeline to the region in the initial hours after Hurricane Rita did her slam-bam-thank-you-ma'am routine and traveled farther inland than weather wizards had predicted— *100 miles inland.* Beaumont, Port Arthur, Sabine Pass, other places in Southeast Texas, and pockets of Louisiana, including Lake Charles, were expected to take the worst of what Rita had to offer. They did. Inland counties, parishes and towns weren't prepared to deal with a Category 3 storm or the agonizing wait for help after Satan turned his attention to other matters.

Jasper County, a beautiful spot of Texas tea I love, had been devastated, the same place Angel and I had met in 1999 while on assignment. Mammoth pine trees either blocked access to once passable roads and streets or rested on 9 out of 10 rooftops. Debris remade the "Jewel of the Forest" into a cleared lumber yard ready to be loaded onto the chained bed of a logging truck. People lined the highway, others slept in cars, bewildered by the discovery that overflow shelters had no room. Or spare cots. Ditto for jam packed motels, inns, and quaint boarding houses. Generators were scarce and Rita wasn't supposed to bash Jasper for almost nine hours with sustained winds over 100 mph. The county was insulated, not a coastal community. Nobody told Rita.

For the masses who "survived" Rita, Saturday's sunshine on September 24, 2005 was a welcome friend. The wind and heat that tagged along wasn't. After the temperature outside soared above the mercury mark, with residents running low on water, food, medicine,

1

and other supplies, all that was left to cling to was hope aided by hand fans that resembled wooden popsicle holders. Texans prayed. Texans cried. A few ambitious folk climbed access poles, miraculously still standing, to phone persons in the outside world, a million miles away, not even 100 real ones in Beaumont, trying to summon help as best they could, reassure loved ones in other cities.

Angel was able to talk with me that weekend because he had stayed at the TV station where he worked and they were operating on backup generator. The power was too low for the KFDM signal to reach beyond Beaumont city limits. Angel knew that few people outside Southeast Texas were getting an accurate snapshot of the devastation neighboring counties were mired in or buried under. Beaumont was doing its best to reach out, but barely back on one wobbly leg with a mountain of pleas for help severely threatening the crutch it rested on.

Appropriately named, Angel is a person of great compassion, and usually enormous calm. But Rita multiplied the urgency in his voice, revealing that even the rock of journalistic mercy was cracking, frightening me more in the process with each syllable uttered. Angel had also been able to communicate with resourceful residents who fought their way out of Jasper, probably with chain saws to cut away trees blocking exit paths. It is not unusual for hardworking people in East Texas to travel with power tools. Many are personally acquainted with thick manual labor back off in the woods.

One man, an aspiring young reporter named Jerry Jordan, had spoken with a tired paramedic based in Jasper, tending to sick and elderly patients with a variety of needs, including dialysis, heart problems, cancer and Alzheimer's, as well as the onset of dehydration and depression for both the well and unwell. The caregiver's words lit a fire underneath all who heard it. I was no different.

"Joyce," Angel said my name again for emphasis, "this paramedic, I'm quoting him, said 'Send help or send body bags.'" There was a long silence on the generator-powered line that connected me to Angel. A rush of faces paraded through my mind. I had seen many of those same faces a few weeks earlier when I stayed at my second home, The Belle-Jim Hotel, right in the heart of Jasper, where David and Pat Stiles, the owners, have pretty much spoiled me rotten, always giving me the biggest room filled with sweet down home touches like colorful quilts and antique rockers. And a key to the place.

Now I could see, in my mind's vivid eye, the hotel, the 100-year old Jasper County Courthouse, the Cedar Tree restaurant, The Donut Palace, dozens of churches with comedic signs for sinners, like "Hell is Hotter," and people at "the mall," Jasper's largest store in town, its giant social hub, better known as Wal-Mart. I could see the little towns around once-serene Jasper, smashed and shocked, torn and twisted.

Feeling helpless, I towed the line between guilty and safety, asking from my bed in Dallas, the only natural question available, "What can I do?" The pause between us had been long enough to see anxious faces, then decide with Angel on a national media strategy to shed light on Rita's unexpected and destructive inland detour. We had a few colleagues scattered around the country at various news agencies and immediately began calling them, just begging assignment editors to let America see people suffering in 108-degree heat, without food and water, without central air, without the ability to brush and flush, without generators and gas, without electricity, and without a confirmed hour that basic necessities might resemble something approaching normal.

Between us, Angel and I called Washington, New York, Atlanta, colleagues in Dallas, Houston, Austin, and beyond. In some cases, there was genuine sympathetic concern. In a few others, people in charge flatly stated Jasper "wasn't a story" or that it was "too far" to be newsworthy. Others, understandably, were consumed by the girl who wore, and is still wearing, the hurricane tiara. No one in Rita's aftermath begrudged Katy her golden crown, but Rita came barreling at them damned angry that she had been chosen first runner up. They were, *they are* separate hurricanes forever bound by year, date, fate, and historical destiny. Many feared Rita was going to be short-changed in the end.

Monday rolled around. I left more messages, on cell phones, landlines, by email, all to no avail, to friends in East Texas. I knew no one would answer these communications for a long time to come, days that would feel like weeks. Emotional torture. *Were my friends okay?* I was grateful for the one voice that connected me to the most accurate information possible, "Angel, have you seen

Mitch?" It certainly made me feel better to know that the sheriff of Jefferson County was okay, but "looking exhausted and drained," more so than Angel had ever seen. He said Mitch had lost weight in what seemed a matter of brutal hours without sleep.

"I'm sure he'd be glad to hear from you, why don't you call him?" Angel suggested. I thought not. Mitch Woods had enough on his county plate with its 250,000 residents. First responders rarely get the credit they deserve, the hours are long and the pay isn't enough. Both Port Arthur and Beaumont are part of Mitch's Jefferson County jurisdiction. As well as Sabine Pass, which initial reports of horror made sound like the whole area had been washed into the Gulf.

The Monday after Rita, I couldn't sleep. By Tuesday evening, my weary eyes were heavy and sleepless still. I called Angel with progress reports each time there was a sliver of potential that some media outlet or influential person might help. At the same time, I was being bombarded with email requests from people who'd read *HATE CRIME* and thought I would know how to move all the tall trees and lead a convoy of supplies into countless communities like Jasper. I was deeply touched by this notable faith in my creative ability for deleting all physical and emotional barriers that stood between Jasper and help. *Or body bags.*

Around 4 a.m., with my 3,200 square foot house offering its own heavy sigh of bricked sadness, one thought stopped me in a nearly silent carpeted pace. There was one man I hadn't phoned, a powerful man who three years earlier had said I could call if I ever needed him. I ran downstairs and tore up my office looking for the number, first in the outdated, wheeled rolodex, then in a loose desk drawer of a thousand business cards, and finally, in my personal phone book of handwritten numbers. The man was missing, his number nowhere to be found. Two hours later, I remembered a neurotic filing system that meant he was recorded not alphabetically or by title, but under a woman's name who worked for him.

The bad handwriting allowed me to make out her first name, "Kathy," but something in a fancy chicken-scratch was substituted for the last. It had been three years since her boss and I spoke at some *Associated Press* gathering and chatted just outside a grand ballroom at the even grander Worthington Hotel in Fort Worth, Texas. He was at the podium wrapping up a speech, and I was scheduled to follow with mine. I looked up, minus the mandatory glasses I was too vain to wear, and remarked on who the faraway man at the podium looked like, to which someone said, "He looks like him because it is him." So it was, so it was.

Sometime after 8 a.m., I dialed the card's number and a professional sounding woman answered. She was polite. She was all business. I was nervously frazzled, half hope, half adrenaline, "Hi, I'm looking for Kathy. My name is Joyce King." She quickly interrupted my spiel, "Yes, the woman who wrote *HATE CRIME*." It was the first time I had ever been relieved at someone volleying the words to me in recognition instead of repulsion for the rest of the title—*The Story of a Dragging in Jasper, Texas.*

Kathy's last name was W-A-L-T, except in my garbled penmanship, I took it for Watt and can't remember if I called her that or not. She was curious so I wasted no time in telling her my concern for friends and neighbors in Jasper County and other devastated areas of Southeast Texas. If I had to guess, Kathy Walt heard much more, unspoken, in my rambling voice.

I think I said something like, "Can you get a message to the governor?" Perhaps it was framed this way because James Richard Perry had been in Beaumont with President Bush in the hours before my call so I wasn't exactly sure where Gov. Perry was supposed to be that day. Or his whereabouts at that moment. It wasn't very likely that the man who had read my first book and said so in a handwritten note signed, "Your friend, Rick," was safely tucked away in his Austin mansion while Texans were struggling along with their shattered lives. Walt listened attentively and pledged that someone would call me before another hour passed. I hung up with one smug thought: *Yeah, right.*

Not 45 minutes later, my phone rang. The caller identified himself as Steve McCraw, Homeland Security. According to the numerical ID he was based in Austin. Somewhere along the way, I think it had been either stressed or assumed that I was "a friend" of the governor's, to which I offered a correction, "I think *friend* is too strong a word." Then again, maybe it wasn't. In 2002, I had stood, after security clearances, on the front porch of the governor's mansion, and inside, there for a breakfast hosted by Anita and Rick Perry for invited authors at the prestigious Texas Book Festival founded by another First Lady who loved to read named Laura Bush. *Okay, yeah, he's my friend Rick, that's right.* McCraw gladly received the information and sources I supplied, welcomed whatever else I could confirm. I spoke about being proud of the job "our governor" was doing, not only in his response welcoming victims of Katrina, but his initial handling of Rita in the aftermath. McCraw was easy to talk to. He went out of his way to be friendly and accommodating, even affording me what private citizens usually are not granted access to—"a briefing" on the situation.

Possessed of either past military experience or intelligence training, McCraw had a smooth authoritative voice which dispensed a calming effect on my nerves. He was not agitated by the request to halt his duties to call a complete stranger in Dallas. Nor was he condescending in any way. This man simply told me what no one else could when he confirmed 1500 National Guard troops would be on the ground, in East Texas, in a matter of minutes, or hours, but definitely that day. I was free to pass this vital information on to anyone who could funnel word back into Jasper. *Hang on, the Texas Calvary is coming.*

Another close media colleague, Bob Morrison, the news director at USA Radio, had already interviewed Sam Bodman, Secretary of Energy, and directly asked about Jasper, what was going on there. *People were suffering.* Bob sent me a copy of the interview. Slowly, but surely, word about Jasper's plight was getting out. NBC had offered a well done network story with rare footage of what the wind is capable of after it breathes down the neck of a region, sitting and lashing and raining, not moving, in the same spot, for nine hours. More people were starting to take seriously the lonely desperation felt by our neighbors in cut off sections of East Texas. The last thing McCraw said was, "Let me give you my cell phone number in case you need anything." I had gotten a message to Rick Perry. With three years and not a word exchanged between us, he sent back a strong, silent message of his own. *They weren't going to need body bags.*

It was an average Wednesday morning after landfall. I suddenly felt like I owed the governor of Texas a favor, or, at least a thank you. My love for a place nicknamed "Jewel of the Forest" wouldn't be diminished by a brazen hussy named Rita.

TWO

After how long it took for some counties to get aid, t-shirts began surfacing in East Texas towns about what FEMA stood for: FIX EVERYTHING MY ASS. I stepped up my frantic search for a Beaumont hotel room, calling area managers to personally explain my willingness to sleep in a broom closet and pay the going rate. Many hotels and motels had serious damage, severely limiting availability.

A Holiday Inn stopped taking reservations, the hotel empty, closed, abandoned, shattered glass allowed air into random rooms like invisible confetti. The few hotels in town that crawled back to anything remotely close to 'normal business' were booked for weeks and months in advance by busy energy crews, insurance adjusters and construction workers who had more important jobs than mine. I hope those assigned the almost insurmountable task of cleaning up and making the lights come back on won't be too upset to learn that I attempted, on more than one occasion, to have at least one of them kicked out of the MCM Elegante' Hotel, where I usually stayed. I specifically wanted whoever was in Room 623 to give back my suite.

Both October and November 2005 defied me with a busy schedule made months in advance. While I gave my all for every lecture and appearance slated, my vexed heart remained in Southeast Texas and much of the Pelican State, with its big-mouthed strange bird holding the contents of a racist past. It is ironic that a bird with such a beak can not speak. I grew up in a parish where racist cops were fond of describing black-on-black crime as TND, Typical Nigger Deal. There are parts of Louisiana where no state line scrawled into Texas is necessary to recognize redemption in reconciliation work that still must be done.

I've always believed that North Louisiana and East Texas should be one state, while South Louisiana and Southeast Texas belonged together. The culture, race relations, so much hope for both. Geography lessons aside, I was also waiting for stamped judicial authorization for a pending divorce on file. A life on hold. Just after Katrina, and right before Rita, I had filed for divorce and was in the eye of my own storm. Rita was the work that saved a soul and gave it a mission to rebuild. She erased numerous temptations to shake hands with Jim Beam, visit Jack Daniel's or Crown some Royal. I couldn't get into Beaumont, Jasper, or anywhere else ravaged by Rita and it wasn't time to stand, alone, in front of a judge. A busy schedule and phone calls about hurricanes saved me from myself. Talking was therapeutic. Pretty soon, a ringing phone was constant and I couldn't answer all the incoming calls. In the frenzy, I missed one marked "private." The message began, "Joyce King…Rick Perry. How are you young lady?"

Stunned is an understatement. I don't know anyone in my circle of friends and colleagues who have received Friday afternoon phone calls from a sitting governor of Texas. I played the message over and over until I believed it was authentic. It sounded like Rick Perry. The words echoed that slight Texas twang he delivered with just the right amount of gentlemanly finesse. After about 10 minutes, I was convinced it wasn't a hoax from one lunatic friend who might pull such a stunt, then feign ooh-ah amazement when I called to brag about the governor nominating me to some board or commission, before telling me *they* were the governor. No, it was Rick Perry alright, with his perfect hair and magnetic charm.

Slightly amused by his flattery—*young lady*—I was only 9 years younger than him, thank you very much, I decided the governor might be trying to get under my vote with that one. But it was the genuine sound in his voice that rewound to our brief past at the same function in 2002 that made me remember the kindness extended that day by Rick Perry, the man. Our politics aren't exactly the same, but I felt like we were on similar pages when it came to hurricanes.

Four days later, my cell phone rang again with the notorious "private." This time, after missing my gubernatorial close-up, I had the phone affixed to my shirt and promptly answered. Reward: another youthful compliment that may have something to do with an old photo at my website. Basically, this was how my involvement with Rita got cranked up—one conversation led to another and dialogue became the savoir that made me feel I was doing something besides feeling sad and lonely about my upcoming divorce. From Gov. Perry's call, I answered my phone day and night to talk with friends and neighbors, people I knew intimately. Many I had never met.

It was nice to speak to Mr. Perry without a third party between us. He made my day, listening to frustrations at not being able to get to Jefferson and Jasper counties sooner. We talked, briefly, about race, people who had been trapped on buses, and our common bond as Texans. He promised to stay in touch. I vowed to never let him forget what Rita did, like Washington colleagues who later developed hurricane amnesia quickly after her landfall. A few days later, I was finally headed to Southeast Texas.

The drive alone to Beaumont from Dallas, first down Interstate 45 to towns like Ennis, Corsicana and Huntsville, is a vehicular trip longer in reality than clock or odometer ever denotes. An Internet map site has always listed Beaumont as being about 5 hours and 20 minutes from my back door, which made Huntsville the approximate halfway point. Rush hour traffic added another hour.

In *HATE CRIME*, Chapter Five offers a sample of the prison research I did on the Jasper dragging defendants. From scary T-M-I (too much information) moments and a prison education afforded me by wardens, inmates, prison officials and eager tour guides, I still harbored an uneasiness related to Huntsville. I never went to a single event where readers didn't point out how "humorous" they found posted signs in Huntsville and near prison units: *Hitchhikers may be escaping inmates.* I didn't see what was funny, not when I wrote the words, not when I stopped for gas that day.

There were dozens of nice people who helped me in Huntsville, a fine place, including two I hope to see again—Salvador Buentello, known far and wide for his prison gang knowledge, and a now-retired warden named Dr. Richard Watkins. Since neither man was at Starbucks, I locked my doors again as soon as the coffee was in place for the second stretch to my native Houston, which pained me to drive over, not one stop to visit two brothers, a favorite uncle, many of my mother's 12 siblings, and 10,000 cousins. Our family reunion could fill up Hermann Park.

Joyce King

Blowing Houston a kiss, I remembered Hurricane Carla. 1961. The baby decade I came of age and the disappearing rabbits we never saw again after the storm. Carla killed 40 people. I wasn't a baby for Hurricane Alicia, 1983, and recalled the devastation more vividly in the decade of young womanhood. I love Houston but gave her a frown and connected with "the Loop" few ever call Interstate 610. Another change of bumpy pavement left me exited onto Interstate 10 and a huge green and white freeway sign. Underneath was one word: Beaumont.

I sung a ton of George Strait, blaring, blowing with me in the coolness and *chill of an early fall.* If there's another black woman in the United States who knows as many Strait tunes as me, she can have all the money in my bank account (that ought to get her to San Antonio) and every photo I have of the cowboy who looks equally handsome in black hats and white ones. When we crossed the Jefferson County line, it was George who reassured and cradled me with the lyrics, "Nobody in his right mind would've left her." He was way down at the Alamo and knew about the pending divorce.

Along the entry into Beaumont city limits were leftover signs of Rita, things not yet cleaned up or repaired. Bent poles and snapped trees posed in open fields. Abandoned buildings and former businesses had partial rooftops with missing or wide open doors. Chewy bites of furniture fed my view. Restaurant signs weren't signs at all. Cracked neon bulbs of air replaced former identification markers, McDonald's arches rested sideways on the ground. For the most part, Beaumont, on the surface, was back on her feet, swept up, nailed down, and ready to carry on, except for adjusting that would require diligence, state and federal dollars. I smiled that the old girl looked pretty good in high heels except for a gaping run in her panty hose. Beneath the city dress there was enormous damage. Beaumont had been pulverized by a green-eyed female named Rita who disliked strong proud women dancing down the yellow brick road in Texas.

Instead of checking into the hotel, I drove past it, continued to record the lingering remnants of twisted metal, charred shotgun houses, broken parts neatly stacked, boxed springs and boxed trash, piled with purpose. Red lights all appeared to be in good working order, street signs up-righted and re-rooted deeper into earth. A few Christmas decorations peaked out from neighborhood shops and

10

strips, signs of hope that life went on warmed me like Louisiana Hot Sauce, the perfect condiment for a cool fall day. It was two days before Thanksgiving 2005. I drove on.

Back at the hotel, I had to sign a disclaimer that stated my understanding the rooms were not what they were when I had visited pre-Rita. They were not 100% repaired and ready. I didn't know what to expect behind the door of Room 315. It wasn't my old suite. Except for a few minor things—there was no ice on the third floor, the silent machine wouldn't say a word when I pushed the brown button for ice, nor would the $1.50 a can soda vending machine accept money. The room was okay, priced higher than before. One stark reminder that Rita had violently checked in and out leaving her bill unpaid made me cringe. Part of the wall near my view was ripped out, exposing an internal shell, the naked construction composed of several two by four slats. Rita had peeled back the wall, a fact that made it easier to hear the person next door.

Downstairs, I stood for a long time near the front desk, frozen to admire a photographic memory of a brown woman in a pink pantsuit sipping a White Russian in the hotel bar. It was a savored moment inside The Blue Parrot days before an intrusion by the drunken hurricane that tore through smashing the bar to bits, throwing chairs, crushing bottles of expensive liquor and hissing through her intoxicated breath. I didn't recognize the Parrot, standing, gawking in the same spot too long. Incoming guests and a few employees soon noticed and fixed their gazes on my face, visibly saddened and angry that the little table I had guzzled the vodka at was scratched and bruised, storm-furniture survivor. Then I remembered no one was hurt. We were all hurt, just not the standard medical definition.

As I drove around Beaumont, eavesdropping on residents preparing for a long holiday weekend of gratitude and family, there was a duality of joy and sadness from one end of the city to the other. I could see it in Mitch's face too when he talked about a fallen comrade and friend. A popular judge named Tom Mulvaney was being eulogized the next day, Thanksgiving Eve. The man was 55, the same age of a media colleague in Dallas who didn't wake up the same Sunday morning as the nice judge.

Glenn Mitchell, longtime public radio host of *The Glenn Mitchell Show,* was about to have his KERA-based program syndicated on satellite radio. If anyone deserved it, Glenn did. He had worked hard over the years establishing himself as a masterful interviewer who was smooth, articulate and well-informed. He knew everything from world affairs to world citizens to bestselling authors to man-on-the-street concerns. In all the times I heard Glenn on the air, I can't recall a single occasion anyone ever goaded him into raising the calm voice he was famous for.

Glenn was gone. Before the rest of America got to enjoy his broadcasting wizardry in motion. The judge had vanished, snatched by the cancer monster all of us have seen visit the ones we love. A death in Dallas and a death in Beaumont, miles away, suddenly, to me, seemed connected. Both men were 55, respected members of their professions and communities, taken in the prime of their excellent lives. Both men had their stories told well, work remembered on the evening news. Both died the same day. I grieved for Dallas and *with* Beaumont, sorry to not know Tom Mulvaney.

A few hours later, I was still at the sheriff's office with his executive assistant, Keesha Guillory, catching up when cell phone music interrupted us. I popped open the caller ID and saw it was Billy Rowles, who had earlier promised to hook up if we could find each other at the end of a long day.

"Hey girl," my good friend enthusiastically greeted, "Where are you?" A knowing laugh when he heard "the sheriff's office." I was always with one sheriff or another trying to get on the right side of the law or beg more peace officers to provide faithful protection. Billy had been a private investigator, a DPS trooper and the legendary Jasper County sheriff who arrested the trio for the murder of James Byrd, Jr. He always supplied an "aw shucks" grin whenever I called him hero.

The sun was setting. Billy gave instructions for the trip to Buna, Texas, which is located in Jasper County about 40 miles from Beaumont. "Call me when you get to Highway 62," the familiar voice hung up. Billy may not be sheriff for the moment, but he'll always be emeritus lawman of that county to me.

A million Christmas car lights later, I finally hit the sign for a road named 62 South only to discover cell phones don't work in thick woods. I was tired, still perched on the connecting highway and stopped in front of a mom and pop store where a dead pay phone ate my last two quarters. I stepped inside to cool indifferent stares and put on my best lost city slicker look, asking a woman and her daughter behind the counter if I could use their landline. Since I didn't favor a robber, had no visible weapon, they could plainly check just over my shoulder to record the license plate of the Volvo, they said it would be okay. They would dial the number. I only had to say Billy's name and any real suspicion melted. *Oh, come on in, why didn't you say so? Take the phone, stretch out, you want a soda?* They told me directions again themselves when I hung up with Billy.

Here's the dilemma. I may be a native Texan, a tough Southern girl, and all of that, but I am, notoriously, one of the scariest people in the state. When I agreed to let Billy grill me a steak, I thought he meant at his *house* in Buna. It was only when I reached the little store in Buna that Billy said I wouldn't be able to find him without someone coming to get me. He was worried that I might get lost in dark woods where I had assumed his house was. It was deeper and darker than that minus any house.

His beautiful bride, Jamie, and their baby-dog, Noodle, picked me up at the Pines Store. Jamie took one look at the Volvo and decided "the little rental" that wasn't a rental would never make it down the roads we were headed. We ditched the white princess and saddled up the Ford for a ride that changed my life. As Billy has often been known to do. Even in the darkness of only the vehicle's headlights, I could see countless giant broken twigs and pines that had once been tall timber straddled in a Rita-produced thinner forest.

Jamie slowed down to point out spots where houses or trailers of neighbors on the route had been uprooted and tossed about or left sideways without occupants who came back in tears at the sight of soaked memories and menacing debris. Jamie showed me a patch of earth Billy had poured heart and soul into "getting just right," their second home, only to have the wind split a giant oak on top of it. Rita's ax had wildly swung at slimmer pines too. We rode on. It was best the scene was so dark. Jamie couldn't note the tears that formed. I was as bad as Billy when it came to crying, the fair landscape worse than I was prepared to accept.

Her twists and turns, for about four or five miles, led to one last curve that emptied us into the driveway of land Jamie called "deer lease" property. I wasn't sure what the two words meant and nodded as if I knew. It was an important detail that I failed to comprehend when mentioned earlier by Billy. He would be cooking at that same property, not at home, but at their hunter's paradise. A houseless getaway they treasured.

Warmed by his gracious hospitality, the cold night air relented a bit when the man wrapped his arms around me. Two notable visitors, one named Jack, the other named Daniel's, met a cup with my name on it. Billy wasted no time in pouring something that would stick to my ribs. With my fiery liquid companion, I joined the group Billy introduced me to around a blaze of breathtaking blue manipulated by bright orange and black embers combining for the perfect glow. Everything in the world was alright at that standstill moment. I didn't know it then, but this was my Thanksgiving holiday, a wonderful commune with big Lone Star pride, our nature at night, surrounded by the kind of people I appreciate more than ever. Lovers of the land and respectful of one woman who was no lady. Backstabbing Rita.

One couple still had on their hunting gear from the day's activities. She had netted a large doe, "not a buck," which our party explained in terms of 'men are from Mars and women from Venus.' Jamie said it best, "It's just like men and women; there are always more does in the woods." Everyone agreed. Billy was back and forth behind us at a huge grill, handsome as ever, with hair on his face this time. Last time I saw him, a few weeks before, he was hairless. Masculine phases I supposed.

"Joyce, how do you like your steak?" he quizzed. When I said, "medium-well," the cowboy next to me moaned something like "Good luck," hinting that Billy was only asking to be polite. "Mooing" and pink would be the order of the day. I think he was yanking a city girl's power tools. A myriad of conversations around the fire scaled the gauntlet from funny to personal, serious to political, and Las Vegas in a kind of unspoken theme of *what happens here stays here.* I met some of Billy's friends, including Craig Corder, kin like cousin Pat Fletcher, deer hunting buddies and their better halves.

None of them knew 2005 would be my first holiday to give thanks alone. My two sons were in Louisiana having a grand time with their father. They deserved to spend some quality days hanging out, eating turkey, watching football and acknowledging the blessings of a good life. None of the people at Billy's private gathering knew the lone black person with them, way back off in the woods, admired them for surviving a hurricane national newscasters had stopped talking about.

Longing to truly belong somewhere my entire adult life, I wondered why the same region I had run from four decades was such a good match, the soothing reality of perfect fit. I wondered how and why I felt at home, at ease, wealthy and needed, protected and loved, appreciated by plain people like me, who were, on the surface, nothing like me. It was the best Thanksgiving I could've had. Moon at my back, a mini bonfire at my face, and strangers who welcomed me as neighbor dropping by after smelling the mingled fragrance of ribs, steak, an upright chicken fully roasted, garlic potatoes, beans simmered in onions and ground beef, succulence unlimited.

I never felt the cold night air again and even walked around some, never brave enough to venture far. It was still East Texas. I hadn't stated any readiness to shoot at Bambi. But any white man that can get me that deep into thick woods is very close to placing a gun in my hand and hunting garb on my back. A dangerous prospect indeed.

When it was time to eat, Billy let me sample ribs hot off the grill. He spoon fed me a sample of the bean concoction, which reminded me of Louisiana and my mom's recipe loaded with all the good stuff—brown sugar, bits of meat, cut up veggies and more. People like Billy and places like Jasper County are the reasons I never diet. Eating is as much a part of who we are as what we are— Southerners with a co-joined history of surviving hurricanes.

That night, the eve of the eve of Thanksgiving 2005, stories were shared, tall tales told, deer doubled in size, and I found the courage to join Billy at the grill for a private moment he knew was coming. I whispered the divorce talk that had exposed nerves and made me deranged over the summer back in his office. He knew, he knew. Enough said. None of what was actually uttered is important enough to share here, given my undying respect and admiration for Billy. The real reason none of what was actually uttered can be shared is, it mostly can't be remembered thanks to Jack Daniel's sloshing around before meat and potatoes joined him in my fat belly.

We were not left alone to whisper long. Billy soon announced, and I was proud he did, that I was almost divorced. Not to see if there were any hunters interested, (not a bad idea though) but to try it on for vocal size. It came out right. Plain people talked. I listened. Ordinary stories of extraordinary courage and fortitude complemented the open air meal.

At an outdoor table that could compare to the finest set at Buckingham Palace, I was in hog heaven, our great Texas element, marveling at the size of a slab of meat Billy called 'my steak' for the chow down. Damn, it was fine, just like the cowboy in the white hat who served it. No television, no cable, no cell phones that worked. I sat, satisfied, warm, laughing with Jamie. No longer afraid of the howling animals that had been pointed out to me earlier, when I wished they hadn't.

Even with the singing pack of wily coyotes in the too-near distance, convened by the smell of bloody meat and human feet, there was enough ammunition to make me feel nothing and nobody uninvited was about to crash my Thanksgiving Party. Billy wouldn't let them. I felt like the guest of honor, finally getting the tasty steak he had been promising for more than five years.

When I mentioned to a friend back in Dallas what a great time I had in the fresh outdoors, he tore right into me. "Are you out of your black mind being in the thick Piney Woods with a bunch of white folk deer hunting and drinking? You're lucky no Klan showed up." Luck had nothing to do with it. I was with Billy Earnest Rowles.

At some point, we have to take each person we meet, black, white, male or female, one at a time. If any Klan *showed up,* they probably would've gotten fed to the coyotes that night. We were having too much fun to take part in any rallies. I am well aware that racism isn't dead and it might never die. The simple truth, my grand oversimplification on race again, is, there are two kinds of people: good and bad. Get with your posse and I'll get with mine, a necessary requirement for surviving powerful hurricanes that ripped our Texas heart to pieces. I don't possess the luxury of discriminating against people who have been nothing but wonderful.

In the truck with Jamie, I said of the husband she has shared so freely, "I want one just like him." That's why Jamie works hard at staying healthy—our little joke about Billy being "my next husband in my next life." She dropped me back at the Volvo.

With foil-wrapped steak, I sped on down the highway crying back to Beaumont. Big happy tears conquered the dim vision of wrecked wilderness and kept alive my fierce love connection, despite evil Rita, to Jasper County, Texas.

It was time to listen and learn. Soon, the daylight would come.

THREE

In September 2005, Gov. Perry appointed 11 people to an Evacuation Task Force comprised of talented professionals chosen to gather testimony from key victories and flunked lessons Rita taught, all given the necessary jobs of establishing better evacuation plans for future disasters.

Not that many residents had attended one of the town hall-styled meetings open to public officials and citizens in Harris County. While Houstonians weren't thrilled at how thousands had to sit for hours barely moving on interstates packed with fleeing Texans, they didn't turn out in droves to offer testimony in October. Jefferson County residents got their turn December 13th.

Jefferson County Judge Carl Griffith, Jr. did not make the opening remarks as listed on the program. The judge wasn't there when the meeting was called to order by task force chairman, Jack Little, former president and CEO of Shell Oil. To his left and right were serious faces identified by customary name plates and impressive positions. Theron Bowman, the only member of the panel I knew, was absent when Beaumont Mayor Guy Goodson referred to low hurricane evacuation moments as "dim bulbs." When I looked again, the police chief of Arlington, Texas, had arrived for the sixth and final state evacuation meeting.

Gov. Perry's purpose for the hearing was projected onto a bright white screen as the theatre audience, a nearly full house, was told that they weren't there to "talk about Hurricane Katrina" but to focus specifically on how to better evacuate. Four major issues on the agenda were mobility, available fuel, identifying special needs citizens, and something referred to as 'command, control, and communication.' On cue, Judge Griffith entered behind the third C.

Griffith used words like "unbelievable" and "unprecedented"

and testified that it took calls from him to U. S. Senator Kay Bailey Hutchison (R-Texas) to get things moving for an airlift of 8,000 special needs patients from area hospitals. The judge stressed urgent pleas, "Hospitals were calling me all the time telling me people were going to die." Griffith called Hutchison, who, in turn, he said, phoned the White House. A man who knew an awful lot about politics told the convened panel at Lamar University that it should not have taken "politics" to help get things moving.

For the next few minutes I listened to local and regional officials. They worked for hospital administrations, city governments, and emergency management teams, offering predictable and unpredictable statements, including the obvious, "We've been through four evacuations—Andrew, Lily, Katrina, and Rita. There are things that need to be worked on." I was a little concerned to hear, "The state of Texas didn't have enough oxygen." I applauded the idea of a better county-to-county communication network. Especially given cell phones don't work well in optimum weather for a few pockets of Southeast Texas. One can imagine how great they work during storms.

Paul Parker, the city manager for Lufkin, Texas, brought his own slide presentation, as if he needed evidence to bolster what everyone in attendance already suspected about a doubled population in his city two days before Rita. Parker admitted, "We were in very dire straits." He said it was fortunate that Department of Public Safety troopers had arrived to help local law enforcement overwhelmed with meeting the needs of not only its own citizens, but thousands of visitors packed in area shelters with more coming. Then Parker mentioned dehydrated Beaumont residents on school buses, "We got them fueled and on their way."

Parker's testimony touched on security, logistics, future solutions for shelter, how to avoid what he called a "yo-yo effect," people leaving and returning, something that created more of a bottleneck environment and issues with fuel. Someone at one of the Lufkin shelters had been robbed. Worse, a woman had been raped. Before Parker knew it, his allotted 10 minutes were done. He gave up the witness stand to a man named John Wilson who identified himself as representing the Center for Safe and Secure Schools for Harris County. I made my exit, doubtful at least one resident would speak before a scheduled 20-minute break. *Where were the 2,000 people who had been trapped for almost 50-hours on Beaumont school buses? Did they want to testify? What about other residents concerned with jobs, food, temporary and permanent housing? Would Texans in motels be put out on the streets?*

Just the day before, a federal judge had added an extra month to the January 2006 deadline that FEMA planned to stop paying for Katrina hotel rooms. The extension didn't apply to displaced Rita victims, creating more talk of a double hurricane standard. However, there was a sliver of good news for Southeast Texans. 24 hours before the evacuation meeting, in the same auditorium at Lamar University, Lt. Gov. David Dewhurst had outlined a proposal by lawmakers to spend more than $70 million to help residents either repair their homes and businesses or help them build new ones.

If housing was the number one issue directly linked to revitalizing the economy, there were a ton of questions. Why hadn't Rita residents been included in the hotel extension granted for those affected by Katrina? Why were thousands of FEMA travel trailers sitting empty and unused at dozens of "staging areas" while residents eager to leave motels were being told they had to wait for available shelter? These were people who desperately wanted to return to work and rebuild ripped apart lives, didn't cotton to the idea of five or six family members all cramped in one room indefinitely. Without work, money, or credit cards, they also didn't cotton to the idea of no choice.

More patience would be required and more time needed for a proposal that set aside $50 million to build decent, affordable housing that might lure Rita victims back to fill service industry jobs. The other $20 million, according to Lt. Gov. Dewhurst, would be utilized to help repair damaged homes. Southeast Texans also learned, the same day, that Gov. Perry had okayed a $2.4 million dollar grant package, the Texas Disaster Relief Fund, money that offered potential. Some grumbled it was only a band aid for hurricane hemorrhaging in Chambers, Hardin, Newton, Jasper, Jefferson, Orange, and Tyler Counties. Mr. Perry had also declared Angelina, Liberty, Nacogdoches, Polk, Sabine, San Augustine, San Jacinto, Shelby, Trinity and Walker Counties disaster areas.

A break in the evacuation hearing was delayed and a scheduled rendezvous beckoned. I left for Woodville, Texas. The drive from Beaumont into Tyler County marked the first chance to vividly record, by the plentiful rays of a gorgeous afternoon sun, a larger view of the damage Rita had left behind. Before that, I had only seen bits and pieces of real estate outside Jefferson County at dusk or in total darkness. Nothing prepared me for the stark reality of teeming daylight.

Some 20,000 call the lovely little county home with a 'Don't Mess With Texas' pride in towns like Spurger, Fred, Chester and Warren, which all sounded, initially, like names of affable cowboys. Woodville is the county seat with its population of more than 2,400.

On the main highway, 69 North toward Lufkin, a majority of homes featured heavy royal blue tarp on rooftops, keeping the chill and rain out until Rita Holes might be repaired. Or insurance adjustors could determine damage not documented in photographs. I later learned that most of the tarp was the same because it was the official color government workers nailed to all those roofs. Another uniform thing, almost instantly noticeable on the drive, property owners had done the backbreaking labor of neatly stacking miles of debris right to the edge of the highway.

Along the route, I saw boarded up mom and pop businesses in need of repair. There were vehicles, cars and trucks alike, that still sat in front yards silently cursing big trees that took seats on the lawns next to them. Or flat out on top of them. In cleared fields, the reddish brown dirt of my Southern youth looked like gummy clay. It held numerous piles of small fires. Purposely blackened. The cooking that added unsolicited zest to a landscape dish. Trees and giant match sticks burned in mounds spread only feet apart. I counted smoke signals that a better day was in the making. We had to have faith in his futuristic day.

Motorists were not agitated by my wacky driving and abrupt halts. Unable to stay in the lines of a coloring book car, it was quick stops, slow down, brake-for-better-looks while in defensive shock mode. Trees poured from inside of see-through forests that had formerly been thick Piney Woods. Un-curtained acreage allowed me to see where animals had lived, hunters had hunted, and lovers had happily gotten lost, no brown and green left, only the redness of the dirt and breathtaking Texas blue sky. I saw once hidden houses and trailer homes owners had deposited in the security of a luxurious wood haven destroyed and reduced to rubble. Some trees, viciously snapped in two, clung to the solid bases that refused to quietly depart earth. Others were uprooted and deposited far from where they once stood.

Another thing that captured my attention were how many American flags whipped high above blue-tarp, damage and destruction. House after house, trailer after trailer, proud Texas neighbors displayed Old Glory in all her glory. Others ran the Texas flag up right beside Miss America. Lives shattered, houses minus soaked carpets, empty freezers, meat ruined, holes next to chimneys in roofs, trees leaning on cars or peeking in bedrooms, yet nothing could prevent the unfurling of too many flags to count that day. She flew high above it all, serving as a victorious reminder that Southeast Texans would not have, and never will have, their collective spirit defeated by a hurricane designed to maim and malign. And George Strait was on the car stereo, "I'll be somewhere down in Texas…if you're looking for me."

In the center of Woodville, I stopped at a Diary Queen, not sure why, during the busy lunch hour and monitored the work environment. Whatever else I could gauge. There was a definite sadness, a frustration, and not enough workers to keep up with food orders. The DQ phone rang and rang while one woman made admirable attempts to take orders, grab food, answer the interruptions, and help a co-worker with an equally busy drive-thru window. After standing there a few minutes, they realized I hadn't come to order a tasty Hungr Buster. Someone politely pointed to my destination down the road, perhaps wondering why an overdressed woman wanted to know where the sheriff's office was. I drove right past it, continuing to stare in awe at beat up buildings and missing windows, then turned around and went back. It looked like the Woodville Inn was permanently closed for business.

Once inside the Tyler County Sheriff's Office, my mouth flew open when a very large man, a very large *black* man, answered to the name of Jessie Wolf. When told there was a visitor, the busy sheriff, who counseled a pair of young men about how to pay a fine and not find themselves in the same kind of mischief that made it necessary in the first place, turned his attention to me. I thought about my criminal past, which included riding free on the Dallas Light Rail and using my affiliation with lawmen to get out of speeding tickets. I stepped right up behind the boys he dismissed like a stern daddy.

Elevated, Sheriff Wolf was made even taller than his 6'8 physique by the intimidating fact that he looked down on me from thick-paned glass that resembled one of those bullet proof check cashing windows. *Thank God this man knew of no crimes from my recently divorced past.* I had only been "free and single" one week. And warned that Jessie Wolf was indeed a big man. Or as one person put it, "He wears a size 17 shoe but is a gentle giant." The gentle part is well concealed from those who know nothing about Mr. Wolf.

His expression did not change when our eyes initially met. "Come on in," he motioned to a side door so we wouldn't have to discuss all the flavor of our Kool-Aid in front of curious Tyler County residents stationed in a small waiting area. Behind the truth or consequences door, where other peace officers did paperwork, I got a closer, level one look at a huge man with a tall tale name for a southern sheriff. Jessie Wolf's story was the documented stuff ready made for legend.

"I've been sheriff for about a year now, I worked as chief deputy for seven years," the baritone-voiced lawman answered my first question about a long, impressive career that totaled 25 years with the department. Wolf sensed that I wouldn't delve into more serious questions without confirmation on what my eyes had already measured and weighed.

The home-grown football player had attended Warren High School and played with the World Champion Miami Dolphins in 1971 and in the World Football League before moving on to Canada. Normally, I don't ask men the bulk of Wolf obvious questions like, "Is it true you wear a size 17 shoe?" or "How much do you weigh?" But he smiled at both, never tiring of, "Yes it is," and "about 410 pounds."

The cassette recorder between us had only been rolling a few seconds before the former defensive tackle displayed remarkably gentle qualities with a particular soft spot—his love for a man named James. "I had a twin brother and we played all our ball here in Warren and graduated from Warren High School and then went on to Prairie View A&M." It was hard to imagine *two* gentle giants. Wolf lamented the fact that they were briefly separated by football careers. It was the only time they were apart. He beamed when supplying one of the reasons. "James was with the Pittsburg Steelers when they won their first Super Bowl."

Wolf lost his twin to Multiple Sclerosis two years earlier in another December that remained as fresh as two days ago. "I miss him, and I sure miss him this time of the year but I know he's in a better place." A baby smile crossed his face when the sheriff explained the non-rhythmic twin handles: Jessie and James were named after the famous outlaw. Both men were not only well thought of, they were law abiding citizens the entire community was proud to say were raised by their little village. 25 years ago, the big football player who never considered himself a city boy, even after logging thousands of miles traveling, missed home so bad he fled the bright lights.

"I always wanted to get in law enforcement and just liked the sticks better," the sheriff remembered his desire to serve the same place that nurtured him. After going through the academy—it was the first sheriff that Wolf worked under—a man named Leon Fowler—who took him aside and shared basic lessons on police work, including a motto that the younger lawman continues to live by today: "Treat people like you want to be treated." By many accounts, citizens in the masculine-named towns of Tyler County say Wolf lives up to his ordinary mantra.

"I've seen a lot of these kids grow up in Tyler County and I've won a lot of mothers' hearts and a lot of kids' hearts so it wasn't a color barrier when I ran." Wolf has a humility about him that complements the people he serves, residents who voted him into office. "It was more the man that was fitted for the job." Color is not the first thing Wolf wants people to notice about him. Nor was it something he dwelled on when Rita bashed Tyler County.

"We didn't lose one life, other things can be fixed." Sadly, there was a lot that needed fixing in the early hours of a total blackout. "We had over 1,000 people gathered at the parking lot of the old Wal-Mart and one Red Cross representative there and I had to tell all of them that particular day that Red Cross help wasn't coming." Wolf credited what happened after the frustrating announcement to the caliber and backbone of people in Tyler County. There was no fighting or raising Cain. The crowd dispersed. They were disappointed that official help did not arrive that day and was so long in coming. They went back to homes without air and electricity, or to property with unlivable abodes. One thing was agreed on up front— Tyler County could use some help.

When the call went out, Victoria County Sheriff T. Michael O'Connor dispatched deputies, along with cars, equipment and fuel to aid Wolf for the next few weeks. He described O'Connor as "the finest fellow you ever want to meet."

With every minute that passed in our "interview," which was really just two Texans shooting the breeze, I found myself liking Jessie Wolf more and more. I wasn't surprised at his admiration for mutual friend, Billy Rowles, "He's just a flat-out good country boy, he's a good man." Not a good *white* man, a good man period, something there are too few of in any color.

"Anything that my people are involved in, I'm involved in it with them. I ain't got one deputy to do anything that I wouldn't do myself. Whatever I get, I share it with my people." His "people" included two Sergeants and 12 deputies who made daily treks over the 960 square miles that is Tyler County, an enormous amount of land to watch over.

With Chief Deputy Clint Sturrock, Sgt. Tricia Ford, Sgt. Aubrey Sturrock and Captain Eddie Fredieu, the sheriff ventured out to help residents after landfall. What they saw was beyond heartbreaking, defied comprehension. "I was just hurt, there was an empty feeling and you know there's nothing you can do." Wolf sighed heavily at the memory of lush rolling hills redecorated into twisted landscapes, rearranged houses, churches bent out of shape, rooftops with gaping holes, mighty trees turned into useless lumber. The beautiful little county was reinvented in a matter of hours by wind, rain, flying objects, sharp glass, and downed power lines that left faithful residents completely in the dark for days.

"One of the things we did was to just get people food, water, and ice because a lot of them didn't have generators and running water," the sheriff explained. "God knows how many game wardens with chain saws were cutting their way in to help people." Officials weren't the only ones who didn't sit around waiting for the government to show up. "Oh no, a lot of the citizens would break out their own chain saws, they would work because we just have good people in this county." Over and over, Wolf deleted anything that put race ahead of simple humanity.

"When Rita hit, it wasn't a black and white issue, it was one people. Everybody just banned together and worked together and things turned out lovely." Wolf had a working thesis—suffering was the tie that bound humans together.

Wolf remembered Texans trapped on school buses. Three had stopped at the Woodville emergency room. "They had more than they could deal with, we tried to treat as many as we could and get them on the road, get them a little further, to a larger facility where they could get more help." No one had ever seen anything like Rita. Playing the blame game in the aftermath, Wolf believes, doesn't do any good.

Wolf let out a thunderous laugh when recalling the lack of one chief amenity. "It was hot during that time so a lot of people told me they were almost about to get used to these cold showers. You never get used to a cold shower, I don't care who you are." When the big lawman put on his invisible "paw-paw" hat, the gentle giant showed all over.

"I didn't have electricity at my own house for about a month." Wolf says Rita left her calling card all over Texas. The likelihood of more evacuations is a given. He didn't lay the entire responsibility at the feet of government officials in the business of emergency expertise. "People will be better prepared *themselves* in case of this type of disaster again. A lot more people know now and are prepared, when before they weren't."

In Tyler County, some residents used the darkness to reminisce about a simpler life that meant no cable, cell phones and computers anyway. You *talked* to your neighbors. In listening to his own constituency, Wolf knew before FEMA and Red Cross ever got to town that he would give officials some advice. "If y'all not going to help these people, just be honest and tell them." The sheriff sincerely believed that if people knew the truth, rather than officials making them fill out a bunch of misleading paperwork that fostered their eligibility hopes, they'd be okay. Instead of waiting to get something that government workers knew they weren't.

A lot of people did get help from Red Cross and FEMA, but

there were just as many who didn't. Perhaps if FEMA had done a better job, and everyone knows this in hindsight, the agency wouldn't be in the embarrassing position of asking Texans who weren't eligible, but received money, to pay back $1.26 million in aid. After Rita, more than 600 people erroneously cashed checks for that amount while hundreds of deserving people got zilch.

"I had to explain to them that the officials had jobs to do and could only send in their paperwork as it was given to them. All I could figure was some residents met the criteria and others didn't." Wolf had compassion for the many who never met conditions set by Red Cross and FEMA. He knew of cases where people got $2,000 vouchers when their neighbors didn't even qualify. Others received slightly more, and checks for each family member when homes were completely destroyed. Wolf found himself in the dreadful position of having to explain he had no control over what the agencies did.

The same day I sat down to chat with Wolf, it was announced that Marsha J. Evans, Director of the American Red Cross, would step down at the end of December 2005. One of the reasons cited was concern over managerial style. Red Cross had collected more than $2 billion dollars for victims of Katrina, Rita and Wilma, but was plagued with issues related to theft of supplies and money allegedly taken by volunteers. A longtime Red Cross volunteer refused to let me use her name next to sorted accusations she made about personally witnessing incidents where fellow volunteers "took things."

Frustration in Tyler County did not discriminate. Everyone had to follow guidelines, fill out paperwork and meet deadlines. While many were denied, the work was nonstop. Trees and trash were stacked at the end of driveways and at checkpoints. It was exactly what FEMA requested for the ongoing cleanup. A humongous "no-bid" billion dollar deal to remove debris had been awarded to a handful of firms while thousands of Texans did the labor of cutting, sawing, chopping, clearing and hauling, at that point, to make homes and yards passable, livable again. Their manual labor was free.

"If you would've seen this county a day or two after Rita, I was just blown away, it was massive trees and telephone poles across the roads." It took the sheriff three days just to funnel his way to his own home, blocked by fallen timber and glass. In the early hours, not many outside of Southeast Texas were aware that Rita's path had taken such an inland route, tearing up coastal cities and towns, not satisfied, then deepening her presence with each inland mile.

"*Dateline NBC* came in and did a good interview, but things were a lot more serious than a lot of people initially realized," Wolf shook his head. He and County Judge Jerome Owens went to Beaumont to speak with President Bush. "About 40 of us were in the room with him and you could talk to him some, he just basically assured us that we would be taken care of." When supplies, food, more ice and M-R-E's (Meals Ready to Eat) started pouring in, Tyler County residents were grateful for the blessing of basic needs being met. Wolf just wanted to get people he cared about something to eat.

Life was tough for Southeast Texans. Three weeks before, thousands had opened their hearts and homes to help neighbors. "There were a lot of Katrina people living at the Woodville Inn, but the storm [Rita] closed it." Wolf proudly talked about his county's response to transplanted citizens and his personal outreach, "I'd make a point to go by there [the inn] everyday and visit with them." The entire county participated. Taking turns extending hospitality to Louisiana neighbors, many of whom had stated they would never return to New Orleans. That was how much they loved Woodville. The best cooks in the county brought them home cooking, "I'm talking beans and rice and fried chicken and dumplings." Wolf abruptly stopped listing mouthwatering dishes because we were visiting right through a missed lunch hour.

Not everything after Rita left was negative. "The hurricane brought people closer than they were before and a lot of invisible barriers in Tyler County have been removed." Wolf seeks to maintain a togetherness embraced in the initial post-storm days when people were forced to work side by side. "I feel bad about what happened, but in my heart, I know the good Lord above always has a reason for what He does. Maybe it was to open eyes to see that everybody is created equal."

We talked about life, about love, about being divorced, new topic for me, old for him, as well as dreams and hopes he has for being reelected sheriff. "I'd like to see Tyler County grow more economically and see things stay like they were when Rita first came through. I'd like to see more people working together to help each other. We've already got a loving county. When one person gets down, everybody goes to check on that person." The sheriff's compassion was part of the reason his twin brother always predicted that Jessie Wolf would someday wear the tin star. James Wolf didn't live to see it, but he knew.

"Oh my God," I started, as Wolf waited to hear what could possibly follow, "all these sevens." Then I attempted to show him connections that might look different in his future. "You were chief deputy for seven years, your brother died December 17th and you were only the seventh black sheriff to be elected in the state of Texas." He jumped right in, "And my unit number before I became sheriff was seven."

I didn't mention his size 17 shoe again or the seven grandkids. I think he got it. Tyler County is the epitome of Texas still standing, her residents survivors, as is their sheriff. They are good people who will make the beauty and wonder of it even better.

Better than it was before Rita. And before they helped Katrina evacuees move in and feel at home.

FOUR

I missed the rest of the governor's meeting, but there were still evacuation stories to hear from three different lives with different perspectives linked by destiny on buses from Beaumont bound for an endless and unknown destination nearly 50 hours later.

"At 7 a.m. on Thursday, my neighbor came and knocked on the door and said there was a mandatory order to evacuate," Carl Wortman recounted tidbits of unfolding drama that required swift decisions. Without personal transportation, Wortman got a ride to the designated location. The wait made things slightly more anxious since he wasn't sure what was supposed to happen next. After four hours, a yellow bus picked up passengers gathered in the gym at Smith Middle School.

By lunchtime Thursday, September 22, 2005, the 44-year old man was headed out. Company included elderly couples, single mothers with children, and uncertain folk like him, alone and disabled. Brain damage prevented Wortman from driving, so school buses supplied by the Beaumont Independent School District were his only immediate and available option. Wortman didn't mind.

"We just kept driving around and driving until I had no sense of what time it was while several towns did their best to discourage us from staying." Wortman was dazed about any destination on the circuitous route and baffled by things he overheard, including, "We can't refuel your buses here."

One explanation made sense. One did not. "They would tell us they were low on fuel, while other people were allowed to gas up right in front of us." Wortman had no idea why it seemed some were afforded preferential treatment and wasn't sure if underlying factors, like Katrina fatigue, played a role or not. He knew some on the buses thought skin color accounted for how they were treated. He squelched that lone theory, "I didn't hear anyone making racial slurs, but some of the towns weren't very friendly."

People who bombarded me with questions trying to secure an admission that Beaumont citizens were ill treated because of race, since most of the passengers on the buses were black, will never succeed in getting me to label everyone in East Texas racist. I just don't believe it, will never believe it because there were too many good people willing to help, as had been so convincingly demonstrated in the days before Rita when a majority of residents welcomed Katrina evacuees into all parts of the region.

Wortman, one of the few white men on the buses, doesn't dare call himself an expert on race. Neither do I. But he firmly believed leaders of the convoy "messed up," a fact that didn't help matters. "There were speakers on the buses so we could hear the radio traffic between convoy leaders and some of the things they were saying." He was adamant that one woman, an unidentified person driving one of the lead vehicles in front of the buses, made things worse "by sounding like a drama queen."

She forever "promised things that never came and raised the hopes of everyone onboard," including passengers who were diabetic, older people who needed bathroom breaks and howling young children who had sat bent over in parents' laps too long.

Each time Wortman thought they were going to be let off buses, another announcement would dash passengers' hopes. "I heard the convoy leaders say things like 'We have to press on, endure to the end.'" Sadly, no one knew where the end of the road led or when it would come.

Wortman was confused about exact locations but remembered finally being allowed to exit buses and walk around for a bathroom break. Too late for those who had already soiled themselves. Buses lined the road across from a Diary Queen, a popular chain known far and wide for its locations in mostly rural Texas. It was at this brief stop, according to witnesses, that 81-year old Charlotte Ranger was killed.

Passengers have told different versions of what happened. Wortman didn't personally witness the tragic accident that claimed Ranger. His voice lacked emotion when he confirmed, "I heard she got thrown in the air like a rag doll." Dead, trying to cross a busy highway after a bathroom break to get back on a school bus.

"I was numb, hadn't been to sleep for hours and was just bone-tired." Wortman was sorry for her family, but consumed by an odd feeling of not feeling much at all from being deprived of too many basics. Buses rolled on.

From Thursday afternoon to sometime early Saturday morning, to describe the ride as uncomfortable on hardback seats meant for kids who only have to be on them for short periods, was an understatement. No matter what a passenger does on a school bus seat, it is impossible to find a comfortable position for an almost 50-hour excursion.

Some had lifesaving amenities. Wortman was glad to have air conditioning on his bus. At various bathroom breaks, passengers were allowed to exit because of what Wortman called "random acts of kindness." Like highway crews who let passengers use portable facilities. Another kindness, according to the soft spoken man, was being given something to eat in San Augustine. Wortman says the food ran out before everyone could be fed.

As for the rumors of blocked exits, dogs growling and private citizens standing on porches with shotguns, Wortman did not personally witness any of the more serious allegations. He heard passengers who had gotten off other buses talking about one sheriff with his gun drawn, *urging* the convoy to keep moving. "I have no direct knowledge of this," he stressed, adding there was plenty he wanted to say to the governor's task force. Wortman didn't attend because he never heard about the public hearing at Lamar University. And getting around was problematic.

"What would you want officials to know?" His suggestions echoed testimony from the meeting: better trained convoy leaders and quicker routes. "We were moving like snails, move, stop, move and stop."

The one time Wortman's voice sounded less burdensome was when he spoke about Canton, Texas. "Those people were nice, food was waiting on tables when we got there. They must've worked really hard getting blankets, pillows, and other stuff, with only a few hours notice that we were on the way." After that, Wortman didn't have much more to say, except a thank you to Canton. A 53-year old black woman named Ella Hill had a slightly different take on things. Her vantage as one of the drivers in the convoy was part of the reason.

Hill had a smoker's voice, raspy and tired from work, from living, from things not going better. The widow of two years volunteered to drive. Officials promised she'd be paid upon returning. Hill possessed a commercial license, the experience, and it was an opportunity to help neighbors. Her transport mission was established and seemed doable—get to Lufkin or Nacogdoches, Texas.

Almost as soon as the convoy struck out, the difficulty in that became very clear, "It was so much traffic, by the time we arrived at Lufkin High School, it was already filled with people. And we couldn't go into stores."

That's when the job of driver turned into something else. She and the others then attempted to keep passengers calm, but they were weary, restless, and upset at the news no one would automatically be allowed to use restrooms whenever they needed. "I think race played a big part because this convoy was mostly black." Hill was scared and disappointed by treatment she'd never experienced.

"One officer got on the bus and told me I had to go because lives were being placed in danger." The man spoke in a well-mannered, professional tone. They complied. "When we stopped in Kilgore, there were police everywhere. I didn't know whether we were going to jail, since jail was threatened." The Opelousas, Louisiana native has lived in Beaumont 34 years and loves Texas. She compared what happened to the bus convoy as something "so difficult to describe" that she was just plain scared. Feared for her life.

"Even living in Louisiana, with how racist it can be, I never felt threatened." Hill wasn't sure why people from Beaumont were being treated so indifferently by other Texans. Until Canton. "The one town that did accept us was so great. They made us feel so special, they fed us, we were able to bathe," Hill's voice relaxed into the memory of a welcome moment. "They were just so kind, so loving, and treated us with dignity and respect." They were "colorblind people" who only saw them as tired passengers trying to outrun Rita. Folk who desperately needed help.

Hill disagreed with Wortman about convoy leaders. "I think they were wonderful, there were three that did stick with us throughout the whole ordeal." Hill personally saw people who blocked exits, refused to let them get gasoline, and was quite shaken when she had to follow the same route earlier driven by the first convoy because they knew an elderly woman had been killed on the highway. Buses were originally divided into two convoys of 25 each. "When we came through, her blood was still on the ground."

A woman who voluntarily left her daughter and two grandchildren to help others was fortunate to be in constant communication with her family while driving the uncertain route. Like Wortman, Hill wasn't able to attend the governor's public hearing but had plenty she would've said directly to him. "I think we need to have places to go if we're going to drive a convoy of school buses. Our destinations should be known and people ready for us."

Much of Hill's family remains in Louisiana. She wished out loud that the rest of the country would look closely at how bad things are for Southeast Texans. "I think Katrina is getting the bulk of the attention, but we didn't have the water and the deaths, so I understand why she is."

Eventually, Hill and about 300 others arrived at a minimum security facility in Dallas to rest. She thought the Decker Detention Center was either out of service or had inmates housed in a different area than where they were placed. "What upset me is we didn't have the freedom to come and go." Hill says Beaumont residents were told that once situated they'd be able to walk around and move freely. Some officers prohibited even small pleasures. Like leaving to get items. A curfew and metal detectors didn't make evacuees feel secure. Hill wanted to smoke, but that too was against policy. "My freedom was taken from me." The only privacy some evacuees had in the jail were thin sheets hung between cells. She spoke to the issue of an unprepared government to handle its own crises, "We help all of these other countries. What's taking so long to help us?"

Audrey and Camille were hurricanes that Hill came of age with, storms she knew through her parents' stories and a child's eyes. They had helped neighbors after each hurricane never expecting that one day they would be the ones who needed help. Hill asked me to hang on the line while she searched for a newspaper article. She began reading snippets, prefacing her reason for sharing—it had happened in the city I lived in. Not East Texas. And occurred at the hands of a ranking law officer.

A Dallas County sheriff's captain, she says, had called Rita evacuees "knee-walking, knuckle-dragging Beaumonters." Then came the words, "apes and monkeys." According to Hill, the officer labeled evacuees "ungrateful" for all that had been done for them. Her voice changed many times during our conversation. When she read from the clipped story, saved, so she would never forget, there was only a weary sadness.

My final question: "Would you be willing to retrace the route with me?" Faint hesitation crippled her 'yes,' but she did agree if I really wanted to. I needed to drive it. Especially after a friend who had evacuated reported that some of the same cities where a handful of residents were accused of being hostile had greater numbers of citizens who made handwritten signs displayed in front yards and on porches and in windows. The signs had unforgettable offers like "Our bathroom available. Need water? Stop and rest."

Remembering the kindness of Canton and its citizens, Hill believed that no one should ever use a single event or an isolated incident to paint a region racist, even if elements of a certain incident are racist in nature. Not everyone agreed with her, but many more were grateful to be alive and willing to forgive. Never forget.

22-year old Aron Agustsson was one of Hill's passengers and he was able to attend the evacuation meeting. The Lamar University student, a psychology major, had already done his share of trying to bring attention to the plight of hundreds who rode buses to evacuate as ordered.

"We were told to meet at Smith Middle School, they didn't say where the destination was beforehand," the young man started. At Smith, they were put in the cafeteria for about 40 minutes and then loaded onto buses. Some drivers didn't seem to know where they were going and told passengers they would only be allowed to take two small bags. "They told us specifically not to take water." This would later prove to be a serious misdirection as thirsty people unable to buy liquid refreshment harkened back to the ill-fated instructions.

Agustsson had only been in Beaumont two years and grew up in Houston. He is not a native Texan. Or American for that matter. When I asked what kind of name his was, the derivation, he knew I was being tactful in trying to pin down citizenship. We spoke by phone. Considering my vast broadcast experience, I was unable to gather a trace of any known region in Agustsson's dialect or delivery.

"I'm Icelander," the surprising announcement instantly put me back in elementary school geography. I had to think for a moment about where Iceland is and what kind of road leads from there to Beaumont. Agustsson must've heard my thoughts, "I was the only white on my bus." *Oh, that kind of Icelander.* It took "33 hours before passengers were even allowed to get food and water." What he saw provided an eerie Civil Rights era history lesson.

"It was a mess when we got to some places, the stores and some of the people were so hostile." At least one store had employees who pulled guns in plain sight, another threw boiling hot water as a warning. Agustsson witnessed law enforcement who came armed with dogs, a photo his mind instantly paralleled with buses and Birmingham and hoses and black people. He recalled several stops on the "nightmare ride," including Center, Nacogdoches and San Augustine, where "they had soup for only 200 people." The environment inside the bus, at times, was nearly as volatile as the one outside at the hands of a few unwelcoming would-be hosts.

"There were so many people screaming and crying. Parents wanted water for their children. People just wanted something to eat and to get off the buses." Agustsson's memory of the odyssey sounded frighteningly compartmentalized. He offered details others had only guessed on. "It was 24 hours before we were even allowed to use the restroom," he flatly stated, then again added, "and 33 hours before we got food and water." A snapshot of the bus Agustsson rode, being driven by Hill, provided a sad visual of Texans who had one thing in common—they were trapped on a school bus together and no longer had the luxury of remaining strangers. "There were three newborns, one blind man and another lady who couldn't walk."

The more Agustsson remembered, the more his voice seesawed up and down between anger and sadness. He had, perhaps therapeutically, placed frustrating thoughts in well documented letters to city and state leaders. Only one Beaumont city councilmember had responded with a phone call. "I told her and the council that they were responsible for what happened on those buses." I never needed to see this young man's face, although I hope to one day, after hearing the hurt in his voice.

"44 hours of driving straight," Agustsson paused as if he still didn't believe anyone could stay behind the wheel of a school bus that long, "and our driver finally asked if anyone else had a commercial license." Hill was good, but she was exhausted. Of the convoy leaders, who were in a small truck and minivan ahead of the buses, Agustsson did confirm things they said over the radio could be heard on buses equipped with speakers. "They would say out loud on the radio things like 'Next stop you'll get to go for coffee at McDonald's.'" But that never happened, which endlessly frustrated passengers.

"We passed three Super Wal-Marts that were open and they just kept on driving." No one, especially given that Wal-Mart is usually a 24-hour business loaded with food and water and other needed supplies, understood the decisions to drive by the huge saviors. At different attempted stops, law enforcement circled buses in an intimidating fashion. Both sheriffs and DPS troopers were involved says Agustsson. Of the handful of residents who didn't want passengers getting off buses in their communities, "I don't think they were 100% honest about being full. I understand people were scared. I understand people were nervous." The Icelandic native says the law-abiding group from Beaumont was also scared and nervous, but just wanted help and the chance to buy things they needed. Most had brought money from home.

One man on the same bus with Agustsson would never make the final destination into Canton. He was too ill. "The guy had just gotten a transplant, they agreed to leave him there on the side of the road." This statement sickened Agustsson, who stopped talking for a moment, reflecting on the weakened man left to wait for an ambulance on the side of a lonely stretch of Texas highway. Willing to take his chances anywhere else but on a school bus he had been stranded on. Agustsson heard from his driver that convoy leaders briefly left in search of gas and more water. With or without them, Agustsson quickly proved he was a resourceful young man fellow passengers could count on.

"I was fortunate enough to have a satellite phone and was making calls for others who needed it," he said without a hint of pride. His voice was matter of fact, the same way one would share extra water if he had it. His family worried for his safety. "They were so scared for me," Agustsson talked about being separated from his parents. They had already evacuated and were staying in their luxury RV in Giddings, Texas. His goal was nearby Austin.

"I had paid for a bus ticket [by Internet] on Greyhound, but once I got there they wouldn't honor it." Before Agustsson made it to the Dallas terminal, there were other things he rewound back to for the start of an almost 50-hour bus ride.

"You know, at first, I was just terrified." He countered a statement made at the evacuation hearing about which day leaving became mandatory. "They came on TV, about 6 a.m. that morning (Thursday) and said it's mandatory, not Monday." Once the marathon journey got underway, probably after 14-15 hours, some of the buses started breaking down. Those running had to accommodate extra passengers. A woman with an autistic child got on his bus. Agustsson could not bear to see them stand. So, for nine hours, he stood in their places.

"I was numb standing in the same position for so long, then on the steps." For some 30 hours, the only seat for the only white person on the bus, the only *Icelander* on the bus was in the doorway. Suffering was issued not based on color but perseverance.

In all, Agustsson estimated there were 60 buses. I phoned the Transportation Director at BISD, but he never returned the call. Agustsson, rightfully so, has questions too. His primary concern, stated over and again, was "terrified children and older people who couldn't be provided for." The Lamar University student, if an evacuation were done tomorrow, would like to see two drivers on each bus and highways opened sooner for outbound traffic in one direction.

"Beaumont has two places assigned to them—Lufkin and Nacogdoches." He didn't finish the rest of that sentence with an unspoken question. *Why didn't things work out for them if they went where they were supposed to go?* By now, everyone knows. Katrina people were already there and others from Rita had beaten them there. Any Texas town that opened its doors and facilities was overwhelmed. There wasn't a break for caregivers between the fresh lessons of New Orleans and the evacuation for Rita.

"In Canton, FEMA and Red Cross never showed up. People had to wait four hours in the line for one hot dog." Like the others, Agustsson was relieved to see Canton and friendly faces. The little town was one thing all three Beaumont residents agreed on. "People were nice, they were helping with whatever they could." For that, he remains eternally grateful. Agustsson connected with his fellow passengers, calling relatives for them, freely passing his phone around, standing nine hours so a woman could sit with her child and trying to preserve some semblance of calm. Even talking with the driver, helping Hill keep woke.

Agustsson downplayed any bravery. Or kindness. A simple act of pooling resources brought a laugh, "We used my phone at the shelter [Canton Civic Center] to order more than $2500 worth of pizza and paid for it." Simple things like being able to get off a bus, stretch stiff legs, use a real bathroom, tell jokes and order pizza were slices of life that Aron Agustsson would never again take for granted. He hated to leave his new neighbors, it was a bus ride that bonded them for life.

"After Canton, I separated from my bus." In all that satellite phone usage, Agustsson had the presence of mind to phone friends in Iceland. They, in turn, reached out to the prime minister. Since no one was being allowed back into Beaumont, it was still too dangerous, Agustsson needed to find shelter until he could reach his parents in Giddings. The Iceland Embassy in Washington went to work. Within a matter of hours, embassy officials found one of its native citizens a place to stay in Lindale, Texas.

Agustsson felt sure no one would charge him $5 for a 20-ounce Coke there. His sense of humor never wavered on the disturbing journey, "If you want to know, this wasn't a vacation."

FIVE

His name came dangerously close to being George Washington Woods, III. That's what his mother, Marcelle Mitchell Woods, was insisting upon. But her husband, G. W. Woods, Jr., wasn't about to tag anybody else with the noble presidential moniker he had lived with, then tucked away for preferred initials and the nickname "Shorty."

How ironic then, that decades from his June 1952 birth, George Mitchell Woods faced another man named George, who really was a *living* president. Fate had spared him from having to do so with the historical 'George Washington' ahead of his father's last name. Long before the commanding moment in September 2005, a man who had been "Mitch" his whole life would live up to the Woods name.

Sheriff Mitch Woods came of age surrounded by men in uniform. He paid tribute to humble beginnings, "I grew up a 2nd generation law enforcement officer. My father was a deputy sheriff for many years. I was real lucky as a kid to have a father that bonded with his son by hauling him around when he wasn't working." But dad worked a lot, starting in San Augustine, then Jasper County to work for Sheriff Tommy Mixon. In 1952, the elder Woods moved his family to Jefferson County, where he earned other prestigious assignments, including Special Texas Ranger. Working was in his blood, Shorty Woods did not retire until he was 76.

"I grew up in a time of innocence and came from a real loving household with a mother that didn't work and was always home and a wonderful neighborhood with a lot of boys my age. Our sole existence was to play from daylight to dark, until our moms made us come inside."

Both parents instilled in their three children, Patricia, Mitch, and Julie, a strong work ethic and values like honesty, fairness, and integrity. "My father and my mother are two of the most caring people for other people that I've ever known." The future sheriff of Jefferson County followed closely in the footsteps they made. He obeyed his mother and watched his father, for years, interact with people from all walks of life. Later on, he appreciated the many demonstrations on respect.

"A big deal for us was to go to the fair every year. My dad would see somebody and I'd hear them address him as 'Captain Woods.' He'd stop and talk, they'd shake hands and laugh." Sheriff Woods says only after the person walked away would his father say something like, "That was so-in-so, I arrested him or had to handle him one time for a burglary or a robbery." His dad, "a real man's man," felt comfortable with rich or poor, and treated folk with respect, even those he had arrested.

When we sat and talked, Woods was closing in on his 10-year anniversary as sheriff of Jefferson County. Everyone I spoke with said virtually the same thing about him, using adjectives like loyal, hardworking, dedicated and fair. "Mitch is the real deal," our mutual friend, Billy Rowles, had told me months before. Not only did I trust Billy, there were fine descriptions contained in my own heart following each encounter with Mitch Woods.

"I like it here," he says when asked if Southeast Texas might always be home. The 53-year old sheriff was born in Port Arthur, the same city his law enforcement career began. Local schools with historic names like Woodrow Wilson and Thomas Jefferson provided the backdrop for social activities like football and integration, both of which he didn't dwell on. It wasn't that Woods ignored race. His focus, with few black students, was squarely aimed on what his parents had instilled: treat everyone the same.

Once Woods left the security of a loving home and community, race finally had his attention. "I went to the Army in 1972 and I think that was the first time that I really began to sense, experience, or feel some of the racial tension that existed." After serving his country two years, Woods returned home to work for the police department. "At that time, I was introduced to a part of Port Arthur I never knew existed."

There were two distinct sides of the city divided by Houston Avenue. Street addresses started with 100 East and 100 West for each section. The east side of town turned out to be where most Anglos lived, while the other part of Houston Avenue became the West Side, popular terminology for "the black community." At its heyday, there were about 70,000 residents. Today, the words have a different meaning since half of the nearly 54,000 citizens in Port Arthur are black.

Eager to prove himself a good young officer, Woods accepted the assignment for what it was—an invaluable learning experience. Little did he realize, the black side of Port Arthur that he "never knew" was about to dramatically alter his life. The innocence of a well loved Texas boy who believed everybody grew up like he did was about to face its biggest challenge. The same little Port Arthur kid who didn't know he was poor because he was happy and nurtured, got an instant education in race that graduated a quick study.

"Early on, I hadn't been with the police department a year, I was involved in an arrest, a shooting that resulted in the death of a black man that I had gone to school with." Woods was not the shooter. The sheriff drifted back to the scene where the incident had started as a very minor infraction, then quickly escalated, by the detained man, into a major deal. Faced with resisting arrest and assaulting an officer, he escaped from the police station. Woods says a gun was "brought into play" and the man was shot in the back as he ran out.

"It caused a huge racial explosion in Port Arthur," one Woods defined as a catalyst, an act that brought a range of emotions to the surface. He was suddenly caught in the middle of a volcano simmering with ill feelings the black community had probably suppressed for years. "I had the misfortune of being involved in that."

Usually, Woods takes his time, is never rushed from the slow Southern drawl. That day, his voice was thicker and slower, accompanied by genuine sadness, as he continued to describe what followed: a grand jury investigation, burned buildings in downtown Port Arthur, huge protests in front of City Hall and the police department, and a $5 million dollar lawsuit. One thing helped diffuse the situation and calm a majority of the residents.

"Looking back on it now, and also having worked in the District Attorney's office, I realize what an unusual and monumental thing it was." When the DA allowed a grand jury monitor to sit in on secret proceedings, it offered the community a chance to understand every phase of the investigation, particularly because the man chosen was a prominent African American attorney from Beaumont. Then-DA Tom Hanna appointed Elmo Willard grand jury monitor. He heard all the testimony, saw all the evidence, facts that served to have a calming effect on the community. But Woods added, "Don't get me wrong, it didn't calm everyone."

The tragedy in December 1974 made Woods seriously reconsider his career choice. The rookie cop had been on the force less than a year and was already involved in a high profile shooting that tore the city right down the middle of Houston Avenue, an invisible racial line disguised as a busy thoroughfare. Woods found his balance. He made up his mind to stick with the job he loved and Port Arthur became a significant moment.

"I think the time I spent working, 13 years, at the Port Arthur Police Department, besides the influence of my father and mother, more than anything else, the experience that I got working there has ultimately defined who I am, what I believe and how I do my business, my profession." Woods spent the next three years working patrol division in the evenings. Ironically, it was another black man who changed his life again.

African American officers were rare, but Port Arthur had a handful, including the man Woods spent the bulk of the next 36 months riding with. An older man who sported giant paws for hands named Arthur Andris. Woods' hearty laugh soon returned, "He was affectionately known by the nickname of Scatterbrain," which turned out to be 'Scat' for short. There was no way to know where the story was headed, particularly after an admission from Woods that he wasn't sure he could make it all the way to the end without getting emotional.

Officer Andris had started his career working in the water department for the city. There was a former police chief named Douglas who had offered Andris the job as officer and he didn't hesitate. After all, Garland Douglas was the same man Arthur Andris had worked for when he took care of the chief's horses. The two men bonded and Douglas kept his eye out for Andris.

Quite often black officers got together to talk about how different their experiences within the department were and on the streets. Woods offered names from another era, a rich history in the Port

Arthur Police Department, Sgt. Wesley Godfrey and Sgt. Corliss Branch, the officer Woods eventually replaced in the detective division when Branch retired. Of the partner the sheriff so fondly discussed, a bomb dropped without warning. "He couldn't read and write." *How did Woods know this?* "You learn everything about someone when you work that close together. When you spend eight hours together in a patrol car, there are no secrets. You learn everything about each other." He knew Arthur Andris was a smart man, one who didn't require book learning to understand people, how to deal with them. Andris didn't need degrees to possess the street smarts necessary for intuitive and demanding police work.

"Some officers didn't like riding with him because when you rode with him, you had to do all the paperwork, all the reports," Woods kept going, "I, on the other hand, would rather ride with him than anyone else because he was so savvy about everything." While 'Scat' couldn't read or write, he was the man Woods credited with teaching him more than anyone else he had ever worked with. "And he was fun, I just loved him. There's no other way to describe him other than fun."

Over time, Woods kept encouraging Andris to learn to read, try night school. He knew his partner was sharp. The big man owned a few rent houses and a little restaurant, a barbecue pit on Houston Avenue. There was nothing wrong with Andris' math skills and people warmed to him, a benefit that didn't hurt. "He knew everybody, as a result, I came to know everybody too." The partnership ended, the friendship remained.

When Woods moved on to the detective division, Scat was finally put on days. His former partner saw it as an opportunity to enroll in school. Finally, Andris did just that. Only he didn't make a grand announcement of it, just quietly set out to learn how to read. Woods called it "one of the most touching things" that ever happened to him as an adult. It was the way Scat decided to tell him that stands as a beacon in the sheriff's mind.

One day Woods was riding in downtown Port Arthur when a big baby blue Cadillac with a white vinyl top pulled up beside him. It was Scat blowing and gesturing for Woods to stop. Woods lowered the bass in his voice and gave his best Scat impression, " 'Hey boy, pull over boy!' He always called me 'boy.'" Woods obeyed and parked on the one-way seawall stretch. Excited, Andris had something to show Woods. Satchel in hand, the extra large man took the passenger seat. He was wearing a favorite dashiki.

Keeping Woods in suspense, Andris first pulled out a fresh can of chewing tobacco, took the lid off and used his mammoth hands to dip half, which was his habit. "He got that Skoal all ready, got it in his mouth and then he pulled out of that satchel a Dick and Jane reader and started reading to me out of that Dick and Jane reader in the car on the seawall." It was at this exact moment, after sharing a preserved and treasured memory, that the sheriff of Jefferson County stopped talking.

A voluntarily muted voice and deep sigh clearly told another story. Mitch Woods had transported himself back to young manhood, stationed on the seawall in Port Arthur. The man who had been his mentor was there smiling and welcoming him home. Then I was there too as seconds of silence between us equaled the patrol days from a lifetime ago for a rookie officer remembering a great brother. *What happened to Scat* wasn't a question that needed words. "He later died with cancer."

This was one story that George Mitchell Woods did not have to tell. Because he did, it only heightened my profound respect and admiration for him, his character and integrity. More quiet followed. More emotion unspoken. No questions. No words, until, "He was one of the best friends I ever had." Woods did not need to offer more proof that Arthur Andris impacted his life forever, but served up another humorous 'Scat' story before repeating something for the record, a fact he deemed important enough to say again. "He was one of the best friends I ever had, a guy that I learned so much from."

What Woods learned has been passed on, multiple times, whether as a parent to his three sons, or mentor to protégées. The proud father lights up most when talking about 32-year old Clint, Jason, who is 28, and 20-year old Tyler. Anyone who has ever noted a striking resemblance between the sheriff and a prosecutor in the Jefferson County District Attorney's office will have passed Clint Woods in the halls, practicing a love for justice and upholding a legacy started long ago by the Woods men in his family.

Another son has expressed interest in a law enforcement career.

Of the youngest, Tyler, Sheriff Woods says, "I'll support him in whatever, but have encouraged him to finish college and get his degree." Jason is the politician in the family, "a man about town" who runs his own business and lives in the region. Woods has his hands on the judicial mantle being passed on to his sons, given by a loving father.

One glance around the sheriff's Beaumont office and a visitor is ushered back in time to an era filled with lawmen who wore hats and ties, cowboys in boots, cowboys in suits and color pictures of the next generation. There is an arresting photo of four men decked out in black tuxedos. Woods and his three sons are at the wedding of firstborn, Clint, who had tapped his father best man.

In the three terms Woods has been sheriff, several things on the agenda have been accomplished, but there are still items he would like to finish. Woods has already decided to run again in 2008, doesn't ever think about retiring and will probably try to break the record set by the not-so-tall man who established the bar. "I enjoy what I do, law enforcement is who I am, it's what I do, it's my purpose." If there's anyone who understands that mission, it's Zena Stephens.

Ask Woods and he has no problem rattling off a few of the reasons he made Stephens his chief deputy over the law enforcement division. Years before hiring her, Woods had taught Stephens at the police academy and was impressed from the jump. Later, when she worked for the Beaumont Police Department, Woods says she "had a lot on the ball" and he followed her career through the media, which was fairly easy since she had made a name for herself as a spokesperson and by doing news segments for Crime Stoppers. When Stephens dropped off the radar, Woods assumed it was a change of assignment.

After being elected sheriff, destiny reconnected him to Stephens, who was no longer in law enforcement. "I think I probably asked if she missed it and she told me that she did." A short time later, a position for an administrative assistant in the Internal Affairs division came open. Woods quickly dispatched Ron Hobbs, his Narcotics Task Force Commander, to reach out to Stephens, maybe dangle the silver badge. "The rest is history. She was interested, I was interested."

When the sheriff hired Stephens, it was with the thought that, ultimately, she'd be an administrator in his office, but certain "law enforcement bills" had to be paid first. Stephens proved herself by working hard and was promoted to captain, working in the Port Arthur office over the warrant division. "She got visibility in that office, in that community," Woods explained. In time, Stephens was brought back to Beaumont, where "she has done a wonderful job."

Woods is adamant that his choice was based on qualifications Stephens had, her diligence and her professionalism. "Zena would've done a wonderful job no matter what color she was. She wasn't chosen for her color, but for being who she is." Being African American and female—a black woman—Stephens has brought a different perspective to her position and passion to the Jefferson County Sheriff's Office.

No matter what Woods tells me, I don't know another white sheriff in Texas who has a black woman for his chief deputy. *And I know plenty of the 254 sheriffs in our state.* The working relationship Woods and Stephens have, the mutual respect, and worthwhile goals for the department are proof that law enforcement in the Lone Star state has come a long way. Still, there is more work to do, more progress that beckons. I have only known Stephens a short time, but she is called to this tough work, just as her boss is. They have a certain chemistry, undeniable in its magnetic ability to inspire 400 employees who work for the department.

Mitch Woods knows more about race than he has admitted. Like the earlier version of himself, he just doesn't dwell on it.

* * *

"It takes about 36 hours to get everybody out of here." An evacuation process is "a trigger that must be pulled" when there is a window of opportunity for that kind of pressing timeframe. Woods' experience with hurricanes comes from on-the-job training and his degree in life. Before Rita, he had been through evacuations working in Port Arthur and as a child surviving Hurricanes Audrey and Carla.

"We should've called a mandatory evacuation 24 hours earlier than we did," Woods revisited tense times when officials waited for Rita to come ashore. There was a meeting late Wednesday, one that

Woods felt sure when everyone left there was little doubt an evacuation would be called Thursday morning. Even in hindsight, the sheriff didn't toss out armchair strategy, just his humble opinion that a necessary 36-hour window was sliding shut. "I don't want to second guess the mayors and the judge, but had I been making that decision I would've called for the evacuation Wednesday rather than Thursday."

As officials gathered information, monitored the storm, made plans for the evacuation, the path of the storm kept changing. "I think any reluctance was holding out hope against hope that sometime during the night Rita would take a turn further west or east and spare us." As the hours neared landfall, odds of that happening were slim indeed. The best thing to do was get people out of harm's way and brace for the worst. Horrible images from Katrina, less than one month before, vividly burned in the collective conscience of Jefferson County residents who fled by the thousands. Work for Woods kicked into a higher, more stressful gear.

"Friday morning, at about 3:30, I got a phone call at my residence. I had already sent my son out the day before, got him evacuated, and I was awakened by the Marine Coast Guard to tell me they were telling everyone the storm had changed directions. They were expecting landfall at High Island, which put us right in the direct path of that thing." He fired bullet-vowels much faster than his normal Texas twang. The significance in Rita's new target was both personal and professional for Woods since he could "throw a rock" from High Island to his own home. He often described his property, located in the Southwest corner of the county, as a place with nothing between him and the Gulf of Mexico but a few barbed wire fences.

Sleep was finished for the sheriff. He got up thinking one thing: "Well, this is it. I'm fixing to lose everything I own here." Woods was convinced, at least at that moment, he would return, after Rita, to find a concrete slab where his house used to be. "It was quite a sobering moment for me." Sure, there were other times Woods had left his house for other storms, left it boarded up, protected, insured, nailed down, and confident that, for the most part, his bit of brick and wood and mortar would weather the storm. But Rita was the first time he had ever gone through the experience of leaving his residence and thinking it wouldn't be there when he got back.

The sickening feeling that sunk in reminded him to retrieve things like important papers, irreplaceable photographs, clothes and other items. Woods packed quickly. His sense of humor kicked in when he recalled some of what he had packed, "Typical male, I loaded up all of my guns." Woods threw the guns, documents, and a few work clothes in his truck and left. Back at his Beaumont office something else "sunk in." Woods always wore a suit to work. In the rush, he had packed a "tactical bag" that contained only casual work clothes.

"It dawned on me, 'Oh my Lord, this thing is going to hit and wipe everything I own away, but I'll still be sheriff, and still be expected to *look* like sheriff.'" With his more expensive clothes in the house he had said goodbye to, the lawman who wears a suit everyday couldn't believe his forgetfulness. "My suits, my dress shirts, my shoes, everything still there." Armed with a large duffel bag, he went all the way back to get them. Sheriff Woods is handsome, but there's not a vain bone in his body. He wasn't worried about what he would look like or have on in the aftermath of Rita, as opposed to presenting a fragmented normalcy to troops who would be monitoring his every move, word, and action—*after* landfall.

Woods surveyed his closet, pulling and tearing items out, mashing suits and stuff in the bag. "As I walked by this room I call the office in my house, I had bought my son a new computer, that computer was just sitting there." Woods paused just long enough to entertain the logic that after Rita, there would still be college and Tyler would still need his brand new computer. "I unplugged the computer and the printer and put all that in my truck." Each time Woods was set to push off, he remembered something else that shouldn't be left behind. He loaded a four-wheeler, thinking it might come in handy for search and rescue.

Back at the sheriff's office once more, Woods rested a little easier. Employees were busy doing a number of preparatory things. He was swamped too. But a baby suddenly cried. Woods heard her purr in the back of his mind, "Oh my God, my Harley is still out there in that garage." The motorcycle, "my road king, my baby," was not about to be left behind. Ron Hobbs gave him a lift to the house, a third time charmed ride had the sheriff Forever Two Wheeling his way back to Beaumont on a Harley. "The people at the Port were kind enough to let me put my Harley in the belly of that ship."

The entire time Woods was going back and forth, doing a thousand things, answering three cell phones that rang nonstop, he was formulating secure plans—one to house department employees and another to relocate his jail population. "That's a big task for us, before Rita we probably had 1100 inmates." Since it had been done before, Woods was sure his team would do it well again. The relocation plan, set in motion ahead of the evacuation, rolled right along.

"Early on, we started preparing a list of all the classifications of the inmates that are in custody, what their charges are. Then we get with the judges and try to release as many as we can on some sort of recognizance bond." Trimming the jail population by issuing personal release bonds did get the county down to 900, the number that would have to be evacuated, along with everything else that needed to be moved, stored, and protected. A few years earlier, Woods and his department heads realized that the "lifeblood of the jail" was its valued computer system. Everything was on computer—records, files, property information—everything. If those records were lost or destroyed, it would be "horrible for us." Enter plastic.

Containers that resembled giant portable vats were built specifically to house computers, monitors, records, the "lifeblood" that was ready on short notice to go with employees. All locked up in sturdy trailers. Inmates moved, computers hauled to higher, drier ground, Woods saved the most precious cargo for last—first responders who work for the Jefferson County Sheriff's Department.

"After Hurricane Katrina and all of that, we wound up with a bunch of leftover cots, so they were stored at the jail. Instead of 'going to the mattresses' like the mafia wars, we went to the cots." Woods ordered those same cots brought to the courthouse and made final preparations to shelter employees there. Everybody got a cot and things from home they would need to survive "for a few days." By noon Friday, in short order, all of these things had been accomplished. It didn't mean anyone could relax and wait for Rita. The work went on, strategies were planned, brainstorming sessions produced positive results, food was wheeled in, traffic was routed, painstakingly slow, out of the path of Rita. The hum in the courthouse was anxious excitement, busy anticipation. Like another George who sang about being a fireman, George Mitchell Woods had baby blazes popping up that needed putting down.

"I called a meeting with the other police chiefs and all the other law enforcement in the county at our emergency operations center and because I knew there was a plan by a lot of the emergency management people to leave Jefferson County and go to Hardin County over to Lumberton." It wasn't that Woods was opposed to moving his department to another county, if absolutely necessary. In fact, Lumberton was a tried and proven strategy utilized in the past for staging equipment and personnel out of the floodplain. There was a solid belief by many that Beaumont would take a direct hit, resulting in a tidal surge that would have Interstate 10 under water.

Apparently, the sheriff wasn't buying it, and the voice of Shorty Woods, never far from his son's mind, hit where he lived: "You just don't leave here during a hurricane." The idea that Woods would abandon his turf and go to Hardin County was not an option. "I'm the sheriff of Jefferson County, and my place is here," he expressed his intentions to those at the emergency meeting. It was his iron way of being true to a legacy of law enforcement. "Cops are not supposed to run."

Woods would not be persuaded otherwise. Nor would he back down from the decision that the bulk of his people would remain at the courthouse, right where they belonged, with him. Anyone who entered that meeting with the notion that Woods had no plans for protecting his equipment, assets, and personnel, left knowing better.

Woods had other reasons for staying behind. He knew, in the long history of Texas hurricanes and storms, there had never been a time when *everyone* evacuated. Woods felt strongly that people who decided to stay, whether or not they made the wrong judgment calls, "were going to need us." When Woods hunkered down, "I'm not leaving Jefferson County," there wasn't a human being on the planet who could've moved him to change positions. He was done talking.

"This notion of shutting down operations to move to higher ground is a relatively new concept," one the sheriff doesn't understand. Every bit of the "cop's cop" came out in Woods' voice when he served up verbal castor oil hidden in fudge to chocolate lovers: "The same people who are proponents of that thinking, that seem to be so concerned about the safety and welfare of these law enforcement officers and firefighters and other employees, I wish they shared that same concern for their safety *everyday*." Officers are more likely to be killed in a traffic stop, when they're out alone, than by a hurricane.

Next, Woods met with administrative staff, supervisors and patrol. Everyone had been placed on 12-hour shifts on the law enforcement side of the house. It was a necessary tool, the ability to "utilize all law enforcement personnel to deal with an emergency." Woods had some of the most experienced and best at his side, including all his deputy chiefs, Zena Stephens, George Miller, Ron Hobbs, and Walter Billingsley. Deputy Brent Weaver handled communications, but also floated wherever Woods needed him.

The Sheriff's Office is comprised of several divisions, including corrections, services, warrants, vice/narcotics and law enforcement. Rita preparation meant redefining chain of command, as she took issue with those who failed to respect equalization skills. "What happens in an emergency situation like Rita, corrections, all our law enforcement people become, those specialized jobs pretty well get put on hold," Woods confirmed.

If a deputy normally worked as a detective in criminal investigations, Rita probably sent him/her out into the community, in uniform, to patrol. It gave Woods and his staff the ability to assign greater concentration of manpower to those situations that required such. Half of the employees took days, the other half nights. Everyone knew the mission statement from Services, which covered everything from budget issues to crime lab, from the K-9 Unit to aviation. And Rita.

"The Jefferson County Sheriff's Office Services Division will provide support to all areas in order to assist each unit in accomplishing their mission." That mission required every man and woman do their best. The sheriff expected no less.

Jefferson County, in the hours before Rita, gathered all its resources and planned for a fight, both during and after the storm. Woods had access to two military sealift ships at the Port of Beaumont, they provided a secure place for rolling equipment and vehicles. Captain Kevin Brooks and crew were also aboard The Cape Victory and crew members were positioned on the Cape Vincent. At the same time, Woods made a series of evaluations on the lives of his men and women. They patrolled all areas of the county, including the more populated cities, up until the time it was no longer safe to remain out.

"I made a decision early on to leave that decision up to my field supervisors on patrol, for them to make the call about when it was too dangerous to be out on the street." When Jefferson County continued to respond to 9-1-1 calls coming in for agencies that had stopped taking them, supervisors would soon make their respective decisions. Besides the sheriff's department, two other law enforcement agencies stayed through the storm: Beaumont Police and Lamar University Police.

"We were responding to calls in Port Neches, Groves, Nederland, Port Arthur, as well as out in the county." Rita hadn't even arrived, but citizens who stayed behind, for whatever reasons—financial, physical, personal or plain stubborn—were deluging the emergency call system for help.

"Late that evening, two of my deputies went to Sabine Pass and got an 80-year old man out of a house down there." It was a daring rescue. The elderly man had run out of oxygen and was still hooked to his breathing machine when officers arrived. "At that point, during the rescue, the storm had already gotten bad." It was one of the few times, in the hours before Rita, that Woods verbally expressed worry. He was concerned about whether deputies could even get into Sabine Pass, because Highway 87, quite often, flooded out whenever the tide got extremely high. Not only did Lt. Todd Richards and Deputy Bruce Koch make it there and back safely, around the same time, the officers rescued another man and took both to Christus St. Elizabeth Hospital, making sure the frightened men were out of harm's way. It was definitely time to come into the house. Pull back.

Half of the patrol cars had already been called in. They were past the danger point. Some did end up in Lumberton where a lot of other agencies had gone. "I sent them up there because on the outside chance there was something to this tidal surge and we did get flooded in, at least they'd be able to respond to un-flooded areas at the north end of the county." Woods sent them with the understanding that as soon as the storm passed and they were able, "to get back to the county." *He meant it.*

Police cars not housed on the ships were moved to an elevated parking garage at St. Elizabeth. "We have an Armored Personnel Carrier that is amphibious." Woods strategically positioned it, along with a Hummer, at the courthouse, in case they needed to ferry deputies to their cars at the hospital. A few school buses remained in front of the courthouse that had been used to evacuate inmates from the Jefferson County Correctional Facility on Highway 69. "I had positioned our boats and one very large boat we couldn't get on the ships, but it was in a warehouse at the Port." Woods, and the entire department, was prepared to greet Rita. Two smaller boats were set to launch, and two helicopters were also positioned on the ships with full crews.

"I had all my SWAT teams at the courthouse. Everybody else, except the crews to operate positioned equipment, were bunked down at the courthouse." The 18-member SWAT team prepared just as it would to face any hostile situation. Rita put everyone in crisis mode, on high alert, and they were ready inside the Jefferson County Courthouse. It was a structure with history, a house with character, happy with newfound attention and respect. The walls nearly spoke. Built sturdy, originally, as a fallout shelter, a designated Cold War facility residents would be safe from if bombs fell. Everyone knew, nasty Rita was birthing a big windy bomb out in the Gulf. The reliable courthouse had weathered a few storms, the sheriff never left his office there. Partners to the end, he looked at his old friend, "I was confident that the building would be here." He had no fears about the safety of his employees inside the Jefferson County Courthouse.

But some of them certainly did.

SIX

"I realized, early on, that once we got all our inmates evacuated and the corrections staff were present in the building, there was a lot of anxiety, a lot of fear. It was evident."

It hadn't dawned on Woods, until that moment, that while he had been through storms and hurricanes before, there were dozens in the department who hadn't. "I walked around in the building and talked to them, tried to comfort those that were in need of a little comfort, just tried to reassure them that everything was going to be okay." Woods could easily see, understandably so, tense faces afraid for their families, concerned about well being, lifelong property, maybe possessions. They were also thinking of neighbors, who had, hours before, evacuated, leaving behind a Southeast Texas ghost town.

Sgt. Dennis Knight, unofficial chaplain for the department, held a prayer service in the jury impaneling room for anyone who wanted to attend. Quite a few of them did. Then, Rita showed up.

"It was dark, you couldn't see a whole lot, but you knew it was bad," Woods says. By then, the electricity was gone. A darkened courthouse and city were being ravished by a scorned woman mad as hell that the welcome mat was pulled inside, not caring about all that was done in preparation for her arrival. "You could hear it," Woods intimately knew from past sounds and past furies. There were probably several inside the courthouse still praying, who wouldn't agree with Woods that it was a little like a serious thunderstorm. Except it "lasted a lot longer." Spoken like a true hurricane survivor.

By 3 a.m. Saturday morning, the eye of the storm "passed right over the courthouse." Woods had been walking around, and knew, instinctively, even in the dark, something just didn't feel right. Then he realized it was the dead calm of a nocturnal silence. It hit. "The wind died down suddenly and I jokingly said, 'Well, it's all over, let's go outside and see what's happened.'" The man he offered a smidgen of humor to, Deputy Chief Ron Hobbs, agreed with the next Woods assessment, "It must be the eye." They went up to the third floor to seek out thick paned windows that hadn't blown out, nor were they likely to, windows that overlooked the front parking lot. "It was pitch black dark."

Woods found the route, blindfolded by only a flashlight, to the District Attorney's office. The two men positioned themselves in front of a scenic view they could not see, but were able to visualize from a working photograph made possible by longevity and habit. At times, when a flicker of lightning gave form to the cerebral movie, the two men would snatch crumbs of sight from a dark vicious storm. Five minutes after they took up their posts, the lying wind, which had been eerily calm, busy contemplating where it would wreak havoc first, came roaring back from the North to assure everyone in the Jefferson County Courthouse that Rita had only paused to catch a more intense breath. The female fighter had not begun to spit and flail and kick and scratch.

"It was like flipping on a switch," Woods recalled. The growling girl that had been blowing in a southeasterly direction before calming down on a mini break, suddenly remembered she wasn't done and whipped back around North by Northwest. Imagine a very large woman, the old-fashioned opera singer, belting out a tune that only she can sing after a tremendous warm up, an exercise of sucking in enough breath to hit the high notes and command respect of all in her audience. Rita was ready to sing to the tune of accompanying winds up to 130 mph.

Woods and Hobbs didn't see much in the turnaround, couldn't see, but their ears provided all the scary sound effects any Gulf Coast resident needed to know it had been more than necessary to evacuate and protect as many lives as possible. "It was ferocious when it came back blowing at us," Woods shook his head. They watched a utility pole fall down right in front of the courthouse. They were only able to see it in brilliant flashes and tiny snaps made by Rita's giant bulb. In her darkness, and in their collective own, two blind men had their other senses instantly sharpened, forced into deeper territory, to vividly record chunks of once immovable items blow down the street. Others crashed hard into the building. Tears of sideway rain begged to be let in, almost as if water craved separation from Rita, the ugly girl it came to the dance with. *She's making us do it.* Every few seconds, here and there, awesome light shows produced eerie fireworks by Mother Nature. They watched a mess in the making, swirling around, but felt the old courthouse hold her unshakable ground.

When Rita's warm breath ran out of Gulf Air, she calmed down, leaving the light work for a trained ally: powerful wind gusts. "At first light, the wind still blowing and raining, our guys loaded up in the APC and Hummer and hit the streets." There was enormous damage, limbs and lines down, not the massive flooding some had predicted. Streets were passable. It was time to get to work and assess the situation. The Sheriff's Office was ready. Chief George Miller knew from early planning sessions, as did, Chief Stephens, Chief Hobbs and Chief Walter Billingsley, that the county's 250,000 residents were eager to hear damage reports and official word on when they might return.

Law enforcement dominoes started to fall. Equipment had to be unloaded from ships. Guys in Lumberton had to hightail it back. The wind had to exit post-Rita, die down a bit before the ships would lower ramps for vehicles to be rolled off. Deputies with vehicles "fanned out" and the sheriff made his way South. He had already gotten word that his house was still standing. "I was relieved, it made me feel good." That feeling sustained Woods for another four days, the time it took to actually go home. See the paradise he had compartmentalized and never thought of again after retrieving the faithful Harley.

"I don't mind telling you I went through some emotional times," he acknowledged, "after seeing Beaumont." At the same time, the sheriff knew things could've been much worse. There was a saving grace that resulted in no initial fatalities. Because Rita came so quickly on the heels of Katrina, everyone had nightmarish images of a grief and suffering that did not discriminate, randomly chose its company. Woods has no doubt that "the fear factor" helped move residents. "It was the largest evacuation of people we've ever gotten out." Folks heeded the message. Houses can be rebuilt, humans can not.

Woods rode around Jefferson County, to take stock, to reflect, to protect, to help, and to document the awe of a hurricane moment that lasted for hours. He saw the violent destruction that spared all who remained behind. There was no time to be concerned with his own house—its missing shingles, caved in garage and other minor brick injuries. He was, however, very worried about the boyhood home his parents still lived in.

"The last place I went was in Groves to my mom and dad's house. I was scared to go there." Woods wasn't sure what he would find and thoughts consumed him on the snail's ride over. They had trees he had climbed and hidden behind as a child—one large pecan tree right near the structure and a huge oak tree in the backyard. "I was so afraid that one of those trees would be on that old house." Woods cautiously picked his way through town, avoiding pockets of water and debris, slowly driving, muddling his way around. Finally, he turned down the little dead end street and held his breath.

"I saw all the trees across the road, and I thought 'Ah man, this ain't gone be good.'" He drove even slower, not wanting to, but desperately wanting to, see. And then he did. The house was fine. The innocence from youth was still standing. Woods was relieved. Like other Jefferson County residents, little things, in the initial hours of an unpredictable aftermath, were welcome blessings they could cling to. Woods sat on the front porch so moved by the moment that a pent up dam finally, and briefly, burst.

Disturbed and delighted by a familiar sound, Woods glanced up to see hummingbirds at home in their feeder. He called his mother, the woman whose maiden name stood between his and his father's, and told her everything was alright. Woods not only believed that, he was confident it was true.

"There wasn't anybody in Jefferson County untouched by Rita," he started, "damage was from one end to the other." Sabine Pass, being that it is located right on the Gulf, did suffer some high water that other places didn't get. But everyone in Southeast Texas had stories to tell, stories of courage, stories of fear, rescue and relief, heartache and pain, joy and grief, stories of tasks performed, tasks shirked. Everyone in counties from Jasper to Newton from Orange to Tyler from Hardin to Jefferson, and parishes like Cameron, cities like Lake Charles, Louisiana, and even a few places beyond those geographical borders, embraced an overriding thesis they could all agree on: Rita had taken her best devastating shot and they were still standing.

Resilient residents, along with the sheriff, with homes and lives in the path of the storm, knew they were going to be alright even if many had no clue as to when they might feel that way. Or if they had homes that weren't flattened or redecorated by trees of oak, pine, cedar and pecan. Others were more secure that they had temporary quarters the state of Texas planned to return them to—900 Jefferson County inmates who had been relocated and cooped up with more than 450 prisoners at a facility designed to house 500.

Without basic services like power and water, the inmates wanted out. A disturbance-in-the-making, described by some as "a near riot," was quelled by the Swat Team before it could develop into a full blown situation. There were no injuries to officers or the inmates. It was critical to move them as soon as humanly possible, back to the same jail on Highway 69 the sheriff always stressed as being run by "a bunch of great people."

Woods knew, like the boy who watched his father issue respect to men he'd "handled" on opposite sides of the law, that same father, now 86-years old, expected him to remember, that as sheriff, inmates deserved respect. Woods recognized his "duty to take care of them, care, custody, and control." Each inmate made it back without incident.

Then our conversation turned to that little matter of what George Woods said to George Bush. The sheriff, according to my sources, has never publicly revealed what he whispered in the ear of the 43rd president of the United States.

"I could tell the way things were being positioned that we were going to get a presidential visit," Woods explained how he knew before the official announcement. Gov. Perry had surveyed damage the Sunday after Rita, it would seem perfectly natural that President Bush check on residents in his home state. The same place a lot of Texans were intimately familiar with "W" from his other titles: businessman in West Texas, part owner of the Texas Rangers, and finally, governor before Mr. Perry.

Even though the sheriff expected to have his guess confirmed, he put it on the back burner, if on the stove at all. A ton of other fish was being fried. And it was hot as hell, weather and stove. At one point, Woods had to stop and ask about the full scale merger not listed on any office calendar, "What day is it?" He was blowing and going, at the helm of a recovery frustrated citizens desperately wanted speeded up. A few others wanted to flat out misbehave, but Woods wasn't having it.

One of my favorite Mitch Woods stories came from Angel San Juan. Right after Rita had slapped and cursed the Jefferson County Courthouse all she could, slinking out of town upon losing the match, the sheriff emerged from the old bomb shelter ready to work. He never looked back. Woods ordered the flag hoisted to its rightful position with six words: "This courthouse is open for business."

The people who kept it open, kept things going are true Texas heroes. First responders who never get medals or accolades. Not all of their names are known. Most of their stories will simply be handed down to generations of family members proud of what they did one faraway September in the year of our Lord, Two-Thousand and Five. I am proud to have met a few of them and heard some of their incredible stories, including one about a woman named Patricia Angelle. Woods is a thousand times prouder, his department went above, around, and beyond, forever erasing the so-called "line of duty."

"Some of our dispatchers had been there for five days," Woods started, "in the heat, with no air conditioning, doing more than anybody could ask." Again, Woods' voice sped up, a rare occurrence kin to a verbal heartbeat that pumped quicker at the pride he felt in what kind of employees worked for his department.

Before Rita, anyone with special needs or dire situations had been allowed to leave and take care of their families. The announcement was made, as Woods would say, "early on," and granted to employees who *absolutely needed to leave.* They were released from the uncertain duty of pre- and post-Rita grueling labor, physical and mental. No one argued that Angelle, a corrections officer, didn't have a unique circumstance that made her eligible for exiting just ahead of Rita's arrival. If she had wanted to.

"It was told to me that her mother passed away and jail administrators told her she could go, take care of family," Woods recalled. But Angelle refused. She said no because her mother had always taught her that when she was needed at work, she was supposed to stay at work. There wasn't even time in a grief stricken moment, born while an evacuation was underway, for Angelle to properly break down. The most normal thing a human can do, as anyone is likely to with the loss of a beloved mother they would never see again in life. Officer Angelle felt sure that her mother would be proudest if she stayed to help co-workers and others who needed her. She expressed conviction in a potentially crippling situation: she could do nothing for her mother right then except stand up for her co-workers. To call her boss impressed would be a malnourished understatement.

"It just touched my heart in a way that I've never had an employee affect me since I've been sheriff," he says. During his "walkabouts" in the building, just ahead of Rita, Woods saw Angelle comforting another young woman who was crying about her father. Angelle unselfishly conducted herself as so many of her fellow employees did.

"It was clear that we all pulled together," Woods says. That camaraderie and spirit of giving has not faded with the months of cleanup and filing away of all things bad and ugly left by the storm. Plenty of good came from Rita too. "If there's one thing I can say I do not like about being sheriff is the fact that the Sheriff's Office is so big," Woods reflected on a career that had always allowed him to get to know everyone he worked with. Until he became sheriff of a spread out 400-person department. Until the hurricane.

"Rita gave us the opportunity to all live together, work together, and eat, be confined together." An amazing law enforcement bond was formed amidst tension, prayers, hope, heartache, and waiting. A strong county circle that Woods witnessed in the making. He doesn't want to ever see it broken, "I'm grateful to Rita for that because it brought me closer to everybody in the Sheriff's Office and I think it brought all of the employees closer together."

Loyalty to their boss, dedication to their responsibilities, these qualities were things not taken lightly. In return, Woods extended the same kind of loyalty to all of them. And to the petite woman with the big heart, Patricia Angelle.

Before President Bush's visit, a Secret Service advance team made a security sweep through town, logistics and all. Navigating their way around, it was discovered that the Sheriff's Department had a hangar at the airport and large narcotics office as well. The Washington suits inquired about using the hangar to store vehicles. No problem, they were accommodated. None of the arrangements were a surprise to Woods, who had put "the feeling" such a visit was coming way in the back of his crowded mind. Finally, everything was in place. The president would hold a news conference inside the sheriff's office at the hangar and there would be time for photos and hellos.

"One of the Secret Service guys told me, 'Look you've been so kind to let us use your hangar, if you'll be here about 9:30, I'll see about setting up for you to meet my boss and have your picture made.'" What came next must've been a mild shock to one of the men assigned to protect the commander-in-chief but not to anyone who knows Mitch Woods. "I said 'Well, no offense to you, but I don't give a shit about meeting your boss.'" Little pause between the two men.

Woods said the first true thing that came to his mind. If the words hit the man's ears wrong, it was only because *he didn't know Woods.* What the sheriff meant, with respect, always with great respect for the office and for the president, was that there were so many other pressing things, at that critical hurricane juncture, more important than posing for cameras. His remark had nothing to do with Woods' political affiliation but everything to do with politics itself. *Political jockeying for position.* No one was going to make Woods say cheese. He has seen too much behind the trap.

"Being in politics for the length of time I've been in it," he explained, "it's just that meeting those guys doesn't mean a lot to me anymore." Woods wasn't attempting to paint all politicians with the same broad brush or lump them into a fixed category. He openly deplored the idea of a photo opportunity being something that should trump the kind of massive devastation that deserved photos of it, and not him. Or photos of all the work done, and done well, under duress. Photos of his finest at their best.

"What my employees were doing meant so much more to me until everything else was insignificant," Woods says. They were busy. It was hot. Residents wanted to come home. They could not. Woods was focused on exactly what he needed to focus on, but, alas, he is not a selfish man. The sheriff knew it was possible his comment declining the photo op might be misconstrued, so he asked the agent, "Can I bring somebody with me?" While Woods didn't embrace the idea of another politically correct picture featuring his person, he knew it would be a big deal, for some lucky person or persons, to meet the American many considered "most powerful man in the free world."

In the initial aftermath of uncomfortable post-Rita days, hours of cold showers and cold sandwiches, no electricity and no air, triple-digit hell for weather, answering calls and questions nonstop, and racing to secure whatever and whoever needed it, there were a slew of employees who met the criteria, who all deserved to meet George W. Bush, or, correction, in Woods' mind, who deserved to have Mr. Bush *meet them.* In an instant, Woods knew his selection: a woman who had displayed such enormous courage, and was still, at that time, unable to tend to a personal storm in her immediate future. Officer Patricia Angelle kept working after Rita left. One of her toughest assignments in life would be making final arrangements to bury the woman who taught her so well.

"The next morning I went by the jail and asked if Angelle was there. She came out, looking all puzzled," Woods smiled. Indeed, it was highly irregular for the sheriff to stop by, request a corrections officer to halt her duties and come out for a conference.

"I said, 'Come on, Trish. I need you to go with me.'" Almost immediately, there was suspicion. Angelle wanted to know where they were headed, what in the world was going on. The sheriff first answered it was a surprise. Then they walked out back to his parking space. Sensing her uneasiness, Woods very calmly stated, "You're going to meet George Bush." Her shock was an appropriate three-word response, "Oh my God." Angelle recovered only enough to ask her boss if there was time for a smoke. Woods answered, "Make it quick."

Headed for the hangar, Woods contacted Chief Stephens and told her to meet him there with a dispatcher of her choice. She would need to hurry. Stephens sent Norma Clubb, an employee who would join them in the receiving line. "Norma, before the hurricane, had had some health issues and weathered the storm with us. She went the extra mile and just happened to be sporting a patriotic red, white, and blue dress." The dispatcher was thrilled, she was a big

George Bush fan. Before Woods drove a nervous Angelle to the hangar, before Clubb met them there, the sheriff had done some major cramming the night before. He had done his Texas homework for a presidential quiz.

"W and I have a mutual friend. This friend used to be a state representative here and was real influential when W was the governor," Woods paused, "they got to be friends then." Woods knew Mr. Bush and the man have always stayed in close contact so he called the ex-legislator to inform him that his presidential buddy was headed to town for a visit, asked if he were going to come down and see him. The man said no. That's when Woods mentioned he might get to meet the president, needed something he could use that would make Mr. Bush stop and really listen. "I said, 'You got any advice for me?'" Without hesitation, the man had plenty.

"We get there, the next morning, we're all in line," Woods says. That's when a Secret Service agent came over to explain how the procedure would work. His strategy was to have Woods and the two women "first in line." When the president emerged from a news conference to board his Hawk, they would be able to greet him and say hello. Woods had intentionally skipped the dog and pony show. He felt sure nobody would miss him. They waited, Woods and his female employees, no doubt, the women trembling in advance of a fleeting star moment. The friendly Texan wrapped up his news conference and walked right up to the first man in line, extending his hand, "I'm George Bush."

Niceties not his first priority, Woods shook hands. "I said, 'Mr. President, I'm Mitch Woods. I'm the sheriff in this torn up county.'" That should've commandeered the full attention of the president. Perhaps it didn't. Mr. Bush responded that it was nice to meet Woods, or something similar. Woods tried again, "You and I have a good mutual friend." The president: "Really, who's that?"

"Mark Stiles," Woods answered, then paused to check out what kind of dent the two words made. There was definite recognition, but the sheriff got an iffy feeling that he was being tested. George Bush wanted to know if Woods had spoken to their *mutual friend* lately, the mini quiz Woods was prepared for. "I said, 'I talked to him last night and he said this is probably fucking your fishing up.'" Yes,

Woods used the "F" word to "W," it left little doubt the two men were acquainted with Stiles and his wicked sense of humor. Mr. Bush let out a big grin, a smile stay painted across his face. Woods, after that, had <u>all</u> of the president's attention.

"More important than that, I want you to meet these people," Woods then pointed to his department personnel waiting in line. It was mandatory that the president know about the caliber of employees who not only worked for Jefferson County, but also the kind of people, Woods told the commander-in-chief, "who work for you." Mr. Bush reached out and hugged Angelle, then kissed her on the cheek and was equally sincere embracing Norma Clubb. It was the best unplanned Kodak moment. Nothing political about it. Which is also the best way to describe Woods' hand around the neck of the most powerful man in the free world.

It wasn't anything he thought about, apparently the Secret Service weren't concerned. No one moved when Woods, who already had his arm on Mr. Bush's shoulder, gently moved it higher to pull the president closer for the now-famous whisper caught in the unplanned photo op. Here's what George Woods said to George Bush, just two Texans, two good ole boys who hunt and fish, put on their briefs the same way, one leg at a time: "I intentionally didn't go into that room and listen to that bullshit in there, but I'm counting on you to help us get this place straightened out and I know you're going to come through for us." The president uttered three words, "What'd you need?"

"Someone told me afterward they were surprised that I did that, surprised that the Secret Service had let that happen," Woods smiled. After all, he was visibly armed. But he never believed trained agents were worried. The storm hadn't taken *that* kind of toll, "They knew everything was OK."

My good friend, Angel, saw what happened and asked Woods' prosecutor-son, Clint, for his opinion on the episode. He told Angel, "I know my dad, and that was not his happy look." Maybe not, but Woods only had the president's ear for a couple of minutes. Like a good cop should, he cut straight to the chase and said what needed to be said.

"There were so many acts by so many people who carried out

their duties unselfishly." When pressed to name individual efforts, the sheriff summed up his gratitude with an inclusiveness that has become his law enforcement trademark. "I'm proud of every one of them." He did mention an employee who wrote a letter about the togetherness of those who "rode it out."

A lot of people signed off on that circulated letter. Together, they are conquerors who wouldn't be defeated by a hurricane named Rita.

SEVEN

Green, red and white splashed onto an easel reminded guests at the MCM Elegante' Hotel and Conference Center that things weren't up to snuff nearly three months after Rita. "Please watch your step…as we rebuild from the storm." The bold tagline at the end read, "HURRICANE RITA WAS TOUGH…but WE WERE TOUGHER."

Beyond sliding doors, two 8'feet tall Christmas trees decorated the entry, tin soldiers guarded the foyer. An overhead banner was consistent with a color scheme and marketing slogan workers were charged with upholding. "Friendliness and Cleanliness: Southern Hospitality in Tropical Elegance."

Red poinsettias did their pretty best to dissuade any notion that a hurricane had ripped through the front of one of the most expensive hotels in the area. Rita jacked up the price. Burgandy leather furniture and wooden tables offered more than enough space for arriving guests or tired employees on break. A woman was busy spraying cleaning fluid onto the veneer. I moved to avoid sneezing.

Down the long corridor, in one of the conference rooms, chairs were being stacked. Long tables of white linen arranged. A room with a hole, with a view, reconstructed, in the hope that no one would notice. Extra help walked around, on-the-job training, and in a hurry too. One friendly older gentleman was doing his work, too many guests needed him, a bellboy, or bellman.

Standing near the festive Christmas decorations, I had no idea what the white man who lived just outside of Buna, Texas looked like. We had exchanged emails and a couple of phone calls to confirm our meeting in Beaumont. Grateful that the hotel lobby was filled with brave witnesses, in case Alan Martin had duped me with his sincerity and gentlemanly behavior by phone, I never asked for a description. I was sure that would sound rude. *What do you look like Mr. East Texas?* It would be a cinch to pick out the stranger wearing a puzzled expression that translated into 'what am I doing here?'

A few minutes after I informed the front desk to put all calls for the 9th floor suite, minus me in it, through on a houseline near the designated interview-couch, a big man came barreling through the automatic sliding doors. I instantly thought he was the "recovering racist." His words, not mine. The man walked by. I was absolutely positive it was Martin. Directly behind me, he paused to ask the same woman who was still spraying that cleaning fluid where the bathroom was. I didn't turn around, but heard his voice and felt sure it was the phone man. Famous for giving affectionate nicknames, the white guy I dubbed 'lumberjack' simply vanished.

Five minutes later, a deep voice traveled over my shoulder, "Are you Joyce?" It was the same tall drink of water that had needed the bathroom break. Maybe he found the courage to go through with our meeting. Maybe he really did need to use the bathroom, wash his hands, look in the mirror and ask out loud, "What am I doing here?"

"Yes, I am," he knew it already. We said hello, how are you, both of us were fine, volleyed small chitchat about the big rain that had fallen the day before. I suggested we sit before all the flown open mouths in the lobby drained the room of any oxygen. Martin didn't seem to notice, too busy watching me with a fierce intensity that initially caused discomfort, fueled by the fact that any violent tendencies in the large man, who resembled a talking teddy bear up close, could be carried out with his bare hands. I decided Martin was real. I had nothing to fear except racial honesty.

Thursday morning. December 15th. 10 days before Christmas and I was back in Beaumont with a stranger who had written in a letter that inside of him was "a man who could easily become something" that sounded regressive and unlikable. Martin expressed strong views on the "immense coverage disparity" between Hurricanes Rita and Katrina. I turned on a mini recorder, gave it to him. Martin placed the gadget in his shirt pocket.

"Why did you write me that letter?" I wasted no time with appetizers.

A smile creased his lips. He thought for a moment, then fired back with the same brand of candor from his letter. "I grew up in an incredibly racist environment as a young man. We had a farm in a little town called Woodville. My parents died when I was about a year-and-a-half and I was raised by my grandfather on my mother's side." Though his adoptive parents were relatively young, late 30's, his mother unexpectedly died from an aneurism. Six months later, heart failure claimed his father, a heavy drinker who never recovered after his wife's sudden death.

"While he [grandfather] wasn't outwardly racist, we couldn't live in Woodville because I would've had to go to school with blacks." The family maintained their Woodville home, but also owned property in Pasadena, Texas, where Martin graduated from Deer Park High School in 1982.

"I can remember, as a kid, the only TV shows in the '70s and '80s that we were allowed to watch that had blacks as the predominant characters was *Sanford and Son* or *Good Times.*" This made me think maybe Martin's grandfather wasn't so bad after all, had racist issues but a soft spot for changing times and legislative integration. I watched my share of both television shows with parents and siblings. Millions still do, thanks to cable syndication. A lovable junk man, Fred Sanford, with his fake heart attacks, set in Watts, and J. J. Evans, famous for saying "Die-no-mite" in a Cabrini Green-like project, aren't characters easily forgotten.

Martin continued his grandfather's entertainment logic for the reason he could watch those shows that starred blacks, and not another highly-rated sitcom. He was forbidden from tuning in to *The Jeffersons* because George and Louise were well to do and, more importantly, Martin confirmed that the successful show was banned in his home because of next door high rise neighbors, Tom and Helen, a mixed race couple. "It just drove, the man I call my father, insane."

Even with this home-based brand of polite racism, not "outwardly" extended, Martin says his grandfather was a good man, one he clearly loved. "I think very highly of him, can't wait to get to heaven and see him again." A silent *but* attached itself to the respect Martin had for the man who raised him. "I fought the whole racist thing as hard as I could *but* I lost for a lot of years." My mind lit up with a flurry of questions. *In what kinds of situations did you lose? Ever use the "N" word yourself? What do you think of mixed-race couples like Tom and Helen? Could you vote for a black president?* I didn't ask right then because it was more important to allow Martin his freedom of expression. He was friendly. His honesty more refreshing than some who have flat out lied about never thinking a single negative or stereotypical thing about black folk.

"Fast forward to now," he shifted his massive frame on the comfortable sofa, "I'm in construction." His brown eyes sparkled as he looked harder into mine, trying to read what I thought of him. "I try to understand, what it is, as a big East Texas white guy, what am I doing wrong? What is it that I don't understand about race relations?" He then borrowed nearly identical language from his grandfather's story to sum up his own: "It drives me absolutely insane." He was still, very much, the man's son.

"How big an East Texas white boy are you?" I hadn't had my fill yet of asking men with hearty appetites in that neck of the Piney Woods their shoe and neck size. He laughed, "I'm 6'5, 300 pounds." *Lumberjack Construction.*

Keeping the bulk of Martin in the back of my mind while we chatted gave me something humorous to balance all the serious dialogue I could sense we were about to venture deep into. I had no desire to make someone his size upset, especially since Jessie Wolf was so far away, ironically, in Woodville, the same place a white grandfather had left so his babies wouldn't have to go to school with blacks. Of course, my Louisiana-born mother had taught me how to drop a man the size of Martin. I heard her voice again, "The bigger they are the harder they fall." A man always has an Achilles Heel.

What I liked about Martin most was he was good at trading barbs. He wanted to put me at ease, and had, as much as me, considered the glaring fact that neither of us had ever laid eyes on the other and hit the ground running into difficult terrain for even the best of longtime friends. Martin was well relaxed from the start. Or did a fantastic job concealing any nervousness.

Eager to understand more about what made black people tick, he had relied, in the past, on a man given rave reviews. Cecil Poole, a black co-worker who lived in Baton Rouge, had worked with Martin on various construction projects. They often "engaged each other in taboo topics." Poole is much older than Martin. The dialogue has certainly helped him understand black people better.

Before I could ask whether that made Poole something of a father figure, he offered, "We used to go to a BBQ place in Baytown when we were working on our project over there and I'd always introduce him as 'my dad,' just for fun." When people gasped at the men, Martin had a great comeback line: "Don't worry about it, my mom's Chinese."

Byron Bankston was another pal who worked for the same company as Poole. Closer to Martin's age, they got along well and he was also credited for introducing Martin to a perspective the "recovering racist" had never considered. "Byron gave me a different slant on everything. For example, I think affirmative action, if I was a black person, affirmative action would piss me off." Martin put a lot of vinegar on 'piss me off,' saying he wouldn't want "preferential treatment" for anything other than what he was qualified to do. Bankston, a Houston-born black man who had dabbled in politics and worked the old-fashioned way, twice as hard to get where he was, offered Martin a little African American logic on so-called quotas.

Bankston first called the view Martin had "fine," but he asked his white friend to put himself in his shoes and attempt to make a dent in what Bankston referred to as 'the good ole boy system' for getting hired. If you're not a member of the club, it's tough to gain entry without network credentials. He told Martin that blacks and minorities simply had something to counter the system called affirmative action. "Now, it's starting to make a little sense to me," the lumberjack smiled.

Martin was 40 years old and some change when we met. He proudly proclaimed the honor of being born the same day as the greatest president of all time. I was thinking Lincoln, until he said "Ronald Reagan" and wondered how many black people he had shared that opinion with. Instead, I asked if he'd experienced any kind of pivotal moment at the Big 4-0.

"Mine was about 35," he began, "I was in Shanghai, China working, and I realized so much of what I was doing with my life was wrong." The reflective mission to change and the events that led Martin down a new path consumed him in the faraway community he lived in for almost six months. He quit drinking and some other habits he didn't want to list. The married father of one son, named for him, says before the Chinese excursion, his family had already started going to worship together. There was genuine happiness in Martin's voice that age 35 was his true "40-moment."

To entering and exiting patrons of the hotel, with piped-in Christmas music filling the ears of dozens who either welcomed it or couldn't block it out, we looked, perhaps, like two coworkers signing off a company party that might be held that evening in one of the large ballrooms down the hall. I was glad Martin brought up family. He had written in his letter how much he wanted to give son, Alan, Jr., a better world. "What would you like to impart to your child about race, particularly race in East Texas?"

Martin had struggled with "stereotypes and classifications" in his youth, probably all his life. "I want him to learn to judge people only by what they present to him, with no predisposed notions about anybody for any reason." Proud papa beamed, "He's in Austin today, beginning a fulltime job with the United States Army as a military police officer." The younger Martin had enlisted in the Army National Guard as a senior in high school.

"One of the things I'm most proud of him for was a very small singlet of a conversation we had out in our backyard, before the hurricane tore it up." They talked, candidly, about the fact that the Iraq situation was a long way from being resolved. Martin offered his only child an option. "Kind of big thing you're doing here, joining the military right in the middle of a war. If you want to back out of this, I don't want you to think I'll think any less of you." Martin will never forget what his son told him. "His reply was, 'Dad I'm 17. You can sign it and let me go join now, or you can wait until I'm 18 and watch me walk away but I'm going to do what's right for me and for what I believe in and for this country.'" Martin and his wife never have it far from the back of their minds that their son might be sent into a dangerous situation. His patriotic light flicked back to upbeat and positive, "We're a Christian family. I believe that I'm better off with him doing God's will in Baghdad than my will in Beaumont."

It was clear that Martin viewed his life as a work in progress with its wet paint. One person has demonstrated boundless faith in the masterpiece and Martin added a theological twist when spelling his wife's name. "Same as Moses' sister." As he spoke about Miriam Martin, a woman I might never meet, she felt like a sister in pink with his very next words.

"About a week after the hurricane, she was diagnosed with breast cancer." Martin called his wife "a strong girl" who was amazing in all that she had endured for the last few months of 2005. His wife, at that point, had gone through two surgeries and was being challenged by ongoing treatment. Martin praised her for being a good woman, better than he deserves. "She should've kicked my ass to the curb about 19,000 times!"

Her diagnosis and treatment has brought the couple closer. They were already on that track before illness announced itself. The lumberjack melted when talking about the girl of his dreams, his son's beautiful mother, as they patiently wait for news that has been prayed for. "The day after she's given that clean bill of health will be my finest moment." I do not tell Martin that the holidays have a bittersweet taste for a most loved relation. My brother, Robert.

Two years ago on New Year's Day, we lost his wife, Laurie, after a valiant fight with breast cancer. Laurie flashed through my mind, her grace and my nephew. People who always ask why I wear pink so much have part of the answer. Pink is symbolic of the wrinkled hospital gown. Pink reminds us to schedule mammograms. We're all pretty in pink, with or without hair.

For the American Cancer Society and the ABC television affiliate in Dallas, I agreed to let my first ever mammogram be filmed for the evening news and shared with North Texans. I believe in the power of pink. Years ago, I had also emceed the Susan G. Komen Race for The Cure and had the honor of meeting Nancy Brinker, the woman whose sister *was* Susan G. Komen.

Martin sensed, rightly so, his comments had struck a nerve, both topics, marriage and cancer. Robert has an excellent new wife, Orbra, and she has thrilled the entire family with her presence. Martin asked about my husband. Never fair, in my mind, for the interviewer to trade places with the interviewee. He recalled the same hesitation from an earlier question on the spouse (ex-spouse) and found the right opening to politely inquire again. If anyone dared ask about Rod, no matter how natural it seemed to them, I always hesitated, rolling over in my mind just how much to tell. I gave a one-sentence summary on a 25-year partnership officially granted its absolution the week before.

That seemed to shock Martin. He had no funny one-liners,

which were in unlimited supply prior to the marital mood killer. My face grimaced in a way to complement the stuttering. A one-two punch made Martin realize race was easy to talk about compared to a former union that had left one partner in the eye of a storm.

"You're a Republican?" was the dumbest question I could've possibly thrown out after the diehard Ronnie Reagan comment. I stumbled badly in a Q&A that turned on me. "Rightwing *moderate* conservative." About the only thing that day in the hotel lobby louder than holiday tunes was the front desk phone. It was about to blow up. 20 rings. 15 rings. I wanted to scream, *Would somebody please answer that stupid phone?* Martin's voice rang out, "As a general rule, I think we're missing a third party."

We discussed the wide gulf that exists between black/white, Republicans and Democrats, rich versus poor, the haves and the have-nots. Martin loved to talk politics. So we danced all over the red and blue map.

"What is it about the 'N' word that upsets you so much?" I interrupted him. "For the life of me, I can't understand why anybody would perpetuate such an obviously negative term." Martin wanted to lead again, "Conversely, I don't understand why so many black people have a problem with the Confederate Flag." *Whoa, big guy, one controversial topic at a time.* He was spinning me around so fast, I lost track of how many sentences he began with 'I don't understand.' Then he did it again.

"I don't understand people who don't understand history, they just don't understand symbolism." There was only one way to slow down a misunderstanding in the making. I fired right back, "Do you have one in your house?" He was truthful. The son kept a Confederate Flag in his room. For a person with such strong convictions, it struck me as odd that Martin didn't also sport one. "Why don't you have one?" He gave a serious look, "Because I don't want to offend people I may want to engage."

A day before our meeting, I had passed an exit on 96 South heading back into Beaumont. The sight of a tall flagpole caused me to feel, not so much discomfort, sheer curiosity at a Confederate Flag whipping in the wind, high atop the pole. From the highway, it can't be missed.

"Do you know why it was there?" he asked. Deep down, I initially thought it was because I had passed a sign with Vidor on it. No matter where a person is whenever the conversation or topic is Vidor, the Texas town is almost always followed by 'Klan Capital of the State.' *Was that flag displayed because I had passed an exit for Vidor?* "No," Martin says, his voice took on its most serious tone. "It was because you were making a curve around a town called Evadale and the Evadale school mascot is the Rebels. That flag flies as a symbol for the high school."

Part of me was glad Martin gave the legitimate reason the flag was posted. Another part might be just as content to have never known. Stereotypes and symbols are hard to reject, to let go, especially when they evoke painful memories. I am probably one of the few black people in the South, that over the years, that flag has been given less power to do as much as it once did. It's a freedom, one only true history affords, when you can, as Martin put it, "understand history." Like Lincoln freeing the slaves, when he did no such thing. I still don't like seeing the Confederate Flag though.

"I think when people have a problem with something like a Confederate Flag, or a song like Dixie or…" At that moment, his cell phone, with its distinctive ringer, went off. He immediately answered, knowing in advance the special ring for that particular caller. "Good morning son," he cheerfully greeted the young Rebel. I reached over in his pocket, took out the recorder and turned it off so he could speak privately. I heard Martin tell his namesake that he was visiting with a nice lady named King.

Martin hung up. We got back to the "N" word with violins adding musical drama to the discussion. A weepy Christmas instrumental felt wrong for the hustle and bustle in the lobby. And for our debate, which ran the gauntlet from heated to passionate from sensitive to sad. I didn't mention to Martin that Nigton is a small town in Texas where black residents never bothered to put on the pressure for a name change. Nigton may only be six letters, but there is no disguising what the name was originally derived from—Nigger Town. Martin and I were trying to cover too much ground.

I did attempt to explain why some blacks used "nigger" to affectionately refer to one another. Growing up, I knew dozens of people who embraced the word to take away any racist sting that had been associated with it, stripping away power to injure them. Martin frowned and totally dismissed that explanation.

In the loving home I grew up in, we didn't use the word at all. Nobody in my house called any family member "nigger," not in jest, not to mock someone white, not ever. My mom hated the word and she didn't think it was necessary for intelligent expression. Yet, she fully understood its use by others who didn't follow the same rule. We were to never judge other black people who privately called each other "nigger." Period.

"Can't we move on?" Martin's voice was playfully exaggerated, as he threw his hands up in the hotel air, garnering the attention of several guests who knew we had been sitting together too long for finishing touches on a company party. Martin was fired up. He threw the hip hop culture on the table in front of us like a trump card that served to prove his point on the word "nigger." I was already in deep shit with a bunch of readers, black and white, for a column I had written in *USA Today* about being sick of hearing the word because abuse had long past the ridiculous limit. I don't know any hip hop artists who tell fans they're using "nigger" to take some of the white man's sting out of it. If that was the reason for such derogatory references, then why, Martin wanted to know, use words like "bitch" and "ho" and "gold digger" to describe black women?

"Nigger" has been uttered so freely and sung and slammed and misdirected until the effectiveness of shock appeal is dead. There are definite situations when the word itself has a place in categories like history, literature, life, that nothing else can be used to substitute when we teach what it was intended to mean. But when a black woman can walk into a Christmas party in New York, as an acquaintance of mine once did, and hear two young white men greet each other with "Hey, my nigger," we're well past ridiculous racial crap.

"The use of that word, there's nothing you can derive out of that that has historical significance or any other thing you can hang your hat on," Martin says. He didn't want me to leave, but knew other conversations were waiting just up the road. "The Confederate Flag, and the Confederacy, had as little to do with slavery as I have to do with brain surgery. It was a component of the reason for the war, but it wasn't the reason for the war. The reason for the war was states' rights." Finally, he calmed down a bit. Martin called slavery "a horrible portion of our history," but added there are elements of history we need "because of its importance to the whole subject of freedom."

We talked about Abraham Lincoln. I have studied much of Lincoln's life, recommend David Herbert Donald's *LINCOLN* and several other worthy books so Americans might better understand the 16th president never "freed the slaves" with that famous document called the Emancipation Proclamation. More debate followed about Lincoln's "idea of America" and Martin concluded that Lincoln "was mostly torn" about slavery because he was attempting to hold the country together, not free the slaves. No, it didn't work, that was one thing we agreed on. My numerical connection to Honest Abe is my date of birth. Lincoln was pronounced dead at 7:22 and even used the same July date in 1862 to offer an advance reading of his not-perfected proclamation.

"Ms. King, you have a phone call," a hotel employee interrupted us. Our debate had produced no clear winner and the race to an invisible finish line was halted. After assuring Angel San Juan I was busy trying to heal Martin, and still alive, I invited the lumberjack to sit again and talk about Rita.

"Where would you like me to begin?" He was home just five miles "east of Buna on Highway 253." When Martin saw that didn't register, he offered a familiar landmark, "You know, that turn right by Joe's Campus Corner." It was the same little store I had, only 24 hours earlier, sipped coffee at with Billy Rowles, watching the foot traffic come in and out like one of the regulars.

Joe's got the right idea. A chipped wooden sign was posted high over tables scrunched together off to the side of displayed food in glass cases, where I got a BBQ rib sandwich on the way out. In faded red paint, the recovered sign, weather-beaten by Rita, had fallen from its nailed home in a tall Pine. It said what I hoped will be true again: "Billy Rowles for Jasper County Sheriff."

Alan Martin stood alone in the lobby. I left a surreal conversation in progress—after landfall. The hurricane brought things out of people that had been buried a long time.

What about Rita?

EIGHT

"I couldn't believe it, how they were treating us, after we treated Katrina people like royalty," the native Texan recounted a hurricane chapter she will never forget.

Maxine Rogers was born in Beaumont, and stayed in Beaumont because it has always been home. The 50-year old single mother of two sons, wasn't supposed to be part of a school bus convoy leaving the Thursday before Rita. She had a car. "I started out, trying to drive myself but didn't have enough gas."

With stations closed and the few that remained open quickly running out of fuel, Rogers turned around and headed back home. Amelia Elementary was one of the schools near her residence. Rogers got on a bus, as a last resort, hoping things would work out.

"By the time we got to Kountze, [Texas] we started to see city and charter buses pass us. My brother was on one of those." The convoy moved like a covered wagon procession trekking across dusty frontier instead of modern vehicles on paved highways. Roads were jammed in one direction and clogged with fleeing motorists, many of whom were taking seriously the order to evacuate, something hundreds of thousands had never done before.

Rogers dodged hurricanes growing up, it was nothing new. But after frightening images from Katrina and meeting New Orleans residents that Rogers got firsthand horror stories from, she decided to leave Beaumont behind. Rogers worked two jobs to make ends meet. Fresh memories of people shell-shocked by Katrina were often supplied in the form of stories she heard at Wal-Mart.

"They would come in crying. I gave one woman my Bible to give her encouragement. We would hug them, talk to them, and I just told all my co-workers 'that could be us.' And sure enough, it was us."

Rogers has compared notes with fellow school bus passengers. Her vantage in the convoy equipped Rogers with unshakable testimony on why things went totally haywire. "We couldn't use the restrooms, there was no food, no water, nothing. It was so chaotic. We were in Nacogdoches, no, Lufkin, and they didn't even want us." Rogers paused, still trying to comprehend the bus ride, "They said we got to keep moving."

As an African American, Rogers was comfortable discussing the role race has played in her life. Any negatives, and there have been some, never overshadowed a belief that racism is practiced by individuals, not regions. "There is still racism, but you treat other people like you want to be treated. I've gone to Vidor and been treated wonderfully, didn't think anything of it." Rogers knows there are black people reluctant to even venture into the town because of its Klan-stigma, because of a 1993 federal order to integrate a government housing project, and, finally, because of its close proximity to Jasper and a 1998 dragging. "Others are real down on Vidor, but my mom brought us up to love everyone, not think about skin color."

Like several passengers, Rogers remembered "random acts of kindness" from people of all hues and what it was like to plant her feet again on Texas earth. "They finally let us off the bus. We were asking for water on the side of the road. One white guy got out of his truck and gave us a jug of water he had." The man was sorry he didn't have more. At that point in the journey, Rogers and more than 2,000 others had been on the bus for some 24 hours without being allowed off.

"The convoy leader in the van kept saying 'We've got to push on' and drivers kept begging the woman to let kids and elderly people off the bus. People were sick." Rogers stopped talking again, then resumed with a question, "Why have all these people and not be able to protect us?" She confirmed that stop after stop, town after town, there was no room. "We met a lot of Katrina people and other Rita people who had beaten us, coming from Ford Park, [Jefferson County] and it wasn't all about race, but a lot of people." Rogers didn't believe it was because towns in East Texas didn't want to help them. With capacity crowds they had to look out for the interest of those who lived there and thousands of temporary guests that town officials were suddenly responsible for. "I understand them wanting to protect."

Any sadness in Rogers' voice stemmed from the fact that "no room at the Inn," as she put it, meant 2,000 people from Beaumont were unprotected for close to 50 hours on school buses. She was determined, as a member of the generation between babies and senior citizens onboard, to help passengers about to give up, encourage them to hang on. "When we finally got to Canton, police came on the bus and told us to keep calm and keep still, but we pleaded with them to take one lady first." Rogers says "it felt like heaven" to get into the small East Texas hamlet. By then, a little white lady, Rogers guessed was about 90 years old, had suffered a light stroke and was either delirious, dehydrated, or both.

"She was so nice, but after all those hours, she was fighting and cussing and speaking a foreign language." The woman kept jumping up, despite police orders to remain seated. A nurse was quickly summoned to the bus, the first sign that Canton was not only prepared to receive them, but more than ready to make them feel as welcome as any Texas neighbor.

"Canton treated us like royalty," Rogers' voice relaxed. "They fed us, we showered and slept. Then we went to a church, it was royalty on top of royalty." Even the memory of lifesaving little town brought renewed happiness to Rogers as she described escorts that were provided to bus drivers, how children of church members unpacked their belongings from inside the buses. "They had towels, issued us everything we needed. It was very orderly."

One of the most touching things was how the kids had made welcome cards, "It was so loving, they really cared about us and what we were going through." Rogers remained adamant that no one had done much for them before the convoy arrived in Canton. The order and organization that has been applauded in Canton began at the Civic Center first. A few of the buses were then escorted, one by one, to a nearby church.

"Gov. Perry needs to go to Canton to see how it ought to be done. They were so organized with unpacking, feeding, and signing us up. We were bus number 20-something." Passengers filed in, one at a time, first to medical tables for information and to see what individual needs were.

Over and over, Mr. Perry was praised for his intervention in calling Canton for help, giving them what amounted to a few hours notice that hundreds of exhausted people, stranded on buses, needed help. The drivers, according to Rogers, were mentally and physically depleted. During one brief stop, she asked law enforcement, "Why y'all letting these people drive without any sleep?" Whenever safety concerns were cited as reasons passengers weren't allowed to exit buses, she countered with her biggest fear that a driver might fall asleep at the wheel. No one outside the buses had expressed much concern about *their* safety.

"In Canton, we had round-the-clock protection, police, medical staff, they stayed with us in the church auditorium." When Rogers and company were moved again, it was to a renovated hospital in DeLeon, Texas, where they were also provided excellent care. That would not be her last stop before returning home. "We ended up in Midlothian at The Salvation Army Ranch. It was gorgeous, neat, very nice. We enjoyed how they took care of us and we were able to walk the grounds." Rogers recalled an exciting new adventure she and some of the other women were brave enough to try. "My first time ever being on a horse and I got the biggest horse there was," she laughed.

If Rogers had to do it over, knowing what she learned from the marathon detour, her outlook was certain. "I'd leave again, even if I have to be back on that bus. I'm alive. I can get over what happened."

Whether I met Texans where they were, spoke with them by phone or they wrote letters describing their situations, post-Rita, I was always touched by their straightforward approach to debilitating circumstances. They will bear them, many confided. Weariness in their faces and voices framed how much these Texans have been challenged. Some worry they might be victims in a future disaster and help would be just as slow. Several expressed grave concerns that they would rebuild or find a degree of comfort just in time for a new hurricane season.

Wanting to beef up my own storm knowledge, I called Frank Lepore at the National Hurricane Center in Miami. He confirmed a period of "above normal activity" has been full strength since 1995 and could last two more decades. Lepore mentioned the importance of awareness before and after any storm. "We must have people prepared, know their vulnerability. Are you in a floodplain?" Residents should heed the advice of local officials familiar with roads and construction and rely on their own advance planning. Especially for an evacuation.

Lepore and I discussed destiny and the long journey that kept bringing me back to Southeast Texas. I wanted redemption for the region I love, and selfishly, for me. "How ironic," I told Lepore, "to be working on this book and find the name 'Joyce' on a list of possible storm names for 2006." We joked about *Hurricane Joyce*, but Lepore was dead serious about strategizing for future disasters.

"How do you plan for the next storm, like thousands in harm's way, when your temporary address is a travel trailer?" I asked Lepore. It would also seem the notion of having enough food and water for 72 hours, as recommended at the Department of Homeland Security website, might need to be at least seven days after what Americans went through with Dennis, Katrina, Rita and Wilma in 2005.

What I admired most about my fellow Texans and Louisianans was their strength of character and grace under pressure, the way they found things to laugh about, even when there was a mountain of work. One of the reasons I was always so inspired by Jasper is the little town has had its share of high-profile heartache. Good people always got right back up no matter how much outsiders expressed shame that Jasper is in America.

No one knew more about hard work, resiliency or laughing out loud than the fine waitresses at The Cedar Tree Restaurant. They were among thousands who assumed Jasper County was far enough inland to be, for the most part, okay.

53-year old Florenda Arabie has worked at The Cedar Tree, off and on, for 18 years. "I knew it was going to be bad, but when they evacuated Jasper we were still at work." Leaving was not left up to the more than 8,000 residents in Jasper city limits, the decision was called by County Judge Joe Folk and the mayor of Jasper, David Barber. Kirbyville's mayor, Jerry Noble, also issued a mandatory evacuation. More than 30,000 residents in Buna, Jasper, Sam Rayburn, Kirbyville and Evadale believed Rita had no meteorological business so far inland—it was about 70 miles from Beaumont to Jasper.

During the evacuation process, Arabie was already hearing disturbing stories about nonexistent accommodations in nearby towns. "People couldn't find anything in Lufkin, they were sleeping on the side of the road." Her family tracked reports about where the storm was headed. First they heard Galveston, then Houston would take a direct hit, and finally, Beaumont was the intended target. No one knew for sure. That prompted two of her three grown children to flee their homes in Liberty and Dayton, along with Arabie's five grandkids.

38-year old Ramona is married to Mike Fay and they have two sons, 10-year old Levi and five-year old Cameron. Arabie's 37-year old son, Richard, and wife Sherrie, soon arrived with their three children, Josh, Kristen, and Justin, ages 18, 16, and 10, respectively. They came running to Jasper, knowing it would be safer. Another son, 32-year old Nolan James Trahan and new wife, Kerry, live in New Mexico. They waited by the phone.

"We were without power for 21 days." Arabie was good natured about the 100-degree heat that stayed after Rita made her getaway. In an effort to keep cool, Arabie slept on a bag of ice. "It was horrible." Arabie had friends in Kirbyville who got hit "really hard," she also knew of pockets in Buna that waited weeks to have electric service restored.

"I could see the military coming in on Highway 63," Arabie was grateful that gas trucks weren't far behind. Almost no one had lifesaving generators. The few that did desperately needed fuel to run them. Neighbor checked on neighbor. People shared what little they had.

Before Rita, in the hours of waiting and watching, Arabie was constantly on her knees. "I've never prayed so hard in my life." The eye, she says, "passed right through Jasper." Arabie's daughter, Ramona, helped her with keeping everyone calm, while son-in-law, Mike, kept mocking them. He didn't understand what the big deal was. After all, it was just a severe thunderstorm. *How bad could it be?* With all the humongous oak trees on Arabie's property, Mike soon had his answer.

When things started to get serious, it was exactly what weather veterans in the house predicted, only worse, and ten times as long. A scared family searched for creative ways to remain calm. "Then, here comes the wind," Arabie remembered the chronological weather pieces to the puzzle. With the house shaking and baking, big oak trees bending in unnatural positions, pines snapping, the mood in the Arabie house changed from Mike's joking to unsung lyrics from a gospel song. *The winds obey my will, peace be still.*

Everyone in the house, from youngest to oldest, knew things had a potential deadliness. Darkness added an extra element to the fear. Arabie kept praying, counting heads, just to be sure everyone was fine. A few windows blew out, letting a vicious wind and rain terrorize them more. Rita inched closer to the humans inside. They shut rooms up that featured broken glass and soggy carpet. The house got smaller.

One of the reasons Arabie didn't want to evacuate was her elderly mother. She had refused to leave, and Arabie wasn't about to leave her. Rita made them question that decision for several frightening hours.

As the stormy confrontation between Rita and Jasper continued, someone noticed that Mike, Arabie's playful son-in-law, was M.I.A., Missing In Action. He was nowhere to be found. "Where was Mike?" Arabie laughed, then provided the punch line, "In the closet." That brought a sliver of humor during some edgy hours, nearly 540 minutes of lashing, crashing, banging rain and the wrath of an angry enemy wind. Arabie couldn't resist, she grabbed her camcorder and taped the priceless closet moment. "He was petrified," she says of Mike's newfound respect for hurricanes.

Arabie felt enormously blessed that many prayers were answered during the dark hours of uncertainty. Not one oak fell. Windows broke. Water soaked carpet. But they all survived to tell the story of Mike hiding in the closet, "He admitted that if one tree had hit that house…" Arabie's voice trailed off, leaving her fellow waitresses at The Cedar Tree to fill in the blank. Every woman, no matter how painful, had a hurricane story to tell. Every woman tried to find the rainbow's courage after the storm. 44-year old Sherrie Markovich was no different.

Like Arabie, the petite brunette had also worked at the restaurant for 18 years, give or take a year, with a break here and there. Markovich had been a June bride, married about three months to Mika when Rita came sashaying into the celebration, bearing unwanted gifts and completely destroying their new home. She and her husband, who drives a log truck, had no insurance. They were still getting things sorted out for a new life when indifferent Rita attempted to erase their blueprint for happiness. The pain was still too fresh for Markovich to say more. Her heart commanded a tear threatening to fall back to its work station. Markovich hadn't come anywhere near terms of understanding how some people were entitled to help, rather easily, while countless others were left to fend for themselves.

If not for family, friends and community, these women might've been bitter about Rita. Again and again, they spoke of being twice blessed with connections. Family. One by blood, the other by their association with The Cedar Tree where waitresses are sisters and the owner, Robert Treat, is more like a father. Markovich didn't look old enough to be a grandmother, but her 22-year old daughter, Kathy, and husband, Ricky, have two young sons, Eric and Evan. Markovich also has a 21-year old daughter, Melissa, who is married to Alex. Their two sons are Brennon and Brandal. Her 25-year old son, Jim, is single and in the Navy. There is a fourth child. Her name was known to me because of tragic circumstances. Small world that Sherrie Markovich is her mother.

Gathered in a circle at my table, were four women, self included, who had never before held a conversation. Until that moment. Suddenly the issue turned to race, always just below the surface in Jasper. I'm not even sure who brought it up, though I believe it was related to the dragging. One of the ladies actually remembered me and Monique Nation, my touchstone-reporter from Houston, coming in during courtroom breaks to eat. I was often embarrassed at the size of Monique's huge plate at the popular all-you-can-eat buffet. For a slim woman so tall and regal, Mo' often told me whenever I asked who was going to help her eat the food she'd piled on, "Girl, I can put away some serious groceries." And she could, never gaining a single pound.

Markovich wanted to say something. I sensed it wasn't about Rita, yet it was all about Rita, about race, about stereotypes, about issues black and white are not good at dealing with. She listened to other hurricane stories first, things about the trials, and how Jasper, the women felt, had been unfairly portrayed by many in the media. Rita was again the catalyst for conversation that ventured away from its expected course. Then Markovich very calmly stated she had as good a reason as anyone to hate blacks, but that she never could. A broken heart wouldn't let her.

Two years before Rita, Markovich's beautiful 23-year old daughter,

Chrystal, was murdered during a robbery at an Outback Steakhouse in Texarkana, Texas. The shooter was a black man. I remembered the high-profile case but not all the details.

That same lonely tear moved closer to the edge of her eye and desperately wanted its freedom. Again, Markovich wouldn't allow it. She was tougher than the tear. I could only be silent at her pain. There are no words one mother can say to another who has had a child violently ripped from their embrace. I admired her courage. The torture I couldn't begin to imagine. She offered the truest commentary, a scathing opinion normally hidden in front of racially mixed company. Markovich trusted me enough to say her reason for hating blacks might be justified if she had chosen to take that route in life. I thanked her for such clarity and poise. We were two strangers who had seen each other, with only glasses of tea between us and plates of food or tips and smiles, mostly in 1999, and visits over a seven year coexistence. Now there was something profoundly tender.

It sounded like the pretty waitress had randomly encountered people who suggested that one man, who happened to be black, was proof enough that no one would blame her for hating the entire race. Her brave admission surely took courage, as do daily efforts to navigate past preferred stereotypes. Markovich touched me with her story and her desire to steer clear of an eye-for-eye kind of racial hatred. She knew all black people hadn't murdered her child. One man did.

"Don't write that," she pleaded with me to stop taking notes, felt her story was no big deal. She was wrong. Markovich had no idea what a big deal it was to all the women working and eating that day beyond more comfortable human walls. Four women exchanging the stories of our lives. I had eaten a thousand meals at The Cedar Tree and never knew the waitresses by name. Until the Rita Conversation.

Brenda Proulx had also worked a long time at the restaurant, but not as long as her two co-workers. She followed the advice of officials, "I evacuated to Oklahoma and was gone for 11 days. I didn't get a dime from them." A letter sent to Proulx by the Red Cross was how the 51-year old woman learned her claim had been denied. The memory of how she was treated and the representative who explained the denial by phone, a rude stranger named Jason in Virgina, made Proulx feel like the Red Cross utilized different guidelines to pick and choose who got aid. "I didn't lie, I told the truth," Proulx started, "the house wasn't livable."

The saucy French woman was married 20 years to a Canadian from Quebec and it sounded like a wild ride with the top down. Proulx shook her head, grateful that loved ones, B. J., age 32, Brian, 26, and his wife, Betty, and baby Phillip, and youngest daughter, Renee, who is 25 and engaged to a wonderful man named Seth Wheeler, were all okay. Proulx counted out loud the blessings of survival, but was emotionally wounded that a long distance voice would assume she was so anxious to get money from the government that she would lie about the state of her house and everything in it, all the meat and food lost that had been stored in a freezer. "I got nothing."

One thing I have learned, over the years, about East Texans is, most are hard working, law abiding folk who don't want anything from anybody, especially the government. To ask for official help took a lot for East Texans to swallow lifelong habits and pride. For those who never got help, after being placed in the unthinkable position of having to ask, it was tantamount to being treated like foreign criminals on weekend visas about to be deported. I heard tales of checks and food stamps being showered on some people with barely an interrogation, while others had routine applications scrutinized. And denied. Who can forget the story of one man receiving aid from FEMA and using part of the money for a sex-change operation? After Katrina and Rita, the government forked over $1.4 billion dollars in sham payments. Many who didn't get a dime, and desperately needed help, find it hard to forgive a government they've always paid taxes on time to.

Like an elderly woman on Medicaid and a fixed income who didn't qualify for food stamps with a trailer home soaked and upside down. What was she going to eat? Her imagination? Some people who wrote or called me didn't want their names printed, they just wanted someone to listen. It was hit and miss in Jasper and surrounding counties, and Proulx firmly believed a lot of the decisions simply rested on who reviewed your claim.

Proulx's daughter, Renee, fared slightly better, "She called FEMA and got the $2,000." Hurricane stories about neighbors and total strangers kicked in. I drank tea, barely eating my regular order at The Cedar Tree: fish, hush puppies and okra. Then we tackled men. Proulx gave the thumbs-up to my infatuation with Canadian men on hockey skates. The other women howled. She knew a handsome Cajun who had a fire about him, no skates, but he fit the rest of my desired bill, too hot for me though. With a name like Proulx, I had no doubt Lady Brenda could trade stories with the best about the male hurricanes all of us had obviously been in.

It didn't feel right to hear their personal dramas without sharing. I wanted to be a member of the girl's club. They were sorry to hear about the divorce. Anyone still left in the almost empty, after-the-lunch-rush diner, would swear we were having double shots on that bit of sad news. Over ice tea, the therapeutic testimony had us near tears, then back to laughter, and occasionally paused for sober reflection. These women had seen me come into the restaurant since 1999 and I hadn't known any of them. They didn't know who I was either. In 2005, Rita brought us together, demanded personal information be stated out loud.

Another thing the sister-waitresses had in common was how much they loved the restaurant and its loyal customers. Sherrie, Flo, and Brenda knew hundreds of people by first names, kids and grandkids, where they worked, what kind of music they liked, their regular orders, where they lived, partied and worshipped. The customers, all the women kept repeating, "are like family."

Another longtime waitress, 46-year old Connie Clark, was off that day. She's not married and has two children, Jennifer, 29, and Shaun, 22. Her daughter and husband, Chris, have three children, Dalton, Marshall and Kinley. They all live in Jasper.

Andrea Fowler is a name I was glad to put with a face. "Ann" was working while we sat and talked. She's the restaurant cook and I'd put the 35-year old woman up against any four-star chef. Ann Fowler can burn. Her husband, Quience, works for a lumber mill and they have three children, Jermany, Quience, and Maria. Like the women out front, Fowler had nothing but praise for The Cedar Tree and her first-class extended family.

Before I came into the restaurant that day, on the parking lot, I noticed an older gentleman pull up right beside me. As is my habit when someone stares at me as long as this chap did, I nodded to speak, and gestured in some respectful way, hoping to inspire the stranger to nod back since he had already decided to rudely gawk. Even through tinted car windows, I had seen the sorry look before. I tipped my invisible hat to the old man and he frowned harder. There was no mistaking the sight of pissed off geezer. My crime was simple—I had the nerve to be a black woman in a Volvo or a black woman period. The decrepit man looked about 75. I gave him a racial pass based on age alone. I never dreamed my new waitress-friends would confirm what I already knew and add a little Dave Chappelle humor.

The man was seated just a couple of tables away from our friendly banter. If I had to guess, the interracial company and Rita dialogue, whatever of it he could hear, was partly the reason for his premature exit. Or perhaps he finished eating faster that day. I do not know for sure. What I do know is the man was enjoying a late lunch, like me, because he missed the noon hour, even the one o'clock hour. I soon learned that he purposely chose to eat when the restaurant had emptied out a bit because it might cut down on the prospect of having to witness too many blacks and whites dining in the same general vicinity, God forbid, some of them together!

All the women had waited on the regular customer in the past and knew that whenever he paid his bill there was something noticeable if the total called for change to go along with dollar bills. "He hates Lincoln so bad for freeing the slaves, if he has to use pennies, he turns them face down." That was a new kind of loathing I hadn't heard before. First, a mini silence, then big noise. We fell out laughing.

I drove away knowing nothing I could do would racially heal a white man who hated a dead president. But the prejudiced old fool ought to consider checking out the kitchen at The Cedar Tree, where a black woman named Ann cooks most of the food that he turns those pennies down to pay for.

I can't wait to see Florenda, Sherrie, and Brenda again, three gals I would team up with any day against Rita. There are some good strong women in Texas. That, next time I'm in Jasper, we'll have a pint on.

NINE

8,000 special needs patients had to be airlifted out ahead of Rita. They were much discussed during the governor's evacuation hearing. Because of red tape and privacy issues in the medical community, many had not been returned home to Jefferson County months later. There was no doubt leaving saved lives. And created dilemmas.

23 nursing home patients fleeing the storm, not as fortunate as three million others who escaped Rita, died in a fiery bus explosion just outside of Dallas city limits on Interstate 45. *They almost made it.* Conspiracy and other charges related to the deaths of those who left the Brighton Gardens Nursing Home in Houston will be answered.

Any Gulf Coast resident or hurricane survivor will readily testify that Rita was no 1969 model Camille, a Category Five storm. 256 people died. Rita should never be compared to Audrey, who bore down on Louisiana and Texas in 1957, claiming 390 lives. Another Category Five storm made landfall two decades earlier in 1935, ravishing the Florida Keys and killing more than 400. Rita's winds did reach Category Five status before dropping back down to Category Three and coming ashore.

1900. Galveston, Texas. 8,000 people were killed after a Category Four storm forever changed the city's affluent social make-up. Every hurricane has similarities, yet each is unique in its destructive course and aftermath, facts noted, largely, thanks to what meteorologists, first responders and generations of coastal residents have gathered over time in hard lessons. No two hurricanes in history have been exactly alike. Many *survived* Katrina, the actual hurricane. But flooding after her exit was a killer residents in low-lying areas couldn't outrun or outwait. New Orleans as we knew her was silenced and shocked. In all, Katrina claimed more than 1600 lives and counting. Let us not forget that Mississippi and Alabama were devastated.

Rita evacuees had loved ones who died before, during, and after the storm. Many were elderly with preexisting conditions. Others were made sicker or weaker by the stress, suffering from a variety of ills, including diabetes, cancer, heart attack, stroke, oppressive heat. Lack of food and water didn't help. Causes of death or causes of increased or heightened illnesses might not officially list Rita, but tell that to loved ones left behind and caregivers who personally witnessed a dramatic downturn in the health of patients and family members directly related to Rita. Some of their stories were so similar the heartbreak ended with the same unspoken "what if?"

According to *The Associated Press,* about 100 people died as a direct result of Rita. Another agency put the number closer to 120. Those are the ones that have been documented, including 23 passengers on the Global Limo, Inc. bus just outside Dallas. The tally certainly included six people, among them four young siblings, who died after returning to Beaumont seeking shelter and, perhaps, any tiny remnant of familiar comfort called 'home.' A generator left running inside their apartment was blamed for the killer fumes that claimed them.

Lucas Elementary School, where three of the four children were students, honored them with a quiet tribute attended by their 29-year old mother, Irene Bean. All except her firstborn attended Lucas. Crystal was a 6th grader at Smith Middle School. I was in town the same December day when an oak tree was planted at the school to remember four precious lives frozen in childhood innocence— Crystal, Demarcus, Emery, and Aaliyah. They were 12, the two in the middle both 9-years old, the youngest was seven.

Countless times, people remarked if these hurricanes did one thing, they brought people together. Total strangers. Entire cities. In the nearly 20 years I've lived in Dallas, never before had the "I-45 Rivalry" between Dallas and Houston been placed on pause, than in 2005 when the state pulled together to take in Katrina victims.

Celebrities like Lance Armstrong and Jamie Foxx made a countdown Top 10 list for *The Dallas Morning News'* Texan of the Year. The winner wasn't an individual. The relaxed rivalry stayed that way long enough for Dallas to name the city of Houston its "Texan of the Year" for abundant generosity and kindness to all, after Katrina and Rita. Amen, Houston, where 150,000 New Orleanians are still living. Because Rita produced the largest evacuation in Texas history, we may never truly know how many lives were saved thanks to Katrina. People talked to one another about ways they would survive once Hurricane Rita left. They wanted to avoid a repeat performance of suffering. In Fannett, Texas, something as simple as opening a store morphed into an amazing band of unity for the tiny community.

71-year old Robert Anthony Thornton comes into the Green Acres Grocery & Meat Market every single day to "hold court" in front of the coffeemaker. Saturday, January 14, 2006 was no different, except for a post-Rita world that everyone has chatted about since her departure. Otherwise it felt like the start of an ordinary weekend. Thornton, who returned good morning greetings after the "Bobby" that followed, stood in chair-less space that doubled as his private office. He never once complained about the hard economic facts—being a rice farmer hasn't been lucrative for years.

"Foreign countries can produce rice cheaper than we can," Thornton says, "I'd like to see rice go up, but I don't know how." To make a decent living producing and selling rice, as Thornton has done for 52 years, a farmer must *overproduce* just to break even. That won't work on Thornton's 400-acre property, thanks to higher prices for everything from fuel to fertilizer. Over the years, he has monitored the skyrocketing costs of farm necessities and supplies, while the price for a bag of rice has remained the same for more than a decade. Thornton counted himself lucky to have something to fall back on, "The cattle is what's keeping us going." About 170 head of cattle have kept Thornton more than going. Everyone gathered in the working man's circle laughed when the store owner chimed in, "And he knows each one of 'em by name."

Tom Jenkins wasn't born in Texas. Men like Thornton have all but adopted him as a native, teaching Jenkins invaluable lessons on Lone Star pride not found in any textbook. The retail price on a bag of rice, according to Jenkins, hadn't changed in the 12 years he and wife, Christy, and their business partners, have owned Green Acres. All nodded in agreement and sipped the strong black brew.

Fannett used to have one school named for it and Thornton's graduating class in 1952 was 14 strong—12 boys and 2 girls. These days, a consolidated school district named Hamshire-Fannett serves both hamlets and includes the community of Labelle, roughly giving the area about 7,000 residents. They have seen slow growth, primarily because of all the rice farms with sizable acreage. As rice properties are passed from one generation to the next, baby boomers and their offspring opt out of farming and switch to real estate, which accounts for the handful of cul-de-sacs and new developments in a 25-mile stretch that residents claim for the triple communities.

Thornton was born two miles down the road from the Green Acres store. Thornton still lives two miles down the road from the store. When asked why he has stayed in Fannett so long, the gentleman farmer gave a two-word summation: "the people."

Jenkins and his partner, Louis Blanda, met in 1981 when both worked for the same energy company. When an offer came, some 15 years later, to relocate to New Orleans with Entergy, the men took hefty severance packages that allowed them to receive paychecks for the first year of ownership, basically a entrepreneurial blessing for what Jenkins described as a grace period to "learn the grocery business."

For the first six months, Blanda and Jenkins, along with their wives, Lori "Peanut" Blanda and Christy Diane Jenkins, worked long hours without a single day off. "We paid $1.2 million dollars for the store and did not have a pot to go to the bathroom in." The first business day under their owners' umbrella was April 1, 1997.

"We knew when we bought this place, it had potential." The first five years, they doubled sales and updated gas pumps to a more efficient computerized system. When the four-member management team could afford to take a break, there were still weighty issues like debt. "A $1.2 million dollar note just doesn't go away, even when it gets down to a million," Jenkins laughed. They had a unique financial arrangement not for the fiscally faint of heart.

An astute businessman named Tommy Saleme, who came from a long line of grocers, had not only loaned them the money, he taught them the Italian way of doing business. Blanda and Saleme are cousins, so it stood to reason the two men would make a Texas *Eye*-talian out of Jenkins, a native Indianan who called the community approach of service "old school," something their reputation has been built on. Business with a firm handshake and a smile later attracted butcher Carl Neel to work at Green Acres.

Jenkins and store employees, were getting ready for Rita when an evacuation for Jefferson County was ordered early on Thursday, September 22, 2005. He remembered the precise moment when fear became more than a four-letter word. It hit home as they were gathered around a television set watching the Channel 12 News at noon.

"They've done the coordinates on Rita and the weatherman was just standing there," Jenkins paused, then added, "this sounds like a made up story but it's true." What the grocer said next, to a longtime broadcaster, could not have happened on live television. "He's standing there and he [the weatherman] says 'It's coming in down High Island, down 124' and he starts getting emotional and he's almost crying." Jenkins says he and Neel were rattled by what the weatherman did next, as his upset on camera, like the storm, intensified.

"And he leaves, he's gone, he left the set," Jenkins voice was notched up by even the retelling of something so totally incredulous. Viewers were treated to silence and a weather map. A camera operator waited for direction. Jenkins says it was absolutely unnerving, "My butcher looked at me and said 'He's gone, he's in Lumberton already. He's gone. He's already in Lumberton.'" Nobody laughed. At that reality checkpoint, Rita wasn't a joke. The weatherman wasn't in Lumberton, a few miles away in neighboring Hardin County. But he wasn't on camera either.

The male and female news anchors, according to Jenkins, explained to viewers that it was "an emotional time" for everyone. Redemption for the shaken weathercaster. Jenkins says he pulled himself together and returned about five minutes later to do another, more composed update. Jenkins had no doubt that anybody tuned in that day saw what he and Neel saw, knew what he and the butcher knew. "I had one thought—'Oh God, this is gone be bad.'" Jenkins sounded exactly like a native Texan.

Customers entered and exited. They spoke to Jenkins as he recounted his movements before Rita came crashing into his life and store. Someone needed Jenkins at the front where Texas Lottery tickets are hot sellers. A ringing telephone accounted for its share of interruptions. Rachel Sonnier, a pretty young cashier, with bouncy hair and cosmetology school aspirations, was easy on the eyes and greeted everyone with the same shine in her locks. Neel, 56, who has worked more than three years at Green Acres, had machines humming a sharp melody for meaty precision. A woman waited on her order at a glass case filled with fresh selections of ground round, bacon, and t-bone.

Neel and wife, 47-year old Cheryl, live in Port Neches. They own The Corner BBQ and Deli located next door to the store. Neel turned off the music of chopping, slicing and grinding long enough to say, "When I was a kid, I remember Hurricane Carla and that was devastating and the other ones that were bad didn't bother me as much. But I've never seen anything like Rita."

Soft-spoken and humble, Neel has worked hard his entire life to carve out a bit of security for his family. It was hard to gain an admission on post-hurricane views. Neel didn't come across as a man who gripes about what can't be changed or done over. He retained the same early respect for Katrina that was present on a busy Saturday in 2006. "I think the reason a lot of people didn't die here was because of Katrina, because they evacuated." But when told a national news anchor had referred to Rita as "a dud," Neel's views peeked out from behind the steely exterior. "Tell her to come around here, go to Sabine Pass or over there in Cameron."

The butcher shook his head, almost in a sadness that he disliked having to own an opinion that media coverage between Rita and Katrina was more than an imaginary disparity. It was glaring. "We were devastated. You're talking 30-40 years before it [timber] even comes back the way it was." Neel described scenery between Port Neches and Fannett as "a third world country." His family, 23-year old Brad, 20-year old Kimberley, and 13-year old Carley, were without power for a month. "People didn't cover Rita," the meat man with creamy long fingers turned his workshop back into a symphony of sounds.

Christy Jenkins had also seen the emotional Beaumont weatherman. It frightened her too. She began packing clothes and money, food and water, important documents, and battery-operated calculators, asking her husband for answers. "Where are we going to go? What are we going to do?" One thing was clear—they had to get out of Fannett and leave Green Acres to, at least temporarily, fend for itself.

As the evacuation kicked into high gear, or high fear, they closed up shop and left the gas pumps on so customers could get fuel.

People paid at the pump, ever grateful store owners hadn't shut them off when they locked the doors that busy Thursday. People kept buying and buying. The gas purchase parade was a frenzy. When he and the Mrs. left the store, Jenkins noted lines of vehicles, in both directions, on Highway 124 "about 50 deep" and coming. People who had evacuated from Houston pulled off the interstate in search of black liquid gold.

After all the record gas was sold, store owners weren't there to add up the day's receipts. Inside a little black box that transmitted credit card transactions was $15,000 dollars worth of sales they couldn't get to, a necessity if they were going to turn money back into cash in order to purchase more fuel after Rita. The reliable satellite that transmits the information was knocked off the top of the store during the storm. After Rita, nothing could be transferred to New York, a fact that caused worry, tears and panic. "We had to write a check for the gas because we couldn't get our $15,000 out of the black box."

The money "sat there" until Christy Jenkins started digging through store hard copies. They sent a stack of paper receipts express mail and finally got the cash needed to pay for fuel and incoming supplies. But the couple had run ahead of their hurricane story. The topic of gas and checks in the same breath, reminded Christy of a city they had visited every year for 30 years—New Orleans, Louisiana.

"The water scared us from Katrina, I cried." She reflected on images of bodies floating, bloated and face down, unrecognizable, caked in ashy toxic mud, images of 26,000 people at the Superdome waiting for buses that weren't coming. They met "quite a few people from Ford Park" and heard the hurricane nightmares, first from Katrina, then doubled by Rita. One woman, living in a car with children, had run from New Orleans to Mississippi to Houston, and then had to evacuate Houston to Beaumont and beyond. She came into Green Acres with nothing but a check.

"I didn't know her from Adam, but I took that check," smart Christy Jenkins knew the stranger needed the gas and groceries badly. The Fannett grocer said silently to herself, "This'll be my good deed, God will put a little star by my name." After Katrina hit, many of the store's regulars plopped down large amounts of money to buy in bulk, desperate to help any way they could. They purchased dog food, diapers, bottled water, toiletries, dry goods, and whatever else they could carry over to Ford Park, area churches and volunteer agencies. When it was their turn to evacuate for Hurricane Rita, residents feared flooding and watery graves. A storm surge washing over Jefferson County would've left several feet of water in the store. But so many things, mercifully, worked out right.

One of the Green Acres cashiers, 51-year old Vicky Lyday, was good friends with Jim and Paula Broussard, owners of Broussard's Mortuary. The Broussard family was worried about its five locations, the 20-foot surge potential, and serving the needs of grieving customers who relied on them, storm or not. "They had a newly built mortuary and chapel in Silsbee, on top of a hill, which was high and dry," Tom Jenkins says. "It was the only mortuary in the area that remained functional during the hurricane."

"They kept getting phone calls to pick up bodies," Christy added, then, "and they were picking them up too." The Jenkins rode out the storm in a mortuary just 20 miles north of Beaumont with 10 living people and two with no worries. Inside the Broussard sanctuary, its accountant and funeral director took calls, made arrangements and did all they could until phone lines went dead too.

As they hid with the two corpses, no one eager to join them, 12 live bodies hunkered down to watch, wait and listen for Rita. Trees snapped and the wind roared. "It sounded like a freight train was coming through," Tom Jenkins was relieved they had strategically placed all vehicles in the center of the parking lot hoping fallen trees wouldn't wipe their escaping transportation out. After losing power Friday night, about 9:30, intensity built, things got scarier—the wind, the trees and a light show. A deafening train noise. Everyone was still. Once things calmed, they knew it wasn't over. Rita's second wind was heating up. On a storm break to regroup, Rita briefly quieted down trying to fool the live bodies that stepped outside to survey damage. Then she turned around.

"We heard more snapping," Jenkins summed up how the wind redefined fierce to crush whatever opponent it encountered. Inside, hanging on to each other for comfort, were 12 living souls and two recently departed ones. The Jenkins were joined by Vicky Lyday, their cashier, her son, 22-year old Nick. Lyday's husband, Randy, worked for Mobil and he was on lockdown inside the company, an experienced member of the "Hurricane Ride Out Team." As a supervisor in production, Randy Lyday's primary task was to keep processing as much as possible with generators, when that became necessary.

James and Paula Broussard were there, naturally, along with daughter, 17-year old Jayme, and son, 22-year old Blue, Broussard's brother and sister-in-law, Tom and Donna. The two employees who worked throughout were the accountant and director, Warren Krute and Frank Ruedas. Christy Jenkins' parents, Ethel and Douglas Davis, were there too, as were pets responsible for the Animal Kingdom appeal, which included Gimpy the 21-pound cat, dogs, a wolf and more. Every pet in the place wanted out of its cage, especially when sustained winds over Silsbee reached 130 mph. Unbound human animals caged by the four walls wanted freedom from Rita too.

"It just stayed on top of us," Christy recalled how wind ripped at the mortuary. At one point, the front doors violently blew open. It wasn't a ghost or some creature from another world trying to stir things up at the funeral parlor. Rita smelled death. Violent party crasher. There was a rush to bolt the doors. Knocking outside, in the deep night, continued to bang and terrorize people and pets huddled together.

As the couple submerged themselves more into shared memory, Christy paid homage to a man who never got the chance to witness Rita in her full hurricane glory. "One of our customers who shopped in here everyday died trying to evacuate." There was a tear intent on joining us, three people lodged on the canned goods aisle, acknowledging Southeast Texas won't be the same. "His heart just gave out." To his wife's comment, Jenkins lowly spoke to no one in particular, "35 hours in an automobile is too long."

Somewhere in the seesaw discussion on disaster, a mini commentary on fires that had claimed millions of glorious acres. The town of Ringgold, Texas, was completely destroyed. 32 homes gone, leaving 200 residents with nothing but each other and family. Yet, they held church service the following Sunday, minus any building, to praise God for their lives. The last few months of 2005 and the start of 2006, provided one disaster after another for Texans. They saw death. They demonstrated amazing fortitude, backbone, courage and compassion.

After Rita left the mortuary empty-handed, the well prepared owners unloaded their chainsaws and cut a way out for everyone inside. "The word came to us that the canopy was down but the store was there," Tom Jenkins says. Even if their home hadn't been spared, the couple knew they would have a roof and a livelihood. They slowly made their way back to Green Acres.

"We were not ready to open," Jenkins emphatically stated. Hiding customers who saw their vehicles on the parking lot had other notions. The "radar" that brought community members out in droves meant the Jenkins had to make a snap decision. They came to check on things in the early hours after Rita. It was only 2 o'clock Saturday afternoon and winds were still gusting around 60 mph.

Once people convened at the store, the Jenkins couldn't say no. "We worked for about three hours in the dark, in the heat, in the stink." Water had blown into the store, but there wasn't time to focus on cleanup. Battery-operated calculators came in handy. Brief smiles at the two hottest selling items: cigarettes and beer. "They also wanted ice, our frozen stuff and the milk still usable at that point." Christy witnessed purchasing habits restructured by the storm. "I saw people buying $300 dollars worth of grocery in a buggy, people who usually would buy $30."

No one knew for sure when or if necessities would be restocked. Rumors flew in the wind. "Remarks from county officials, one judge in particular," the couple agreed, "set off a firestorm of panic and people were buying." Customers had heard that they'd be made to leave and all businesses forced to close. The Jenkins knew a curfew was necessary and that Beaumont was locked down. If not for state police, who allowed them through, they would not have made it to Fannett and their beloved store. If authorities hadn't let them pass, Tom and Christy Jenkins would not have seen the raw devastation of rubble, dangling stoplights, mounds of debris, glass everywhere, nails in the streets, countless unhinged shingles, dried leaves pressed to the ground in a blanket of crunchy carpet, uprooted trees and downed power lines too numerous to count. The city limits looked like a war zone. They maneuvered, first, to their house, and then to their store.

A double blessing meant their home had been spared. The two trees Tom and Christy Jenkins assumed would be on their roof were still standing. The structure had been beaten up pretty good and there were a lot of limbs that needed moving to physically open the door. A fence was gone. Girl Rita had played sidewalk hopscotch in the neighborhood. Three houses across the street were "totally smashed."

After Green Acres was open on Saturday afternoon, the Jenkins decided to try again Sunday, knowing people who stayed behind would need supplies and food. They stayed open from 11 a.m. to 5 p.m. Instead of loyal customers popping in and out to buy goods, the community rallied around the little store.

"We had customers mopping up the floor, it was a total community effort," Tom Jenkins beamed. 21 years together has manufactured the completion of marital sentences and the expert reading of thoughts. "Remember George Dearborn?" Christy looked at her husband who seemed about to say the very same thing. "He was in the cooler putting beer and milk in but not knowing where to put it." Customers worked wherever they were needed. It was their store too. "They were just so thankful we were here," the couple again finished the same sentence. *Were they worried about looters?* Not really, not after the community came to their aid and "took care of them" as Jenkins put it. They called loyal shoppers "the guardians" who protected them and watched over the store. I didn't have to ask because this is still Texas. The guardians were armed.

In those rough initial aftermath hours, the Jenkins had been told it might be a full month before electricity would be restored. "I've never seen so many power lines down in my life," Christy fully prepared herself for the reality that they would have to make due for at least 30 more days. Primitive days. The volunteer fire department had been piling ice over meat contained in a huge freezer located at the rear of the store.

"We had 1800 pounds of meat that we saved. There was brisket, rib-eyes, chicken, pork, we had everything back there." Jenkins wasn't sure what to do. Instead of letting the meat thaw and ruin, ice in short supply, they decided to get a gigantic barbecue pit from one of their customers. Carl, the trusted store butcher, and Valerie Casburg, who had worked at the store for 12 months, fired it up and started grilling.

The decision to party, rather than pity over their situation, was made on impulse. It was one store owners have never regretted. People smelled the food. They lined up for the free block party. The Jenkins threw in two slices of bread, great for pressing the meat between, along with condiments, giving substance to the phrase, "All that and a bag of chips!" They gave each person their own snack bag.

"We cooked 300 pounds of meat every day for six days, until it was gone," Tom Jenkins knew the food was more than appreciated. He not only heard it over and over, he had seen with his own eyes people surviving on candy bars and Vienna sausages in the can. People lined up at lunch time each day to get something sizzling, hot and delicious.

"Do you know where Cheek is?" Christy asked. Apparently Cheek didn't have a store to go to immediately after Rita. A large chunk of the community is black. Its residents were the same as the Fannett regulars. Folk who lived in Cheek needed to buy gas and supplies. Some also came for the meat. "You wouldn't believe all the hungry people."

Green Acres won a slew of new shoppers. The couple agreed that a barbecue felt right. It allowed them to share what they had in the store with others, open the store for business and reach out to an area filled with caring residents who had always been their lifeblood. "With all that was going on, we didn't think about black and white," Jenkins says, "just people." His wife nodded, "No question, Rita brought people together."

As we walked outside, Jenkins expressed dismay at how Rita zig-zagged her way across Texas and Louisiana on a wild D. W. I ride. "90 miles inland is the longest hurricane on land." We photographed leftover damage and chatted about the small circuit of arenas that once welcomed bull-riding cowboy talent. There was an arena in Cheek, another in Fannett and off main roads.

"Down 124," Jenkins pointed, "past Hamshire, is another big bull ring that's right outside of Winnie." Robert Thornton had told us that young men who came up with him, didn't "go into town much," a reference to Beaumont. "You worked, you rode bulls, you courted girls, and knew cows and rice real well."

I ran back inside Green Acres to do one final thing—check the price for a large bag of rice. It was $1.89. Farmers deserve better. Then I tallied up the total for 1800 pounds of premium meat.

Priceless.

TEN

Carl Neel, the Green Acres butcher, had facetiously stated the weatherman with frazzled nerves shot up to Lumberton from the live Beaumont television set in a nanosecond. By car, it took a little longer.

My mind still on steaks and chips and long gas lines, I pulled into a driveway where a woman I'd never met invited me to visit. A man who didn't notice me cruise up, sporting white t-shirt and jeans, was doing yard work.

Linda Hale appeared on the front porch and waved. Her jet black hair was big and pretty, her face welcoming and friendly. I never had a single reservation about entering a single residence in Southeast Texas. I was home.

Hale's kitchen table became our chat headquarters. Barely seated, the 59-year old woman didn't wait for me to hit the record button. She was off with an energy that rivaled melted chocolate in a cup. We were meeting to talk about Rita. But Hale was a fireball who first zapped me with her love for history and how the truth can be buried under a thin layer.

"Supposedly, the story was a white woman was raped and killed and this black man was seen hunting in the area. The whole town went berserk." Hale went, in a matter of seconds, from a modern day hate crime she had read about, penned by an author she was suddenly seated across from, to a lynch case that happened in 1933. I wasn't prepared for the transition. Hale had all of my attention the way she burst from the racial gate.

A member of the Hardin County Genealogical Society, her passion was obvious. Two years earlier, the group president, Floyd Boyett, had done an oral interview with a black woman in her 90's who still remembered names and highlights from the lynch case and crime. That's all Hale needed to begin her fill-in-the-blank quest.

Club records had a brief mention in its historical record. Next, Hale went to the Death Index for Texas, where she looked up the date the white woman had been murdered. "Then I had something to go on." A day later, hot on the trail, Hale took off for *The Beaumont Enterprise* to search for articles.

"What this lady [the black woman] had remembered and what the whole black community knew was that her husband, [the victim's] on his deathbed, confessed to the killing." Hale allowed me to turn on the tape. I took mental notes as she pulled out a brown evidence folder crammed full of articles and other items. There was a summary of events that Hale had written, I suspect, therapeutically so, to bolster a strong timeline and key facts. Her voice kept speeding up, it and she, highly agitated, "This black man, they burned him, they dragged him, and it was just horrible." Hale had taken me back to the scene of my own life-altering crime with three words: "They dragged him." Surely my face must've showed some sign of how unprepared I was to hear the gory details.

After her research, Hale wrote something to place in club archives utilizing Census records on the victim's family to give the entry more substance. Another club member, a black woman named Meka McDaniel, she discovered, was kin to the lynched man. McDaniel often heard snippets of the case growing up and knew what others in her community believed. Hale was genuinely shocked at her own father's admission, though he was a child then, to faint knowledge on some aspects of the story. *Why hadn't she ever heard anything about it* was one mystery that multiplied her determination.

An inviting aroma from something slow cooking on the stove wafted all through the cozy abode. We continued down a dark path. "This was the first thing I found," Hale placed a document right in front of me. She was sincere, a sturdy woman made so by nature and honest labor—23 years as a Tech I operator with Arco Oil and Gas. I barely had time to glance the short history of Hardin County before another piece of paper was added. It was a story on the posse that hunted for suspects.

"They shot him in a bell chapel here in Lumberton," Hale gave the man's name and he was more real at that moment. A racial movie unfolded in my brain, its familiar scenario with an end I knew by heart. While Hale talked, I glanced more articles she had copied. Her account was so fast-paced it made me dizzy. Words merged together like "mutilation" and "mob," "bloodthirsty" and "sheriff." Hale continued on, "He has no birth certificate or death certificate and no grave. They burned him." She used one word repeatedly, "horrible," and the *horror* of even its pronunciation easily carried me back to December 1933 and the center of injustice for David Gregory, a man who never saw daylight again. Or his family.

"I am so into the history of Hardin County and I had never heard this story," Hale again sounded shocked that such a thing could've occurred and not been discussed in front of her over the years. Her legal summation continued, "This is what made me sick to my stomach—nobody was arrested for any of this, nobody was brought to justice." Hale finally took a breath. She sat back in a quaint kitchen table chair, relieved to have spread all of the proof in front of a visiting researcher from Dallas.

Exhibit number three was from the *Beaumont Journal* and dated Monday, December 4, 1933. The headline featured big bold capital letters: **SECOND NEGRO SOUGHT IN KOUNTZE KILLING.** According to the story, 100 more men had been added to a burgeoning posse, even though three Negroes were being held for questioning. I marveled at the other news of the day, which included stories about a man who had been killed in a car crash near Nederland, how opponents were planning to hang Huey Long in effigy, voting tactics under scrutiny, an approaching deadline to reach an agreement for fixing oil prices, funeral plans for Judge Will Carroll, and the 9th annual "Community Chest" drive was underway with its ambitious plans to raise more than $97,000 dollars. Half the money collected, deadline was only days away.

The Kountze Killing lead started as follows: "Belief that a second negro [sic] was involved in the brutal slaying of Mrs. Mellie W. Brockman, 30, near Kountze Saturday, was expressed by officers at Kountze Monday noon as bloodhounds were kept on the trail and three negroes [sic] were held in the Hardin County Jail under close guard for questioning." The story went on to clarify that none of the three men being held were considered the murderer of Mrs. Brockman, but one had told authorities he saw a man about 30 minutes before the woman's burning body was discovered. The detainee also told deputies the man they were looking for said to him, "I've got to leave town quick."

Sheriff Miles Jordan was following a multitude of tips on the crime. A white woman, the mother of three children, viciously attacked and murdered on her way to Kountze to "exchange some baby shoes." She never made it. Brockman was discovered ablaze that afternoon right beside her truck just west of town. Investigators believed the vehicle was torched to hide the crime. The young mother had been shot in the head. A history file on Hardin County described the big thicket as "an armed camp. " Texas Rangers were called in for backup, including a man from Buna named Hamer. Their intent clear. "The rangers dared anyone to cross the Santa Fe Railroad tracks dividing the white part of town from the black community."

Not 24 hours later, while "Armed Louisiana Citizens" burned ballots, a $700 dollar reward had been posted for the arrest and conviction of 24-year old David Gregory for murdering Mellie Williams Brockman out on the Honey Island Road. The county's top prosecutor, B. A. Coe, had wired the governor a request for two special state officers to help with the investigation.

By Thursday, December 7, 1933, the *Beaumont Journal,* had another front page of local, state and national headlines jammed together onto an oversized page. Top news of the day: **3 SLAIN IN BORDER RUMRUNNER BATTLE.** Out of Washington D. C., rankled feathers at the leaked information on a Miss Francis Robinson, an NRA assistant to Hugh Johnson, being paid a healthy annual salary of $5,780 as a "traveling" employee. The investigation, supposedly initiated by *Washington Post* reporters, uncovered Miss Robinson's meteoric rise in the agency. She had started her short career at $25 dollars per week as a clerk.

The Community Chest had raised $93,612 dollars. Campaign workers were confident the goal would be met in time for a victory dinner the next night. An exhaustive manhunt for the "Hardin Killer" had expanded to Houston and Beaumont, where law enforcement had received a tip that David Gregory might be hiding out in one or the other. A Texas Ranger assisted Houston officers in probing the "negro quarters" of that city. Back in Hardin County, a thorough search continued in wooded areas near and far from the crime scene just to be certain the suspect had not "eluded their dragnet." *What did readers know about David Gregory?*

The answer rang out in the next edition of the *Beaumont Journal* on Friday, December 8, 1933. **KOUNTZE QUIET AFTER BURNING NEGRO'S BODY.** David Gregory was dead. There wasn't going to be a trial. Three pictures accompanied three front page stories. One showed the Mt. Zion Baptist Church where Gregory was shot by Deputy Ralph Chance. A tip led authorities to the tiny hamlet of Voth. As they approached the church building, according to the county record, Sheriff Jordan called for Gregory to surrender and come out. He refused. Deputy Chance then shot into the church belfry hitting Gregory in the head.

Another photo was that of Sheriff Jordan, coat collar turned up, cigarette hanging off his lower lip. He wore a hat, white shirt and tie. The man beside him in the newspaper's third photo was County Attorney Coe. His serious expression matched a dark suit. The lead was one that had been written about, or not, more than 5,000 times in documented lynch cases across the country, but mostly, in the South.

"Mob violence was quieted here Thursday after the body of David Gregory, negro [sic] ex-convict accused of attacking and murdering Mrs. Mellie Brockman near here, was burned in the negro [sic] section at 1:30 a.m. by a bloodthirsty mob."

The predictable conclusion, after a nearly weeklong manhunt, didn't surprise anyone who knew that after Gregory was shot from a "church steeple in Voth," the torture for a lifeless body wasn't over. A message engraved to an entire community had to be hand delivered. Before the gang could snatch Gregory, the sheriff had taken him to the Hotel Dieu. He feared mob mentality would prevail.

While Gregory—a black man described as being 5 feet 8 inches tall, weighing approximately 150 pounds, dark brown complexion, bushy hair, marble eyes and "extra white teeth," with a Charlie Chaplin mustache—was being transported to Orange, he died en route. Lawmen, according to the brief summary in Hardin County's historical record, decided it would be best to take the body to a funeral home in Silsbee. But the mob got wind of the plan. They waited there, forcibly taking the body. There was little doubt about what would happen next.

Gregory's corpse was dragged through town and then to the black community, where his heart was carved out and shown to his mother. The black man mutilated for remaining souvenir parts. Then, and only then, was Gregory set ablaze. Cruelty reached a feverish pitch when, according to county information, the frenzied mob first tore down the fence around Georgia Gregory's home, using lumber, along with debris and trash, to make a roaring fire to burn her son's body. "There was never any proof that Gregory was the murderer," the written historical segment abruptly ended.

As a precaution, the three men who had been sitting in the Hardin County Jail were taken to another location until things could calm down. No reward was paid. The family of David Gregory, even after what they had seen, requested his remains for burial. The burned up shell of a corpse had been discarded. There was no body and no funeral.

One line in the article was particularly chilling. "Citizens have returned to their homes to get some sleep after the night's events." And the Community Chest drive was going to wrap up Friday evening with a victory dinner at the Hotel Beaumont.

People who knew the story well had said Gregory and the white woman were friends, they lived in the same precinct. Case closed. Case solved. Except in a black section of town where an elderly woman named Versie Fears Johnson recalled a footnote to the story. She claimed that a white man named William Brockman, on his August 1978 deathbed, had confessed to killing his wife. There was never any written or supporting proof. Brockman, according to a Census record, had last lived in Jasper. Johnson's husband recently died in 2006. He was 103. Floyd Boyett, the Hardin County Genealogical Society president, and wife, Bobee, attended the memorial.

Linda Hale was obsessed with the Brockman murder and uprising that followed. She never wanted to publicly share details, not 70 years later, not at all, for fear it might "stir things up." With Hale, I sensed it was personal. She certainly never intended for me to write about the case, but I believe she knew I would. Nothing was off the record. The tape remained turned on.

Our conversation was not what I expected when showing up to chat about Rita. I also believe Hale worried that I would think badly of Hardin County. No county in Texas, or anywhere else for that matter, can have all of its citizens judged by a single event. Folks in Hardin have always welcomed me and treated me just fine. I like it there. Not looking at or acknowledging history has a way of stirring things up anyway.

Everyone I met in Rita's wake had some profound reason for allowing me into their lives. Hale was a fascinating woman who reminded me of a true southern survivor with Mother Wit. She embraced her place in Texas history.

"I was so blessed to grow up in Beaumont on Pierce Street," she closed the 1933 page, "and there was a little half lot behind us." Only tiny brush separated her house from a black community that Hale learned from by observing. "I grew up being taught by my momma, she's dead now, but she taught us 'you see what's in here,'" she pointed to her heart. "You don't look at skin color."

Our conversation meandered some. We visited two days before the King Holiday and compared notes on why many considered it something "for black people." I had just studied an AP/Ipsos poll that surveyed whites about the federal holiday. Only 15% of those questioned planned to do anything special to commemorate the civil rights leader or his life. One of our greatest American heroes has a holiday named in his honor, and sadly, some believe it's a day primarily for black folk to celebrate.

Hale had her copy of *HATE CRIME,* she let me sign it, along with another one she purchased to send to a friend who worked at Scotland Yard. This opening gave us the chance to talk about my canceled December visit to London. She was sorry to hear I had been very ill, but impressed about the Progreso Fair Trade Coffee Bar that I had contacted on Portobello Road. The manager was gracious enough to invite me to read there when I finished my London business. I was ecstatic. It was the same store British actor Colin Firth was part owner of. That was probably the closest I was going to get to Firth. He once surprised customers, helping serve their coffee one morning. Hale thought that was something. Then we switched gears again to tackle Rita.

"We evacuated," she started, "to my mother's lake house in Toledo Bend." Hale and company were right on the border in Sabine County, 21 people, seven dogs, three kids, all with one thing in common—wait it out. Hale was quick to stress that hers was not "a sob story." It was an ordinary deal, the same hand thousands of Texans were dealt. "The minute the storm was over, I wanted to come home."

Hale heard horror stories about Silsbee and Woodville. She felt sick sleeping in a different bed, being on the road, away from her most prized possessions. "Someone else might take china and crystal, but my books and my research—I have 25 years worth of documents—if I lost them I could never start over." Hale suddenly paused, the magnitude of what she said sank deep and resonated all through her being.

To protect a quarter-century work, Hale had placed everything in Ziploc bags and hoped for a miracle. It was an unnerving few days for the full-time history buff. 24 hours after Rita, the Hale family hooked up their camper, which was never used at the lake house because it "was rocking and rolling." They made it to Buna, "The highway patrol was turning people around." What Hale did next even surprised her.

Before her husband, William "Bob" Hale, could roll down the window, she leaned over and took control, "We're trying to get to sick people in Lumberton." They signaled the Hales through the barricade. Hale laughed at the mini fib, which turned out to have some truth to it later. "I just wanted to come home."

When they finally made it to Lumberton, the couple couldn't travel down the street they lived on. "Every telephone pole was snapped or broken in two. We went on the next street and got as far as the corner nearest our house." Neighbors did the same thing. It was a hodgepodge of curiously dazed people weaving in and out, always careful about where they stepped and what they stepped on. "The wires were all hanging in front of our driveway, plus trees," Hale says. "Neighbors got chainsaws and they cleared us a path."

The next step was to buy survival items. They got a generator first, living in the camper for six weeks. But it was better than a tent, better than being outside in the heat, and better than nothing. The camper was sufficient. Not designed for extended living. It provided the benefit of watching their permanent dwelling. "I don't know if you remember how hot it was."

Because of the stifling mercury, for days, they ran the generator only at night. Another reason made it necessary. "It was so hot the first day my husband had to stand in line for nine hours to get gas." Countless others were sweating it out for a few gallons. Fuel was one of the only things residents have admitted to getting into loud fights and disagreements over. Especially if someone thought the person ahead of them was being allowed to get more than them. *Gas favoritism.* The entire time we had been talking, the same nice looking fellow doing all that yard work, was finishing up. Hale pointed in his direction through an open window, "He was in line for over nine hours with every gas can we ever owned or any containers we could get to fill up." To keep the generator humming cost about $45 per day.

"I would've paid anything, I would've sold whatever to run it." Hale smiled, and kept repeating her weather mantra, "It was hot, plus we were working like dogs." There was water damage, the carpet its biggest casualty. Hale was delighted her Ziploc idea worked, doing a marvelous preservation job on history records.

For the first two days, it was just Hale and her husband. Her worried family was frantic to reach them. "The next thing I know, my grandson—a big 'ole husky guy—and my son-in-law, flew in from Pennsylvania." Later, her 36-year old son, Delbert O'Haver, and 14-year old grandson, Devin, made it in from Lufkin. Hale has 11 grandchildren and spent a few minutes doting on every one.

"They just started working like Trojans," she animatedly declared, without missing a beat. Her muscular 25-year old grandson who came first, Jason, told her he would be going to Houston to bring back a friend who wanted to help. That *friend* actually turned out to be Vance Davis, the son-in-law who is married to stepdaughter, Patricia. The next morning, Jason brought back the surprise, more help, more family. "I didn't know the friend was really my son-in-law," Hale says, then stressed how much "step" has no place in her combined family. "I love Patricia as my own."

The makeshift crew worked nonstop, clearing the yard, helping the couple move "every speck of furniture" from all the bedrooms and everything out of the closets. Hale was shocked at the amount of stuff accumulated over the years in those closets. "I had carpet in my genealogy room, two desks, 10 filing cabinets, a Xerox machine, and cabinets on top of cabinets." All of it was moved in order to rip out soggy carpet so mold would not make itself to home. "Everything had to come out of that room, plus the ceiling had a leak so that entire room had to be gutted."

Rita forced Hale to do something she had been begging her husband to do—change the location of her genealogy room. She had always wanted company to have a back bedroom and that another spare room, closer to her own master space, be where she housed the gem of a collection more special than crystal or silverware. "My husband would not have done it." So Rita did.

Visitors to the Hale Home, will, in the future, occupy the larger bedroom, with its privacy to the rear of their spacious one-story home. It meant downsizing and giving away some files to her cherished genealogical society. Hale didn't mind. She could still see them anytime she wanted at monthly meetings. "We open every Wednesday, all day, and one Saturday a month."

Hale was then holding double duties as cemetery and program chairman, but has also served as president. "This is my biggest project that we do, a brand new cemetery book for Hardin County." The arduous task required Hale to inspect every cemetery and record every piece of information on every grave "in a uniform way." Members always started in the southwest corner from where the gate is located, the easiest way to find listed and unmarked graves.

"According to the Historical Commission and according to a book that was done 30 years ago," Hale explained, "there were 47 cemeteries in Hardin County." She always believed there were more. Hale ran advertisements in all the papers with requests that any hunters, residents, or anyone hiding in the woods who knew of any graves, come forward. Now, thanks to Hale and society members, there are 69 known burial sites.

"Oh, I have trumped through every piece of wood in this county," Hale laughed. That was enough to garner the attention of an official from the State Historical Commission who came visiting in 2004. Hale personally carried the woman around, determined to provide necessary geographical documentation. They went to every cemetery in the county, "She took a GPS [Global Positioning Satellite] reading on every corner and they're doing a new atlas for Texas. All of these cemeteries are going to be protected."

Each time Hale discovered a new cemetery, no matter how

small, she would rush home and do the genealogy to locate descendants from those families. Hale preserved whatever records she found for interested parties. For a woman the age of Hale, her energy and commitment to Hardin County and history was boundless and inspirational. *When do you sleep* I wanted to ask. Hale's East Texas twang kept going and going, the spirited Southern energizer belle.

"My other big project that I'm doing right now is," Hale says, "I bought every single Civil War pension application filed in Hardin County." People who served in wartime, back then, were allowed to apply for pensions. Hale wanted those applications for the priceless information contained in them. "They had to name where they were married, birthdates, and a ton of other information." At first, ownership seemed a pipedream. But Linda Hale was patient.

"The Texas State Archives won't let you buy but 10 at a time because it's a lot of copying." It took her almost a year to get them all. 167 veterans had applied for pensions in Hardin County and Hale knows them all by name. A friend, Sandra Stiles, scanned the applications onto a disk and the CD's can be purchased by anyone from her club. Hale doesn't get one dime. Proceeds go back into the Hardin County Genealogical Society, which is part of the masterful Gen Web online project.

Briefly, we discussed the white great grandfather I had been tracking, a man born in England but reared in Canada. I saw the genealogical wheels in Hale's head start to turn as she processed the little information I had gathered from a most unwilling, only child—my father. Sure enough, a few days later, Hale sent me what she had learned on men with the same common name. She wanted me to continue searching. Hale's desire to help has always been extended to ordinary people hunting for ancestors, across the country and in her own backyard. She loved to work and be of service.

Hale and I popped back to our earlier discussion of 1933 and David Gregory. Her pained face, she reiterated a desire to not stir "old wounds." Then out of nowhere, Hale hit hard with a question of her own. "You know when things are going to change?" I really didn't but Hale was sure, "It's going to change when men that are my husband's age are gone." Considering the source, the fiery woman had made a rather stunning conclusion. I told Hale that might be a tad harsh given that some white men her husband's age weren't the problem all by themselves. The problem is prejudiced people all ages. "But I've met a bunch [her husband's age] who do need to change." Point match to Hale.

Bob Hale did finally come in to check on smells tickling his nose, get some liquid refreshment and meet "the guest' who had occupied his kitchen table for more than an hour. I can't be sure, even though my book on white men has provided some foolish notion that I am on expert on the species, but it looked to me like I was the first or second black person to visit that kitchen. I must remember to ask Hale. She would like that.

Hubby was handsome. His salt and pepper hair neat, sideburns long from another decade, silver rimmed glasses fixed, suspiciously in my direction to gauge what the interloper was thinking. He was friendly enough, awkwardly attempting to even grant me a snippet of conversation. I think he peeked in the oven, the same place Hale had remembered a few minutes earlier she needed to check on something baking too fast. He was hungry. I hadn't been divorced so long that I didn't recognize the *where's my supper* look. Mr. Hale, on hold for a moment, retired to an easy chair and remote in the next room. Thank goodness, white men all loved me.

Mrs. Hale got back to Rita, the reason for my visit. Or not. "This little lady that lived down the street from me, her house was almost totally demolished and the house across from me, a tree went all the way through into their house." Hale watched the rebuilding process, with empathy, from her camper. "Another house was also gutted." The hurricane played its hit and miss design through every Texas county that Gov. Perry declared disaster areas.

As our time together wound down, Hale summed up her Rita devastation by "thanking God" she didn't have to wait for insurance people. She had cell phone numbers for contractors and immediately began calling for placement on the "early lists" for repairs. The strategy worked. Hale took pictures, she knew her coverage was better than most. "The insurance man came out the very first week, on a Wednesday afternoon. I had my check on the following Monday."

The post-inconvenience didn't seem to bother Hale much. She did seem kind of testy that Time Warner Cable didn't have things back up and running sooner. Hale had to do without her trusty

Internet service for one month. "People told me, 'Linda, you're going to go into shock.'" She almost did, unable to log on and do the kind of research that has been her mission. Hale spent the time, not looking for names, but getting to know ordinary survivors in her own neighborhood.

"I know Rita brought people closer together," Hale says, "we had some friends over the other night and that's what we were talking about." Rita conversations woke everyone up. Hale knew folk on her street well enough to wave when groceries were being unloaded or mail taken out of the box, but Rita forced them to go deeper, learn more than just names.

"After Rita, I'm telling you, everybody in this neighborhood immediately stopped what they were doing to come over here and get us into our driveway." A kindness Hale won't forget, the same act that has continued to be paid forward. A woman whose house was "crushed" stayed with the Hales in their camper for days.

"We were all sharing food," the former Arco "roustabout" says. *What's a roustabout?* Hale may be retired, but the job at Arco started her helping wherever she was needed—on engines, pumps, in the field. Today, Hale might still put on her rig boots and jeans and head out to the oilfield to check on relief pumps owned by friends who have a lease on some wells. Her 34-year old daughter, Monica Sweeney, doesn't like it one bit.

Sweeney and her 15-year old son, Michael, live in Spring, Texas. They were so concerned about Hale, they begged to be let through one barricade after another to reach Lumberton, armed with a generator, ice, gas, food, and extension cords. Like her mother, Sweeney told DPS troopers, she needed to get medical supplies to the woman. It took a toll. Sweeney was exhausted and sobbed uncontrollably, breaking down several times at checkpoints. Hale relaxed momentarily, reflecting on how blessed she was to have a loving family. She bounced right back, chuckling at the concern over her outdoor activities. "It's in my blood, I can't help it. I have to smell that oil."

My last stop in the Hale Home was that back bedroom remade by Rita for company. A large quilt took up an entire wall. It was breathtaking. Hale won the homemade beauty in a raffle from 500 sold tickets. She had the winner and every woman there was jealous.

The amazing hand-stitched quilt was the work of sister-members from the Texas State Genealogical Society gathered for a big meeting in Austin. Each of the 20 districts represented in the Lone Star state was a unique square gracing the quilt. All were connected to make up the colorful swath of one huge Texas ornament.

For a little while, we stood in silence admiring the quilt. Several have offered to buy or take it off Hale's hands. I felt bad that hubby had to wait a few more minutes on that well deserved dinner.

With a tear in her eye, Linda Hale remarked on the prize. "I am so proud of this quilt. It is so me."

ELEVEN

A man who had a lot to say about Katrina was on his way to Port Arthur, Texas. Given his penchant for inclusion, I knew he wouldn't neglect Rita.

Years before, Tavis Smiley had endorsed *HATE CRIME*. His name is on the jacket. During a phone interview with Smiley in 2003, I finally got my chance to say thanks, but never met the man vis-à-vis. As the months piled up after our long distance connection, I kept having near misses with the television commentator and best-selling author. We were in the same city at the same time, but never the same function. Of all the places I could've predicted it would happen, Port Arthur was not on the short list.

An unforgettable Friday the 13th. January 2006. I had just arrived at my Beaumont hotel, eager to answer a few emails. After the first couple congratulated me for some unknown honor, I plowed through a few more hoping to find out what the achievement was. Finally, someone included a link to see that a Washington-based columnist named Richard Prince had written something about the 15 books he believed Martin Luther King, Jr. would enjoy reading were he alive at that moment. *GROWING UP SOUTHERN* was one of the 15. I didn't know Mr. Prince personally, but knew he was reading GUS. His flattering column was posted at websites for both the NABJ (National Association of Black Journalists) and the Maynard Institute. I was humbled, particularly after I saw some of the literary company.

Two days later, Angel San Juan called while I was reading the Sunday paper at Barnes & Noble downing Starbucks Coffee. He had a woman on the phone named Hargie Faye Savoy. 20 years earlier, at the personal request of Coretta Scott King, while the two women were chatting in her Port Arthur bedroom, Mrs. Savoy founded the

Dr. Martin Luther King Jr. Support Group of Southeast Texas, Inc. Angel confirmed she was putting finishing touches on a big celebration for the national holiday and Smiley would be the guest speaker.

Back at the hotel, someone stopped me at the elevator. "A fan," she referred to herself, wanted to pass on some information. "Tavis Smiley will be at this hotel," the woman smiled, "I know you know the man and thought you'd like to see him." Her face had a hint of Eve's blush in the naughty declaration. I knew why the stranger was excited. Smiley is one of the most eligible bachelors in the free world.

Most black women, and plenty of white ones too, have followed his career and are on a first name basis with *Tavis*. Not so much for his debonair looks and single status, but because of what the man stands for. Smiley has come a long way since the first time I laid an ear on him, when he had at least two jobs—that of social commentator on *The Tom Joyner Morning Show* and at night, host of his own Black Entertainment Television Show, *BET Tonight*. I'm thrilled that Smiley has slowed down his delivery some. He used to spit out more words in 10 seconds than the average person could in one minute. And he pulled no punches, his trademark banter the epitome of the old-fashioned tell-it-like-it-'T-I-IS.

Armed with Smiley's hotel room number, early Monday I called the front desk and requested a bellman come up. I tipped him to take a handwritten note to Smiley's door. It was 7:30. Maybe he was up for breakfast, that free coffee that comes with the room or logged onto the Internet. Something. I had to try. Too boring to "try" anything rated R, the note was a scribbled thank you, hey, hello, can't believe you and me are in the same hotel, a this-is-fortuitous-kind-of-thing. No key card or suggestive message. Since I knew the room Smiley was in I didn't need the bellman had I really a mind to "visit."

After the 'Welcome to Texas,' and 'Happy King Holiday' greetings, I felt like it might be my only chance to hint at an appearance on his PBS television show. We had done the phone Q&A, *why not make it LIVE on the interview couch?* Predictable, I sent the man a book, hoping to secure a second interview. A few minutes later, I left Beaumont for its next door neighbor, Port Arthur. The bellman knew I required no response. Nor did I expect one. Tavis Smiley and me in the same hotel. The woman at the elevator hoped I would take a shot. Sending a book probably wasn't what she had in mind.

The Carl Parker Multipurpose Center on MLK was filling up. A 10 a.m. brunch featured ballroom tables, purchased by various high-profile individuals and agencies and elected officials from the area. The theme was appropriate: "Embracing the Beloved Community Before, During and After the Storm." From what I could see on the drive into Port Arthur, it needed embracing. Palm trees saluted me down a stretch called Woodworth. I turned onto Proctor.

A few structures looked like they were already in pre-hurricane disarray. Some were still boarded up, homes and businesses. Not everyone had returned. Nor did it look as if they might anytime soon. The big Trinity Lutheran Church had a hint for backsliders: "Worship Every Sunday." As if to drive the point home, not far away was the Gabriel Funeral Home, next stop for faithful parishioners and wayward sinners, "Established in 1977." I soon past Gateway Baptist and a Buddhist Temple. It was definitely an equal opportunity religious lane with Lutherans, Baptists and Buddhists in close proximity to the angelic-named funeral home.

For several minutes, I drove around a neighborhood that had seen better days before Rita showed up to wipe out any potential many had worked hard to entice. A Port Arthur police car slowed down to see what I was doing, stopped at a light, talking into a square thing no bigger than the palm of my hand, which made it look like I was whispering into my thumb. *Bond, Joyce Bond.* Taking notes and driving at the same time, forced me, a long time ago, and a near fatal crash, to travel with tape recorder and T-W-D, Talk While Driving. To fellow motorists, it may look hysterical, but is a lot safer.

A light drizzle was more an annoyance than anything else. Not enough rain to turn the wipers on, but enough to hit the auto wipe button every few seconds. A weather nuisance. Election signs almost outnumbered dwellings, it was hard to tell who endorsed whom with multiple markings in the same yard. *Re-Elect Rose Mitchell Chasion Justice of the Peace.* There were boats, trailer homes, and unsteady houses, a high percentage adorned with the familiar governmental tarps of royal blue. Men were on rooftops. Women had on work gloves. Both sexes hammered away and piled debris they were feverishly trying to stack before a deadline. One thing Rita produced was a lot of damn deadlines.

I hit a four-way stop, not unusual in busy neighborhoods, at least, not until I noticed how stunted in growth the red signs were. *Had someone re-buried the signs so deep that they were a full three feet shorter?* It might've been comical to see stop signs for the vertically challenged, had Rita not been the reason for them. One guy, perhaps he didn't see them, never bothered stopping at 7th and Woodworth. I inched out, when it was my turn, hoping other motorists would heed the abbreviated traffic command.

The Port Arthur Fire Station Number One looked fairly new, a beautiful tan colored building, spiffy on the outside, hardly a clue of the work these men and women were called on to do months earlier. A loud yellow and white building stood out like bright sunshine itself. At first glance, S & S Shrimper's Supply was in business, had fared well under the pressure of Rita. On closer examination, it had taken some hard licks but appeared to be servicing a few customers. The hurricane had left its calling card everywhere accessible to the naked eye. Damage had come to Port Arthur to stay. Enveloped deep inside a thick depression that hung in the air, there remained something so vibrant and hopeful about this city.

I liked the multitude of color and character present in older homes and neighborhoods. I saw red, green and blue paint on fading, weather beaten wood. I saw white houses, trimmed by a fruit rainbow. Peaches, oranges, apples and bananas. Shutters wanted to speak from dangling wood next to taped over windows.

A restaurant called *This is It* promised "down home cooking." Too bad brunch was set. I zipped by the Channel 4 "Hometown News" studio. No one was around to cover breaking news. This slice of Port Arthur life made it difficult to determine which muted businesses and buildings were made so my Rita, or already in trouble before she pushed them over the edge. I saw a sign for "Time Out Food Mart," twisted and torn, one loose nail and the whole store would come tumbling down. Probably sturdier inside.

Signs and advertisements were blown off or into oblivion. Unless a traveler was intimately acquainted with Port Arthur, having street markers for this place or that was of little use. Stores stood like homeless people with unreadable banners. I drove beneath a small bridge. Overhead was the Kansas City Southern Railroad line.

As in countless other communities, my love affair with Lone

Star strangers always had its romantic palette adorned by state flags over heartache. It was a profound and silent statement, the red, white and blue with its shiny star. *Oh say can we see by the dawn's early light,* was the beauty next to all her Texas might. We would go on no matter what. I saw it again in Port Arthur, a very poor city rich with possibilities.

The Gulf Coast Health Center was open. They were busy taking care of people with Medicaid and without. New China Restaurant and Larry's Discount Liquor seemed an odd combination. They were open, but the liquor sign was bent out of shape. A fairly new Shipley's Donuts tempted a growling stomach. I imagined a jukebox inside a nearby lounge with another blown off sign. No-name owners waited for Happy Hour or Lunch Hour, whichever came first. The Relax Inn had been battered and played host to a few cars and company, impossible to tell whether anyone was inside *relaxing.* I doubted it.

More boarded up windows on homes. Wooden slats crossed X's on numerous front doors. Some residents, months later, had not returned to pockets of Port Arthur. A small building that doubled as a volunteer fire station was in decent shape. Cars behind me honked, wanted the talking-into-her-hand lunatic to speed up or move out of the way. I needed to turn around. Months and months after Rita and Port Arthur's damage seemed fresh and surreal. Probably because some of the damage was left behind by the previous storm of neglect and abandon.

About 14 palm trees with torn arms once beckoned to tourists who used to frequent this area. Maybe The Driftwood was called by another name then. Damaged, still standing, its island appeal erased beyond receiving guests. I turned into the lot for the American Legion Rudolph Lambert, Post #7, not a lucky number. There would be no one stopping for drinks or to meet anyone anytime soon at The Driftwood. *Was it closed by Rita or before Rita?* Economic devastation in Port Arthur began before the storm, and she certainly deprived the city more upon her exit. I had no proof at that point, only what my eyes recorded and fed my mouth to say—first impressions—into the tiny device.

A Walgreen's, not the old model, but one of the newer ones, had not reopened. Will it ever, I asked into the microphone. Other questions had no answers. How many counted on this store to fill prescriptions and pick up a few staples like milk and bread? It was a black community in a black city.

Joe Deshotel, a state representative, had his office information posted not far from the Memorial Baptist Church's reminder that its food bank would be open 5-6:30 p.m. for one day only, 48 hours from my drive-by. The church suffered heavy damage from the exterior. Men were working on a Scotch Tape roof, blue tarp in spots, not one huge piece, but several pieces of the blue stuff. The tarp was enough to make one weary of anything to do with the color. Rita had pricked holes in the church's heart. God would fix it. I could see, in my futuristic eye, a long line forming later when Memorial opened for 90 minutes to hand out groceries.

Another blank lot. It was once busy and bustling on Saturday afternoons. Not one steel buggy remained at the Lucky Seven Market Basket. Empty. Quiet. I didn't get a vibe that registers would hum again, groceries would be loaded into trunks again. Jobs gone. Lives interrupted. Exactly like the ones at Central Mall. Stores had struggled to reopen, stores like J. C. Penney, which reminded me of childhood friend, Ron Brown, who was a vice president back home at the Plano-based headquarters for the retailer. His grandfather, Frank C. Brown, baptized me when I was 11. I wore a lime green suit with a ruffled white blouse. I would ask Mr. Brown about Penney stores in Port Arthur and Beaumont.

There was an engulfing sadness about poor Arthur and I was instantly sucked in. A death in the family kind-of-feel. Town down, town down, a radio dispatcher might say. I felt helpless and shocked, angry and overwhelmed. What must happen next? I wondered if powerful beings could see the potential. One only needed to look.

A Comfort Inn was filled to the brim with residents who had no homes to return to. Unlivable. Unfixable. Uninhabitable. All the other Un-s of post-Rita life for the poorest among us without credit cards and forced to voucher their way into places that had the nerve to employ people who acted like the government's money wasn't good enough. No room at the Comfort Inn. People waited for word with cabin-feverish children crowded in twin beds and small arrangements. Many businesses and homes neighbored to Comfort appeared abandoned. Owners gave up after one too many knocks, perhaps they knew the insurance game was winless with or without a policy.

The Tire Warehouse was a black and white rubber conglomeration. Tires everywhere. Outside, inside, on the sidewalk and decorating glass windows. A handwritten sign was posted. "Praise God While You've Got A Chance." How telling that none of the goods needed advertising, but salvation free for the reading, more words— *Let God Handle Your Problems Today, Mine Also.* Ironically, just as I approached the tire store, my car hit a major pothole that made me say a bad word. I wondered about the strategically placed concrete. More blue tarp. Missing signs. A city in need of love and work for its residents. Hope, on the Port Arthur surface, was in short supply. How many people have packed up never to return?

Normally, the Port Arthur Civic Center was where the MLK Celebration took place. Rita canceled that too. The center was crushed, flooded, void and vacant, some contractors slowly mulled about. The year before a 2005 sellout crowd had cheered the speaker on. Mr. Smiley, I had no doubt, would be Standing Room Only, just not 1400.

I returned to the Parker Multipurpose building with its clean architectural lines and combo stone and brick, breezy Texas and American flags. Huge plants, more palm trees. It was too windy. Umbrellas around me popped open. Drizzle-mist died. Light rain followed. Same nuisance. Faces sprayed. Hairdos ruined. The two story tan building was user friendly, designed to be easy on the eyes, not the Port Arthur Civic Center, but the next best thing. Adequate parking outside was front of the building in neat straight lines. Security present. Radios impressive. Celebrity Smiley on his way.

It had been arranged for me to sit with Jefferson County Commissioner Bo Alfred, but lack of table-number knowledge, according to committee members manning the entrance, held things up. Finally, a woman named Nicole Parker escorted me to an empty table where I could sit until someone made me move. We briefly discussed how Rita had ruined many things. She had a sister and her children living with her and her kids. It was crowded, but they were alive. Nicole went back to the door where a man offered to purchase a ticket. He had only heard about the event that morning. There were no tickets.

Angel San Juan was on his way. We were always joined at the hip by a phone line. It was a working assignment for my friend, he would get to interview the one-name hunk. Daydreaming and waiting, the room around me zoned out, I was visualizing Quiche Lorraine and a cold Mimosa from The Adolphus. I was famished. Angel appeared and zapped me out of the fantasy cuisine, introducing me to Michael "Shane" Sinegal, nice Port Arthur city councilman and good pre-brunch companion to quiz on my impressions from the front seat.

We talked about evacuations, racism, people trapped on Port Arthur school buses, underlying storm issues, and residents who called him for help. Each time Sinegal and I got cranked up good, someone would stop to shake his hand, pat him on the back, or inquire after his wife, who wasn't there. He was friendly. I liked him instantly. Good host, he remembered my name, politely telling every person who came to the table for 10.

Like Beaumont, the Port Arthur Independent School District had allowed residents to evacuate using school buses. Similar stories made their way back to Councilman Sinegal, "I heard they had guns drawn on them, telling them they couldn't stop there." Things like Katrina fatigue and overcrowding were mentioned. After what he heard, Sinegal was adamant, "I think a big part of it was fear and race sometimes feeds off fear."

Clanking from silverware. Glasses added to the symphony with clinking. Background classical music gave the room a holiday in the mall ambiance. We chatted about 41 buses in easily identifiable convoys—P. A. I. S. D marked on the sides. Almost on cue, the school superintendent passed our table. Sinegal stood and made the introductions. Willis Mackey gave me his card, said call anytime. My real table host, Commissioner Alfred, whizzed by and I waved at him. He was busy and I was free to stay with the councilman.

I asked about the empty feel along Woodworth and had some things confirmed. A bit of the avenue looked that way *before* Rita. But not all of it. "We did lose quite a few businesses," Sinegal explained, "we lost a grocery store. In the African American community, we only had a Walgreen's and a Lucky Seven Market Basket store." He wasn't holding his breath that either was enthusiastic about returning. Looting by a few after a previous evacuation may have left a bitter taste in the mouths of some business owners or chains. It was hard to know. Stereotypes got a lift from Rita. Images. Beliefs. Negatives. Excuses to Exit.

"Racism is alive and well in America," Sinegal says, "and we perpetuate some of those fears by some of the actions we take." It was a difficult public admission for a man who is black to make about black people. We talked about the N-word, both of us close in age. Neither use the word for sport. His two daughters, my two sons, surrounded by culture that freely tosses the word around like candy. Sinegal was enormously proud of his girls, "You can't make them say the word."

Another councilmember took his seat, halting our discussion on the changing use of a racial slur to one generation and a weapon to another. "Jasper is my hometown," Councilman Tom Henderson says when told I wrote *HATE CRIME*. After that, Angel rushed back to the table, practically removing the chair from underneath me. *I needed to hurry to his side of the room.* Trying to follow Angel and scanning the large hall, I hadn't noticed myself running straight for Tavis Smiley lined against a wall.

We were not only in the same room for brunch, we were suddenly eye-to-eye and I didn't know it until I was right up on the man. Nothing prepared me to see Smiley that close, a name I knew as well as my own for the past 10 years. Angel primed me like it was the 60-yard dash and the wall was where runners hit to stop. I almost mowed Smiley down, hitting the shoe brakes hard after I finally realized the reason Angel had been in such a hurry, always looking out for his friend.

Soon Smiley would be onstage. The wall encounter my only opportunity for a private moment. He saw me coming. A tall black woman minus her Smiley Radar and marketing potency. Awkwardness supreme, no words came. I did the unthinkable and grabbed his hand, "Mr. Smiley, I'm Joyce King." He said, "Good Morning Miss King," or something close, looking at the hand that wasn't eager to release his. Unspoken words followed, *Lady, let go of my hand.*

A young assistant or publicist or whatever traveling employees prefer to be called, was at his side, half-grimacing, half contemplating an arm wave to flag down security on the other side of the hall.

Angel watched. If the Smiley handler had jumped, my buddy would've made a move too. "Did you get my note?" I sounded like a lovesick female. As soon as the words escaped, I wanted to get them back. I really wanted to know if he had gotten the book and could chat after his speech. Smiley was notorious for not being around after speaking, he kept a tight schedule. I could easily picture Smiley L-W-E, Leaving While Eating, to make the next planned stop.

"Yes, we got it," the assistant said while someone prepared to give the invocation. I got to stand next to Smiley during the prayer. He bowed. I liked that he bowed. I think he closed his eyes. One might've remained open, like Civil Rights-era prayers, where black men had to monitor those good white Christians with ammunition and hoods. Smiley kept one eye on the persistent woman he still didn't know standing next to him who wanted something he wasn't going to give. And then I finally had the right female response. Hmm, *taller than I thought.* Tall and handsome, employed and single—fine black man. I could clone Smiley and I wouldn't have to sell books anymore. I may have said one last thing to him. By then Smiley had his game face on. He was deep in thought, focused on the waiting crowd. Our circle was complete enough—same city, same hotel, same brunch, seal the deal. Handshake. Goodbye. We'll meet again.

The "Word for Today" was especially uplifting and rocked the house. 900 people turned out and plenty of them knew the Rev. Lloyd Scott of Eastern Star Baptist Church. He fired up the crowd with a Business 101 message. Scott called for changed attitudes, to help "change altitudes" that would make it possible to rise and dream. "The Psalmist said 'Yeah though I walk through the valley of the shadow of death' we'll fear no evil." Lloyd finished by adding, "Port Arthur, supporters, God is with us."

City Councilwoman Deloris "Bobbie" Prince and her grandson, Charles, took seats to my right. A solo from Dwight Wagner set the tone. He didn't yell or scream, he sang. Mr. Smiley sat not far away, in the center of the big room at a VIP table. The program had an "In Memory Of" section for Rosa Parks, Johnnie Cochran and Sergeant First Class Brandon K. Sneed. The Galveston native had valiantly served his country more than a decade receiving the Purple Heart and the Bronze Star. Sneed was a squad leader and Bradley Commander for Bravo Company, 1st Battalion, 30th Infantry. He had a kind and remarkably steady face.

Johnnie Cochran's name brought back a memory for me in Dallas that actually began in his native Shreveport, Louisiana, where he had agreed to speak at his old elementary school. Also my former elementary school. My mother, and biggest fan, had made up her mind she would ask the prominent lawyer to do a Q&A with me. This wasn't long after the O. J. verdict. One thing kept getting in her way. Cochran was heavily flanked by protection and she couldn't get near him. As the event wrapped, he walked past a line of people. My mom pushed through the pack for a front row glance. Cochran felt someone put their hand in his coat pocket. A brazen thing for an experienced pickpocket to do. Except it wasn't a thief. The hand belonged to my mother.

Startled, Cochran stopped walking and turned, demanding to know what had just happened, who had touched him. He looked right at my mother, who said, "Call my daughter!" Cochran ran his fingers inside the same pocket this bold woman had placed her uninvited fingers and lifted my CBS Radio business card. Having his own daughter in the same profession—a newscaster—he nodded a forgiving parental okay and smiled. He was tickled by such love.

Not two weeks later, I was invited to hear Cochran speak in Dallas. When it was over, handlers cautioned people not to touch him, not to take any pictures, just be ready for the man to say hi and hand back a signed book. Well, I am surely my mother's daughter. Placing my hand on top of Cochran's got his attention. Initially, his head was down as he prepared to write. He wisely decided to focus on what was happening right in front of him. One of the bodyguard-types pounced and counselor held out his hand in a calming way, as if to say, "No, let's see what she has to say."

"Mr. Cochran, a few days ago, you were in Shreveport and a woman came up and put her hand…" Before I could finish, he laughed out loud, "Call my daughter! That's you isn't it?" He told me how much I favored my mother. A photographer, seeing the shared connection, snapped our picture. I apologized for my mother placing her hand in his pocket and he said it was okay. He still had the card and no harm was done. Anyone who has ever met my mother

127

can have little doubt about where my spur of the moment aggressiveness comes from. I have never once, though, stuck my business card down the coat pocket of a man I wanted to interview. I send books to hotel rooms.

Tavis Smiley glided to the podium. "I can not imagine, on this particular occasion, any place I'd rather be as we celebrate the 20th anniversary of the King Holiday. Give Dr. King some love." Thunderous applause. Courage, conviction and commitment were the attributes Smiley says it took for MLK to rise in his short lifetime to such stature, a man who ultimately changed the world. A man who was worthy of a national holiday.

"Dr. King is the greatest American we have ever produced." Agreement was as clear as the love shown moments before. Not everyone clapped though. A few people had to roll that statement over in their brains.

Smiley touched on a number of topics, including the fact that King's oldest daughter, Yolanda, would be a guest that very evening on his PBS TV show. He offered a few of the interview highlights, primarily what it was like when her family was invited to attend the White House ceremony where President Reagan signed the King Holiday into law. Smiley sent his prayers to the family, and of Coretta Scott King, he shared with the audience, "I'm told she is doing well and recovering as we speak, so that's a blessing, to still have her in the land of the living even on this 20th anniversary of this holiday."

Smiley first set the inclusive table with stirring content of character questions. He cited the popularity of a multi-society, "Stevie Wonder can tell that we live now in the most multicultural, multiracial, multiethnic America ever." Smiley encouraged the crowd to look behind layers of talk on diversity, inclusion and togetherness. "How might I put this?" Smiley asked in jest. "Don't get it twisted. Don't get it twisted." He made it, as many a church-going grandmother would say, 'plain' that America had not come close to "sincerely embracing what King was talking about."

"When I got in late last night, I didn't know what it was I wanted to share until I got in my room," the commentator started, "and something hit me like a ton of bricks." The epiphany cemented itself at the hotel register. "They handed me a room key with a piece of paper that apologized for the condition of the hotel, asked us to be patient with the repairs that were underway, etc. etc." Smiley stressed hotel staff was very kind to him. Naturally, he knew Rita, the hurricane-decorator, was responsible for the new look.

"In that moment, I saw very clearly the parallel that I wanted to draw between 20 years ago and 20 years later." The arc first landed at the campaign of a Hollywood actor named Reagan that Smiley says announced his bid for presidency in Philadelphia, Mississippi. The room went stone quiet. Surely the ghosts of Goodman, Schwerner and Cheney took their places next to a dreamer. One woman leaned over and said a few of the white attendees had pained expressions. At least one had a visibly shaken look like Mr. Reagan was her president.

"I'd like to stand behind this podium and tell you that I'm feeling better and better and better and more comfortable and more resolved with this notion that in this multicultural, multiracial, multiethnic America we have finally come to a place where we embrace the dream of Dr. King, but I, I, I can't tell you that." When Smiley saw what the hurricanes did, he was reminded of a King quote that summed up the situation best. "Now is not the time to take the tranquilizing drug of gradualism."

Like a minister concluding a Sunday sermon, with three main points, Smiley says the first thing people learned, those who got it, was that racism "is still the most intractable issue in America." Applause from the black people. Most of the white minority sat silent, perhaps wondering how much of Smiley's speech on Reagan, Bush, politics, terrorism, and hurricanes they would have to suffer through. Then Smiley went where almost every black person in that room knew he would.

"For starters, it took the president too long to get there," he attempted to continue over cheers that rang out, followed by more approvals of Amen. "You got the hurricane bearing down on New Orleans and you down here in Texas chopping wood," Smiley sent comments to a sitting president via a roomful of people in Port Arthur who wanted him to keep going. Smiley cited a memory of Mr. Bush, post-Katrina, not on his way to New Orleans, but to a fundraiser. "I'm in Texas, I wouldn't lie to the president in Texas."

Smiley says several elected officials acted indifferently toward

Katrina, her aftermath. He listed a few. None drew more hisses than the name Richard Baker, a 20-year Republican state representative from Baton Rouge. "The member of the House representing that area had this to say, 'Well, we've been trying for years to do something about public housing in New Orleans. We couldn't do nothing about it, but thankfully and finally, God did.'" The Parker Multi-Purpose Center was smoking after that remark.

"He's good," one woman behind me said out loud. Others nodded, some yelled back, straight out of Sunday service when the room feels a little like hell, my favorite curse word, because it isn't really a curse word. No hand fans or central air could shake the heat of truth or media recorded quotes from politicians who ought to know better. Smiley says the president had plenty of non-responsive company "20 years later" after the King Holiday was first signed into law when everyone was encouraged to embrace the dream. Of New Orleans, Smiley spoke a kind of Port Arthur patois, "If you ain't gone get no love in *this* situation, [the hurricanes] you ain't never gone get no love."

Smiley says another politician suggested, in front of the media again, that the U. S. Government prosecute, to the fullest extent of the law, every person in New Orleans that did not evacuate. Then Smiley remembered someone he hadn't mentioned: "I forgot Condi, y'all know where she was, right?"

Smiley says the first black female Secretary of State, Condoleezza Rice, was at a Broadway play, then later spotted shopping. "There was a woman who was in the Ferragamo Store on Madison Avenue in New York shopping when the Secretary of State was in there buying some shoes." Secret Service was at every exit, doing what they do. "This woman looked up and saw Condoleezza Rice buying some Ferragamo shoes, shopping for shoes, while folk was sitting on their rooftops in New Orleans." The stranger walked right up to the secretary of state and "cussed her out." That comment drew the longest applause of the brunch. Many people stood up and pointed like my Big Momma used to at her minister for saying something nobody else wanted to talk about.

Smiley noted government officials hadn't paid much attention when it was widely reported by the media that 100,000 people in New Orleans didn't own automobiles. "Anybody ever been to New

Orleans before? It is a *walking* city, a walking city, a working city, a poor city." Smiley poked serious fun at the order to evacuate, "In what?"

20 years ago. 20 years later. The King Holiday became law. The King Holiday still seeks its dream come true. Smiley didn't leave out FEMA, its corruption, the media, a new definition of "refugees," or the descriptions of two separate photos that left some journalists seething.

One was a black man in chest deep water with a caption that noted he was "looting food." A few hours later, Smiley says, an editorial decision was made by the same international wire service to run a photo of white people, again, in chest deep water. The caption described them as "finding food." *Why was a black man with bread a "looter," while white people in the same water merely labeled as "finding" food?*

"You can't rely on government, you can't rely on media," Smiley drew to a close, "in the spirit of Dr. King, 20 years later, we can rely on the people because it is, after all, about *We* the people." A newly published study, on the 20th anniversary of the King Holiday, concluded "we" live in two fundamentally different Americas—one white, the other black.

"71% of black folk," according to PEW research, "believe these disasters, Rita and Katrina, show that racial inequality is still the order of the day in America." 56% of whites polled disagreed. More than half of the blacks surveyed said response would've been faster had the victims not been black. 77% of white Americans disagreed.

Smiley lowered his voice, no longer the fiery pulpit minister, he needed to leave the audience with a whispered point. "If we are ever going to create what King called the 'beloved community,' we've got to stop the talking and try to get folk to believe what we are saying and start doing the work." *Will Port Arthur do the work?* Smiley got a raucous standing ovation as he dashed out. Brunch was next on the program.

I left without eating, but didn't leave hungry. The assistant saw me at the door and had one question, "How did you find out what hotel we were at?"

TWELVE

"My friend Rick" started 2006 with an unexpected invitation to Austin for a special King Day screening of the movie, *Glory Road*.

With Southeast Texas neighbors expecting me, there wasn't a conceivable plan for an evening film in the capital and turn around trip back to Beaumont. I had an early interview scheduled the next morning and sent sincere thanks to the governor, requesting a date to interview him on Rita. Initially, the answer was yes.

I left Port Arthur the same time Tavis Smiley did, never saw what was on the menu, to keep a Tyler County appointment with a mother and daughter. The proud parent had written a touching letter about a child who sounded like she could inspire anyone.

It rained all the way to Hillister, a hamlet of about 200, with a post office, a store, and a restaurant. As it turned out, Cathy Perry was married to a man named Dennis (Dan) Harold Perry who was born in Athens, Texas. His father, Audie Joe, had a brother named Ray, and Ray had a son named Richard who went on to become governor of Texas. That made Dan Perry and Rick Perry, first cousins. Small world for sure.

Cell phone music played. The voice at the other end of the line was 19-year old Kendra Billiot. She apologized for a "running late" mom who was driving hard and fast to meet me. In a steady rain, no problem, I could grab some lunch and wait.

A speeding motorist could easily drive past Hillister, but Kendra warned me that I'd gone too far if the Ivanhoe Fire Station came into view. I saw the marker and turned around. Not a quarter mile back was a store, a semi-hidden post office in a separate building, and The Tree Restaurant and Grill.

A pretty hostess greeted me. Tables were plentiful. Close to the entry sat a pack of working men who stared at me like I was crazy or lost or both. Lunch was finished. News of the day, possibly over Tequilas and beers, was discussed. News and gossip. I don't believe the plaid-shirted, Wrangler-wearing white men, most of whom were under 40, paid attention because I was black. My guess would be stranger in a foreign vehicle for that part of Texas. For what honorable person who truly belonged in "the sticks" would be caught driving a Volvo?

2 p.m. My waitress' name was Ashley. She had high praise for the grilled chicken salad. I would've eaten deer quiche if someone had suggested it. A sign posted in the eatery welcomed company to the kitchen: "Please feel free to visit our grill and select your own steaks." Billy Rowles would love the place.

Buck watched me. A deer head, not a man, was mounted high on one side of The Tree. A few eyes monitored the situation. Too many newspapers and a briefcase, none of it fit—clothes or car. Framed pictures of chickens lined the wall, I didn't get that one. And curious cowboys couldn't get me. So we were even.

Cedar tables. Four chairs at several of them. Other seating accommodations included benches with picnic-style tables. Light fixtures were old fashion wagon wheels dangling from the ceiling, held by braided ropes securely tied, very western. Décor screamed beef and portraits of chickens squawked alternative for wimps like me. A man with local ties, John Adams, had his fine work on display. A struggling photo print artist who could use a few sales.

Tired of sitting, I walked around the homey grill. All the hats turned. I nodded to one handsomer than the rest. A woman, no matter where she is, appreciates a good looking man who looks like a man. Sports fans had posted a favorite page from June 12, 2005 and *The Beaumont Enterprise*. The headline read: "Class 2A State Championship Woodville outlasts Holliday in pitching duel to win first state baseball title in school's history 2-1." There was a photo of a clean cut kid Tyler County was proud of—Braeden Riley.

Lunch came. Lunch could not be finished. It was the biggest grilled chicken salad I had ever seen. After tea, more papers were sifted through, more men watched the clock and the working girl who could afford to take such a leisurely late lunch. Two cowboys left. Others would wait it out and learn my true mission for dropping by The Tree. Suddenly, a dark-haired beauty came straight to my table.

I followed Kendra home eager to see if personality matched everything her mother, Cathy Perry, had written about the high school senior. Before Rita, Kendra and her classmates at Warren High were having a fairly normal year. She was an A-student, had spent four years as a member of the FFA, Future Farmers of America, and was especially proud of being school mascot. She wasn't always proud of how that mascot was depicted.

Kendra described the insensitive motif as an Indian wearing a leisure suit topped by a huge head. She set out to bring the Warriors into a more culturally enlightened era. "I went to the school board and told them, 'Look, I'm Native American, I'm registered and everything and can show you paperwork from miles back on what I've done. If you allow me, I will give you a tradition to start.'"

As long as the creative senior remained within guidelines of the school dress code, board members were okay with the concept of updating an outfit Kendra considered stale and offensive, nearly a caricature. "I bought my own headdress, bought my own outfit, shield and everything and it's all authentic." Her enthusiasm made it easy to believe Kendra in the role of vibrant mascot urging others to demonstrate spirit. "I can't tell you how proud I am of this, it's been like my baby for three years now." The leisure suit was permanently retired.

"Our tribe was originally the Choctaw Tribe from Oklahoma. When the white settlers came in, they branched out and broke down into five. We are actually the Biloxi Tribe," she explained. Others may know it as United Houma Nation. Kendra's biological father, Antoine Louis Billiot, was a full-blooded Native American. He died in 2002. To get the male perspective on a woman wearing headdress and other aspects of her costume, she did not have to look far. Kendra's stepfather, Dan Perry, knew things from his personal legacy. His mother was full Cherokee.

Usually, the practice of wearing headdress, something not encouraged in the Native American culture, is reserved for chiefs, a symbol of masculinity or fighting. Kendra decided to blend components from all five tribes in her heritage and family history to come up with the outfit she personally designed. "We got a little bit of Apache, a little Navajo, a little of each and went to powwows to talk to different people. We wrote to my tribe and let them know what I was doing and they blessed me."

Kendra taught lessons few ever hear in public schools—none of us can afford to live in cultural cocoons. She was having fun cheering, raising her animals, dating a cute guy named Richard, volunteering, and just enjoying senior year. Then Katrina showed up. Three weeks later, her ugly stepsister joined the madness.

"Before Rita, my chief [John Paul Feeley] at the fire department called, at like two in the morning, and said, 'They're saying it's going to hit us and I need you at this fire department *now*.'" A school night, Kendra did not hesitate to join everyone for the emergency meeting. They were briefed in the wee hours Monday before Rita.

"When I got there, the chief said it was going to be a big one and that Jefferson County was probably going to be evacuated." Kendra had the option of evacuating with her family or staying behind. She chose, at that moment, to tough it out with her firefighter comrades.

Next door to the Perry home is a wood frame house. Eggshell white with a large front porch. Rockers and old-fashioned touches gave it character and appeal. The house was built in 1881 and originally belonged to J. P. and Cordia Phillips, who operated a sawmill behind the property and were considered a prosperous family. The land changed hands in the early 1900's. Mittie and Rufas Hatton raised watermelons and continued to chip wood on site. Everybody in the area referred to the place as the Hatton House, until it was bought by a lawyer few people ever saw. Not much on visiting, that same lawyer sold it to Kendra's maternal grandfather, Elvin Daulton Cooper, Jr.

The history of the land and the plank board house with its 12-foot ceilings wasn't known until Cathy Cooper Perry started sifting through courthouse records and deeds. While she searched for evidence on previous owners, Kendra and her stepfather discovered things in the original design underneath sheetrock. She played around the attic and found a separate door, which led to a room where servants had stayed. There was a usable fireplace. Then Kendra stumbled onto another clue.

"That's when I found these old wooden shingles, we brought

them outside where we sat on the long porch just rocking and talking," she says. They had the shingles with them when Kendra's mother arrived and was fascinated by them. "She took one and wiped it off with a dust cloth and that's when we found *John Davis, 1881.* He may have been one of the builders." Davis, they thought, had etched his signature, proud of workmanship. Kendra's sister, 24-year old Ashley Bednarik, and her husband, Ricky, live in the house with six-year old Nicolette and five-year old Richard, Jr.

Kendra had her niece and nephew when she picked me up at the restaurant. She doted on members of any team she belonged to, whether the unit was comprised of family, friends, cheerleaders, firefighters or her stable of animals. "I had a goat here during Rita and I was so worried. We lost a bunch of animals." Kendra knew from raising goats for the Tyler County Fair that they were a pampered lot, not accustomed to stress or storms. "My goat's name was Baby, it was the littlest goat I'd ever raised."

The last day of school before Rita made landfall, Kendra's agriculture teachers, Ken Cauthen and Rex Currie, were cautioning students that animals had a tendency to behave strangely during storms and what they could do to survive with their pets. Cauthen had told them rabbits, chickens or anything smaller could be brought inside, left in cages or sturdy coops, but larger animals might be lost. Kendra worried about all her goats—Roo-Roo, Roo-Roo 2, Joe-Joe Dot, and especially Baby.

Animals raised by students were kept at their individual homes. The last thing the teacher said was "animals will run with the wind." Those who had lambs and goats were advised to release them from holding pens before the storm. They might have a higher rate of survival. Busy with the fire department, Kendra called her father to free the goats so they might roam with horses. Not all her classmates heeded the warning. "Some kids didn't let their animals out thinking they'd be safer in their own pens. A tree fell on one. Another lamb was running around the pen so fast, it broke a leg." Kendra had to deal with her own sad news about the tiny goat, "Baby never came back."

As she wiped at a tear, a woman came in the door, "I am so sorry." Cathy Perry had been at a job interview that ran long. Shortly after, an attractive man followed, "This is my husband, Dan." Both

Perry and Kendra wanted to know if I detected a resemblance to anyone. Clueless, I had to admit I was totally stumped. I had never laid eyes on Dennis Perry before and was caught off guard—an obvious family trait.

"The governor is his first cousin," Kendra blurted out. As I looked closer, yes, I could see little things that made them kin. That's when Dan Perry had enough of three women gawking at him, "I'm prettier." We all howled at that. His hair wasn't as perfect as Gov. Rick's. But then, whose is?

"There were a lot of people who didn't heed our warnings to leave because they were thinking this is so far up from the coast, we're not going to have bad damage," Kendra resumed our evacuation discussion. Volunteer firefighters took their jobs seriously. They told residents, right to the last minute, to leave. Get out. Many without cars were offered rides from volunteers who promised to drive them away. The closer Rita got to landfall, the Ivanhoe Fire Department split up into crews. Teams might be able to cut their way out and make it to one central location.

Friday night, September 23, 2005, Kendra bunked down with other volunteers at the home of Lt. Charles Singleton. His wife, Linda, was an auxiliary firefighter. A daughter, Jamie Carroll, was there, along with Jimmy Goodman, another volunteer. Singleton had a big brick home, it seemed like a good place to ride it out since the storm had already started to get bad. Volunteers were content to remain inside and brace for the worst.

"At 9 p.m., the pagers went off, and when pagers go off you're supposed to go," Kendra rationalized. After Rita began to bear down, everyone knew to stay in the house and not go out. When that alarm went off, able bodies, all trained to respond, looked at each other and said, "What do we do?" It was a natural thing to suit up, dash out and go into rescue-help mode.

"Finally, we just all ran to the truck and we got in his [Charlie] truck, got our gear on and we're out driving in it. The truck was just swaying," Kendra demonstrated with her hands a rocking motion. That's when Singleton radioed Lt. Harmon to ask what the procedure was for racing to a scene in pre-hurricane winds. Singleton had the lights, sirens going on his POV (personally owned vehicle) as they attempted to make it to whoever had put out the urgent plea for help. Kendra was scared, "Everything was moving." They were trying to get down FM 1013, a farm-to-market road. Kendra started to pray, "Dear heavenly Father…"

The big emergency they had bolted out of a safe shelter for was unfathomable to all in the shake-and-bake Chevy Silverado half-ton truck. "What it was, a tree had fallen in the road. Somebody called because a tree fell and Rita hadn't even got cranked up." Then Kendra, in a flash of facetiousness: "We're all thinking, 'Do you not understand there's gone be more than one tree coming down honey?'" Again and again, this 19-year old girl was made over by maturity. She kept saying the same five words. Kendra knew it and her colleagues at the fire department knew it. "It's going to be bad."

At times, Kendra fought back tears and did an admirable job. Others refused her attempts to wrangle them in. "We all had chainsaws in the truck," she cried, "and everybody just stopped for that one tree and started hacking." The team, at least, made quick firewood of one tree that wouldn't block FM 1013 anymore. Unfortunately, it wouldn't be the last. After leaving the scene, emotions running high, people were making efforts to shore up spirits and necessary energy for the long night ahead. Kendra embraced her coworkers when the teams that had arrived split up again after moving the tree. She told everybody the same thing, "I don't know if I'm going to see you again." It was then that she realized any one of them might be in a house crushed by a tree or worse. "I love you, call me in the morning."

Back at the Singleton home, not 10 minutes later, Rita's fury heated up. Rain banged harder. Trees snapped like old pencils. The angry wind howled at them for daring to think they were a match with their chainsaws and emergency training. What they heard next was crazy—pagers went off again for help. A woman trapped in her car. This time the call wasn't specifically for fire department personnel, but for "anyone who could come." Kendra and company sat glued to the radio wondering if the stranded motorist would last long enough for someone to reach her.

"One man radioed back that he was only two miles from the woman and would try to get her," Kendra says. The savior managed to rescue the frightened lady. She had to ride the storm out at his house, total stranger to his family. "Where her car was," Kendra started, whenever they finally made it back, "it wasn't there anymore."

"Lights were flickering, the winds were higher and we were trying to stay sane and calm." Kendra had brought her little dog, Toby, and a cat named Salem. All the volunteers had pets camped at Singleton's house with them. Nothing about Rita made it any easier to hold fast to sanity or serenity. Pets and people alike were jumpy and frightened. *What was Perry doing while her little girl was out waiting for a hurricane to enter and exit?*

45-year old Cathy Cooper Perry was raised in the Port Arthur-Groves area and years ago her family made a hurricane pact. "If ever a bad one came, this was our rendezvous point." Perry's parents had owned the land and everything on it since 1969 when her dad bought it from the lawyer. In the hours before landfall, everyone agreed Rita was the bad one they had locked pinky fingers on years before. They expected a little wind and some rain, but "never anything like Rita."

Perry talked about the eerie feeling she had pre-Katrina as well. "I have a daughter that lives in Florida and we're all familiar with hurricanes and have evacuated and done everything." Perry told her mother before New Orleans was devastated by floodwaters, "We're fixing to have some problems." This from a woman who had dodged bullets since a girl named Audrey wreaked havoc on Texas and Louisiana. In the ABC's of hurricane ladies, Audrey was awesome, Bonnie was a bitch, and Carla was cunning. No one who lived in the region ever forgot their insults, inconveniences or intimidation.

"They had not called for evacuations here [Tyler County] so I had gone down there [Jefferson County] to help board up my mom's house and bring my mom here," Perry says. She knew it was the right thing to do. Her mother, Nelda Cooper was 73-years old and had lived alone since her husband passed in March 2002. Relatives trickled in, remembering the designated haven.

"This house was full. I had my mother, my sister, her two girls, my dad's old secretary and her husband. And the house next door where my oldest daughter lives, her husband and two children, and my brother and his wife came up, his cousin was with him because Houston had called for an evacuation." Perry took a breath and thought for a minute. It seemed like she had left somebody out. A mental headcount. Oh, there was an aunt and uncle on the property in a third house just up the road. In all, there were nine humans and five dogs in Perry's home, nine people and another large dog next door at her daughter's place, and in the third residence, Uncle Tom Cooper's house, there were six more people and several more dogs. Then the unthinkable happened.

"Everybody gets here, and they [officials] called for an evacuation of Tyler County. And we're like, 'Where do we go?'" The roads were already choked with people, gas was low to nonexistent. As far as Perry could see down the highway, "it was a parking lot of people." She was dumbfounded. Panic. Fear. Perry had horses, goats and other animals she didn't want to leave behind. They had made no provisions for shelter. There were three houses full of people she felt responsible for. Everyone had followed the plan and come to Hillister. All vehicles had less than half a tank of gas, not enough to venture out and get stuck in traffic. They were paralyzed.

"We understood we needed to evacuate." Perry had another reason for not embracing a swift exit, "I also had a daughter that I didn't want to leave behind." That daughter was a volunteer firefighter. It was fine that Kendra knew what she was doing and had received excellent training, but Perry's maternal instinct would not be assuaged by such logic. The eagle wasn't about to leave capable baby to guard the nest alone. She would worry about Kendra no matter where they evacuated to.

"So we discussed it with everybody and we didn't think the higher area of Tyler County we lived in would flood." They agreed things might get a little rough but knew everything would be alright. They anticipated lights out. Nothing major. They were all dead wrong.

"We hunkered down, everybody had brought in food, we had plenty of food but we didn't have a whole lot of bottled water," Perry says. There were cell phones. They kept them charged and ready. It was the only way to later check on everyone, back and forth, between the three houses. Perry laughed at some of the people she had holed up in the compound. The third house, for example, included her ex-husband, his wife, and her ex-mother-in-law. "We had an emergency, that's what family is for. You stay together." And so they did. Ashley's (her oldest daughter) father, Charles Terrell, and his wife, Janice, and his mother, Bessie Terrell, were grateful the tie of friendship was stronger than ancient history divorce.

Perry knew it would've been even more difficult for Terrell to hit the road at the last minute since his wife relied on a wheelchair, so she told him, "Y'all come on up here and get out of harm's way." When they were packed to leave Groves, Bessie Terrell suddenly bolted from the car, "Hold on, I forgot something." She ran back into her home, returning with a large pot and bag of rice, "I can't go anywhere without my gumbo pot." Perry says in "true Southern Cajun form," her ex-mother-in-law put "her foot in it" and made a huge pot of chicken and sausage gumbo Friday night before the lights went out.

"That night we all kind of settled down to go to bed and the cable started flashing off and on, then the lights." Perry knew Rita was hovering over. "Alright here, we're fixing to go, here comes this rollercoaster ride."

They tried to rest. They couldn't rest. Everyone was tense. Everyone was uneasy. Almost everyone. "Finally—my husband slept through the whole thing—I brought her in here (she pointed to grandchild) and she slept through it too." But Perry's mother remained on a sofa throughout the night with her head crouched down on her lap. It was awkward and looked uncomfortable to Perry. She monitored her mother for hours and was extremely worried, "I sat in a chair." Everyone gathered in a large family room at the center of the home. They had lined mattresses up to cover windows. Perry stopped talking, her emotions took control. We sat silent for a moment.

Like a good daughter, Kendra moved in with a different memory that she knew her mother would be proud of. The young volunteer had met a couple from Holland at the Woodville Inn. They came dashing into the lobby to inquire after a room. Frustrated and exhausted, the man told how he and his wife had driven all over creation to search for a place to stop. It was August, they had evacuated New Orleans, and there were no rooms left anywhere, pre-Katrina. Not Rita.

"Did you say Holland?" I needed to confirm. Was it destiny that placed this scared couple right in Kendra's path? She was there at midnight waiting on a mother and daughter that the Silsbee Police were sending over. They too had been in the hunt for shelter before Katrina made landfall. Then a Dallas twist to the story.

The Hollanders had arrived at Dallas/Fort Worth International Airport to begin their fantasy vacation. He'lena and Rene Thaens rented a car for the drive to Corpus Christi, where they would stop, then leisurely travel the coast up to New Orleans before going back to Dallas and flying home. They wanted to see old fashioned Southern charm up close. They had always dreamed of touring Texas and the Gulf Coast, tasting the food, being entertained by the sights and sounds.

When they arrived in New Orleans, it was the proverbial "vacation from hell" that awaited them. Evacuate was the first order and they were caught in the thick of chaos. Geographically, the Hollanders were at a complete disadvantage not knowing the area well enough to find evacuation routes and shelters. Plenty who found them in time were turned away. Advised by authorities at every stop to "keep going west," the couple drove and drove, until the man said he couldn't go any further.

Hearing their sad story, Kendra felt compassion for the strangers with accents. "I have an extra bedroom in my house and if y'all don't mind staying at my house, promise you I won't kill you." Kendra jokingly laughed to the man and wife, then added, "and don't kill me." Kendra knew they had a room without checking with her parents because they had already offered it to a mother and daughter who never showed up. Silsbee Police called to check on the two women. That was an opportunity to let authorities know the women never arrived and that the Perry family had taken in a different pair instead.

The Thaens were from The Netherlands. They had no family, no friends, and were on a dream vacation that wasn't going to be salvaged. The couple looked upon the kind invitation and recognized the best offer they were going to get. They followed Kendra home. They talked about their ordeal, why they were in America and how important good neighbors were. By 9 a.m., they were gone.

"They wrote a long message about how they were going to go back to Holland and tell people in their native land about Texas hospitality," Perry picked up the story. They wrote of only hearing stories of Southern hospitality and being shocked to find themselves experiencing it in the middle of disaster. Even though the couple was disappointed by some aspects of their vacation, they still remembered to ask about cowboys and boots. "They will talk about Tyler County all the way over in Holland."

Perry resumed the story about her mother that had silenced us before.

Trying to keep their spirits up, everyone at Perry's home told jokes and stayed upbeat, even remarking on how good looking a distant cousin was. His TV job had brought him from New York to cover the storm. They saw him one last time before power blanked out leaving the family to sit in a circle for marathon prayers. At times, Perry felt like Dorothy in *The Wizard of Oz,* "Any minute the house or roof was going to go." Her mom kept her head down, for hours, resting on one hand, a fact and position that took its toll. Whenever Perry would ask if she were okay, all Nelda Cooper would say was, "I'm just praying we make it through this."

With a battery-operated lantern in the center of the room for shadowy light, the scene could've passed for a slumber party, except for a crasher named Rita. They talked about singing hymns, that prompted Perry to remember one in particular, *I'll Fly Away.* For several hours, the relentless wind beat down on the three houses, terrifying its occupants. Saturday came. Wind gusts stayed. Hellish heat arrived. Over 100 degrees. No power, no air, no water, and none of the everyday comforts. Perry and her sister had to get their mother to someplace cooler.

Carolyn Kendrick, a cousin in Friendswood, had lights and things were well enough there to accommodate a few people. The plan was for Perry's sister, Karen McDaniel, and her two teenage daughters, to accompany their mother to Kendrick's home and stay there until Jefferson County gave the okay to return. Not long after they arrived, Perry received a frantic phone call. One minute, while drinking coffee at Kendrick's home, her mother was fine. Seconds later, her eyes rolled to the back of her head and she passed out. Nelda Cooper had suffered a heart attack. They called 9-1-1. She was rushed, by ambulance, to the nearest facility.

Emergency surgery included a pacemaker. Perry was in torment the entire time, not being able to get to her mother, a woman who had just survived Hurricane Rita. Perry wanted to be there to support her sister, lean on her too. Later, she felt enormous gratitude that her mother wasn't in Tyler County when the attack occurred. The local hospital had been turned into a triage center. Patients were being airlifted out. Perry's mother celebrated her September birthday in the hospital. Since then, she has had two more surgeries on her pacemaker. Perry cited the stress of evacuating, boarding up her 3,000 square foot home, and the aftermath, as reasons for her mother's deteriorating condition, and, ultimately, the heart attack.

"My mother is 74 years old now, a cancer survivor and now she has a pacemaker. She had to evacuate and Jefferson County couldn't let them come back." Perry's voice turned from concern to frustration. "She was in the hospital and called Red Cross." Perry says they didn't bother to show up until January 2006 to see if her mother was even *eligible* for assistance. "She got not one red cent."

It was later determined that the woman's suffering didn't qualify. She evacuated. She followed rules. She wasn't eligible. Random people, seemingly, were chosen to benefit, at least that's how some survivors say it looked on the surface. "I do not know this person, at least not personally, but they live in Austin and never changed their driver's license from a Port Arthur address. They applied for the FEMA $2,000 voucher and got it." Perry stressed the ease of their post-hurricane success, *and got it.* "That's what makes me sick."

At least one family member would never have to see the devastation that wiped out a business he spent four decades building. Her mother had sold the business, name and all, in 2002 and had one thing to say about Cooper's Automotive on the corner of Main and 25th in the Groves, after seeing the damage Rita caused. "That would've killed my dad."

While the auto parts store, wrecker service, gas station, u-haul and mechanic shop the size of a city block was now another man's worry, the sentiment was evident for Cathy Cooper Perry. Her father had gotten the keys to the business the day she was born. Perry's dad believed in the old school approach to business, a handshake and heart. Then Kendra interjected, "Everybody in the family has had a job there."

When Ray Cooper died, there were people who showed up for the service Perry didn't know, and the family had never seen. They told stories about how he often didn't charge folk who didn't have money to pay. It was the largest funeral ever conducted by the Clayton Thompson Funeral Home. There were over 750 names on the register alone, and dozens of others who paid respects without signing in.

"They placed him on the back of a flatbed wrecker," Perry smiled, "because he was like the grandfather of the wrecker business down there." More than 250 wrecker drivers, from Louisiana and Texas, in a show of solidarity, lined up for the procession with their lights on. A local station televised the funeral. All of this, Perry remembered, for a man she described as being "small po-dunt." *What did that mean?* Although her father, Perry says, was from a dirt poor town he had a class about himself that was based on "respect, honor, hard work and handshakes."

More memories hit Perry hard. Like the woman named Charity she was always in the family kitchen with. Charity Coleman Davis was the family maid and Perry had learned from her how to cook things other white people never heard of until soul food restaurants began opening for business. "I can remember not wanting Charity to leave in the afternoons, this was the '60s and she'd say to me, 'Oh no girl, I've got to get back on the other side of the tracks on the *other* side of town.'" Perry, as a child, never understood what the black woman was trying to tell her. Later, it was well understood. Perry held strong to her racial conviction, "You treat a person the way you want to be treated."

As her voice softened, Rita unearthed more family tidbits. "My mother got very heavy into genealogy a couple of years ago and she traced her family all the way back to Scotland." Perry says on her father's side, "the Cooper side," they had someone the rest of the country would probably count as famous. "One of our distant cousins married Gloria Vanderbilt." *I was instantly drawn back to perfume and designer jeans.* She confirmed it was that Vanderbilt, then asked, "Do you know Anderson Cooper?" I wasn't about to flunk that one. "On CNN?"

"That's one of my cousins." Gloria Vanderbilt is Anderson Cooper's mother. The Perry home was full of surprises. Her husband and Gov. Rick were the sons of two brothers. And she was distantly related to a designing millionaire and a CNN television star who had reported live from Beaumont during Rita. In fact, Anderson was one of those journalists nearly blown away. Small world again. He was one of the few national anchors who even gave a damn about Rita.

I started the King Holiday with drizzle and Tavis Smiley. It changed to light rain that beat down in big fat Texas drops as I sat with Perry and her daughter. How appropriate that as we concluded our conversation on Rita, the wind outside picked up, blew harder, and a scary bolts of thunder quickened my departure. A gray day punished the fading light and made the wet drive back to Beaumont long and slippery.

Perry was a stranger to me. Until our cherished conversation. She had written a letter about America not understanding the enormous devastation Rita visited on people who lived it, survived it, and were endlessly frustrated by it. She was thankful for those who showed up to help—workers from Michigan to Mexico. Most toiled for weeks and were away from their loved ones. Most of them made it safely back. Ricky Lynn Whittington did not.

Whittington was an attractive married father of five. The native Texan and Army veteran was employed by Broadband Cable. His wife, Cheryl, feared the early news coverage on Rita was minimal outside Southeast Texas. People had no idea how bad the hurricane made things. Perry attended Whittington's November 2005 funeral in Texarkana, Texas. A statement from the company described what happened:

"Ricky Lynn Whittington, 37, of Wake Village, Texas, was apparently electrocuted just after 12:00 noon Tuesday, November 8, 2005, at a job site at the corner of Brook Wood and FM 418 in Silsbee. Mr. Whittington, a member of a four-person crew, was in a large utility construction vehicle (bucket truck) when he was apparently electrocuted by a high voltage power source."

Whittington was later pronounced dead at St. Elizabeth Hospital in Beaumont. We gave him a moment of silence on a rainy day. An ordinary working man gave his life to help after Rita. All I would know of him was the sad ending and handsome face with its black cowboy hat. He wore a plaid shirt in the memorial photo and looked friendly. My heart goes out to Cheryl Whittington and their five babies.

Every time we moved near the front door for me to leave, during those breaks where the rain had slowed, we talked so much, drops would pound harder again, leaving us with more time to contemplate other hurricane stories. "You should talk to the Vidor Fire Department," Kendra had a list of names who'd be familiar with how the building was crushed once by Rita and again when insurers handed down their hurricane verdict. They weren't going to pay, according to Kendra, since it was determined only 30% of the structure was destroyed. Kendra called it the largest 30% anyone in Vidor had ever seen, "Their fire department was leveled."

The storm outside kicked and churned. It was too dangerous to drive. We sat a spell longer. Rain or not, I was in no hurry to leave. We flipped through photo albums and talked about life, marriage and divorce. I loved that this mother was so incredibly proud of a daughter who watched her life restructured by Rita. Perry had written in her letter, "Your senior year is the last year of innocence. How did this storm affect them?"

On the page, Perry feared that Kendra might be forever altered by what she had witnessed—a woman who died in her arms, another man with a bloody head injury and no one to help, classmates without homes. The trees, hunger, death and destruction, the long lines for gas, life without power for weeks, and Kendra on nonstop duty helping carry food, water and ice to people. Perry knew there wasn't anything innocent about Rita's aftermath. Because of a hurricane, Kendra's senior class memories are more than football and pep rallies.

There were 76 kids in the Warren High School Class of 2006. Only one a volunteer firefighter. Kendra planned on attending Lamar University, maybe work in forestry as an agricultural public information officer. She wasn't sure. "When we were deciding on our senior class shirts and senior memorabilia, we were like, 'What do we put?'"

For other kids, "Best Year Ever" might seem appropriate. Rita redefined a fun mission and senior year. Kendra says issuing shirts and key chains with "best" anything felt insensitive, making light of a tough situation when some had lost homes and possessions. Finally, the committee of seniors knew the right words.

"Our senior shirt says 'Things We've Overcome' on the front and on the back of it, we put a bunch of stuff. In big letters in the center, it says 'RITA.'"

THIRTEEN

Sunshine a day later accompanied me on the trip to Orange, Texas, where Cheryl English seemed surprised that I managed to arrive at her workplace early.

A little after 8 a.m., English began, "We bought land and started building ourselves, the house was actually our dream home." Nightmare Rita split open the new brick beauty and shattered a devoted husband-wife team who designed, poured heart and soul into and constructed side by side home and hearth. They did it, barely out of their newlywed attire.

Cheryl and Mike English had done an amazing amount of work. Married in late 2002, the mission began a short time later. They cleared land. They drafted plans. They worked weekends, nights, holidays, any free moment the working couple could find went into measuring, hammering, and hiring subcontractors to do assigned chores. None of the grueling labor, especially given that she was 52 and he, 51, was easy. The house was a testament to their relationship, not the first marriage for either, but they determined it was going to have a solid foundation that put the union in the running for best and last.

After about a year, the red, black and white brick home, just under 2500 square feet, with grand white columns, was completed. "It was wonderful," English started, "I had never lived in a new home, brand new, according to my specifications, my colors." The couple continued finishing touches and moved in February 2005, celebrating Valentine's Day, the sweetheart that English dreamed of all her adult life. A slew of windows, big fireplace, island kitchen with centered stovetop, all signature upgrades they included for a lifetime of entertaining family, friends, and bible groups. For nearly eight months, they enjoyed a much deserved honeymoon. "Then the hurricane came."

Less than a month before Rita, graphic images from New Orleans and Mississippi were still fresh in their minds. "I was a child when Audrey hit and can remember evacuating in 1957, we'd been pretty safe all these years of our lives and felt untouchable because we'd never had a big tragedy," English says. She'd evacuated several times for other storms too, including Andrew, but the complacency of dodged hurricanes left survivors totally vulnerable before Katrina. "Unimaginable that it was going to happen to us, we felt untouchable," she shook her head again.

After the Gulf Coast was ravished by Katrina everyone sat glued to the television. "We were horrified by what happened. The Louisiana native waited for word from loved ones who lived in Slidell, her husband's brother and his wife. "They [Carrie and Sandy English] had a brand new home also. It was on Lake Pontchartrain with a little boat docked there." The 35-foot Chris Craft Cabin Cruiser sank. There were eight inches of standing water inside of the home once they returned. "They had to remodel, they had to move and just remodel, of course mold went up to the wall. They stayed with family and friends and fared okay."

English was heartbroken for her relatives, their brand new home had to be gutted. A total loss. Never once did it cross her mind that three weeks later it would be her turn. "When we saw the devastation of Katrina and heard about Tropical Storm Rita, when it was on the other side of Florida, my husband decided we needed to change our insurance premium." Before Rita made it to the Gulf, Mike English had the presence of mind to make adjustments to what had been a very high deductible to a much lower one. "He was tracking it [Rita] and called our agent that Monday morning before Rita hit." English told the agent he wanted the deductible they had originally chosen, to save on insurance premiums, changed from $9,000 to $2,000 dollars. Later, the quick thinking caused a raised eyebrow when it was time pay the claim. It was changed with five days to spare, but everything was in order, legal and tidy.

After Katrina, and just ahead of Rita, Cheryl English was busy juggling two new situations. She had a job as an inspector with the

Orange County Health and Code Compliance Department and was looking for the best way to support local groups tending to the needs of Katrina victims. English volunteered at a church, but knew she wanted to do more, "We contributed a rather large sum of money because we were like, 'Okay, this could be us.'" And then the familiar refrain heard from every person in Rita's path, "And then it was us."

Cheryl and Mike English have three grown children from previous marriages, she has two sons and two grandchildren, he has a daughter. 31-year old Tyler is father to babies Madison, 10, and Connor, 5. His wife, like his mother, is named Cheryl. They also live in Orange County and initially considered evacuating to Houston so Tyler could spend some time with his father in Sugar Land, Texas. It was hard to know where to go. Meteorologists worked overtime tracking Rita. Each update meant a change in plans for the masses. "The weather was reporting it [Rita] was going to hit, possibly Corpus Christi, Padre Island, or the Houston area, so they backed off going there." By Wednesday, English says people were antsy. On Thursday the multitude fled.

"My younger son, Bret, and his wife, Jessica, live in League City and if Houston was going to be hit, League City was going to be hit." English paused to think on her 26-year old man-child, "At that point, we were praying long and hard and seriously." Again, she paused. Co-workers continued to shuffle papers, answer phones and stare into computer screens. English rallied her emotions, but her voice cracked almost as soon as she did. "I told God, I said, 'God whatever you do, take my house but don't take my sons.'" English was crying as I struggled hard not to. *I have two sons.* No mother, no parent, anywhere, ever, wants to outlive a child. English remembered the rest of her walking and thinking prayer. Her boys were just beginning. She didn't want them to lose what they had. Financially speaking, English knew, "Mike and I are more able to go on with our lives."

None of them had flood insurance, it suddenly hit as they packed to leave, again all that New Orleans had taught. "Oh why didn't we?" she animatedly looked at the office ceiling. Much of the anguish that English felt in the before and after of two very different hurricanes unleashed itself in front of a complete stranger. At the same time her facial expressions kept changing from sadness to joy, from relief to anxiety, from worry to wonder. She confessed that evacuating left everyone with a crippling fear on potential storm surge. It was a concern being played up big by forecasters. Her faith was bigger, "I knew that God was sovereign, I knew that He would take over. Whatever happened, we would go forth from there." With heavy hearts, they evacuated.

"As it turned out, on that Thursday, Jessica, Bret's wife, her parents lived in Athens, Texas, which is near Tyler, not Tyler County. They were on a cruise and have a brand new home," English says. Everyone who wanted to was invited to use the home of Jesse and Gwen Richardson as their own. That same day, both of her sons left for Athens. Cheryl and Mike English decided to secure dream house and possessions before leaving Friday after "the traffic had cleared out." She had to laugh when asked about the traffic being clear, "No, we know that now."

They stacked furniture and electronics high off the floor just in case. They taped the windows and boarded doors. Furious work, frantic hours, the countdown pace was frenzy itself. English packed up photos and mementos and books. She found important papers and boxed them for the short road trip. They discussed which car to drive, his or hers. They took both. "We set out Friday morning at 4 a.m., it's only a four-hour drive to Athens." English laughed as if to mock herself, "It turned into a nightmare."

Eleven hours later, they arrived safely. But not before witnessing the long gas lines, people stranded on roadsides, arteries choked with motorists, and frustration so intense it could be plainly read on the faces of fellow passengers inching along. "Thank goodness for cell phones," English perked up, saying at least she could communicate with her husband on the tedious journey. When they weren't trying to keep their spirits high, the couple frequently phoned their children letting them know the state of the evacuation process as it unfolded.

"At one point, we decided to reroute just to get out of the way of traffic," English says, "but once we got to another point there was always traffic again." Always traffic. Everywhere and as far as the eye could see there was traffic. "You couldn't get away from it." In the days before Rita, English hadn't slept and was desperately ill. A long ride behind the wheel made her worse. But the sight of her two children, daughters-in-law and the grandbabies worked like a tonic.

"We enjoyed each other's company, stayed glued to the TV, it was a nice big home and we all had our own bedrooms and baths because the home was built for entertaining," English says. Indeed it was. Five full baths. Even with the amenities and comforts, there was no rest for the weary. Or the sleep-deprived. "That night, I stayed downstairs and never slept at all." English flipped channels and waited for Rita.

During the brutal hours, English described the atmosphere as frustrating because the national media "said very little about our area." She continued to surf and prayed that someone might provide an update. "All they were concerned about was New Orleans and they talked a lot about Houston." English never saw anything about their part of the world in Orange County, while waiting in Athens. They didn't know Rita had torn up the place they called home. "We heard Sabine Pass, Louisiana," she smiled, "which they got the name wrong. We heard Cameron Parish, Johnson's Bayou and areas like that," English explained, "so we weren't thinking Orange County."

The hours merged into daybreak. They waited and watched TV. By afternoon, nothing had been said, at least, not by various media outlets they were switching back and forth to. "My oldest son and his wife decided to leave and go to Sugar Land to stay with his father there." Four words echoed throughout the borrowed home: "It was over with." Waiting for word that wasn't coming made them hopeful about a return to uncertainty. They were eager to check out what had happened in those surrounding areas mentioned on newscasts. There was no one to call for more details "because they had all evacuated."

Saturday evening, brown clouds swirled over Athens. Rain was steady and falling. The wind was gusty, leftover activity from a hurricane that they didn't know had torn up the place they were headed to. It was 6 p.m., on Saturday, September 24, 2005, way too dark, another gift left by a lingering guest named Rita. The dark got darker still. The English family headed home. A cruel reality hovered alongside them and they didn't drive too far south of Athens before getting the idea that something was terribly wrong. "It's usually dark at night driving, but not that dark," English says. It was sinister because they had driven into the zone, a swath of Texas land, far and wide and without power. They refused to turn back.

"Early on, we saw some trees down on the road, we were just

following the headlights in front of us," English shrugged her shoulders. They drove nonstop and made it all the way to Jefferson County. "I was exhausted." But the Department of Public Safety wasn't letting anyone into Beaumont. They couldn't enter the city. They couldn't go back. There was no place to find available shelter. A cell phone strategy emerged.

"I told Mike, 'Let's try going up north and cutting across, maybe another route.'" English suggested to her husband, in the lead vehicle, that he hightail it up to 105 around Silsbee and sift through Vidor, which would give them another option—Highway 1132. "We went in from back roads and when we got into our area, we saw more devastation." Scene after scene of headless trees and stunted trunks soon made it evident why people weren't being allowed into nearby Beaumont. "We were shocked, mobile homes were turned over, metal was everywhere, power lines were down."

With every mile, her heart sank. English felt apprehensive about what they would find on their street. Tormented by how the dream home might be their nightmare in waiting. "When we got to Vidor, 1132, pine trees that were 12-inches in diameter across, were snapped off up high, all across the roads, and power lines across roads, a lot of headlights and a stream of traffic." They had no choice except to get in line behind the traffic. It was surreal. A hurricane had reduced high tech lives to primitive resourcefulness. Men with chainsaws exited their vehicles and cut thick trees in sections, clearing blocked roads allowing traffic to pass. Slowly pass.

"We could see someone with their RV [recreational vehicle] and so we just decided to follow them in." English held tightly to a theory of strength in numbers. It was scary. The wind shook otherwise sturdy objects of steel and skin, timber and tissue. "It was so very, very dark," she recalled. Tiny lights that flickered in the wind and night were almost respectful. Like those at a concert to light up a love song or remember a friend by. "We'd pass homes and could see candles, flashlights and kerosene lamps," English smiled at the sweetness of unplugged lives and battery-operated lights. Her nocturnal moment, she promised, would never leave hurricane filed thoughts, "It was like driving into a void."

Finally, they arrived at the interstate where lanes were fairly clear. The same could not be said of Highway 1442. "We started driving down the road and there were lots of trees, we were having to go around because no one had cut them out of the way." Toward Bridge City, there was a stunning metallic show. Large electrical power lines crisscrossed. "They looked like big metal robots," English described the toppled wires. Fallen giants strewn across the street. High voltage very real, not toys.

"My first thought was, 'Oh my God if we drive across those, we're gonna be fried.'" Her voice was high and exaggerated. It didn't immediately register that there wasn't any remaining power surging through the monster lines. "We drove across." She released a comical sigh and a few tears mixed in with past relief. "God this could be it," she had said as they prepared to connect with the first line. After not being "fried," Mike and Cheryl English were only two miles from seeing their love nest.

"We live down in Bridgeville and turned off our street and we go about a fourth of a mile and couldn't go any further." A tree across the road. The torture of being so close and a world away. Initially, all was quiet. They didn't see anyone. They had no power tools like the men with no names on previous roads. Then they noticed a neighbor whose truck was stopped. He had attempted to drive across his property and got stuck in a ditch. He grabbed a ready alternative. They talked with David Riley, knew his substitute transportation solution was also the answer to their dilemma.

"We rode his tractor, he drove us to our house, which was just around the corner." Armed with prayers and flashlight, they braced for whatever. It was dead dark in the subdivision. "When we shined it up, the first thing we saw was a tree through our foyer, the front entry." English thought that odd since there were no trees in their front yard. A closer examination provided tearful and shocking geometry. The big tree peeking out of their new home had come from the backyard. "It went all the way across our house and just sliced through the middle of the house," English couldn't believe her own words, not even months after Rita. It was the gunshot, a fired lumber bullet that entered and exited, except in this case, the house remained mortally wounded because the tree was so huge it could only exit part of the way. Complete withdrawal meant a second target.

"I have pictures," English offered when she saw the skeptical look, "I'll show you the pictures." She recognized difficulty in comprehension and started again. "The bottom of that tree had some rotted decay where ants had gotten into it and was probably 30 inches in diameter." Huge oak. Solid oak. When the tree snapped and came crashing indoors, all of its weight was on the house, which broke the fall. The departing bullet needed to finish its exit and find a resting place, maybe a thud all the way to the carpeted ground. Their greatest fear was such an impact would completely doom the structure.

"It [the tree] brought the chimney down inside the house, just opened up the whole middle of the house," English says through faded voice. In some rooms the ceilings were nine feet, and as high as 12 in another. Then English thought of an insult that would've been funny if it weren't so sad, "On top of that Joyce, the tree was full of bees, there were honeycombs all in it." A disturbed queen and her workers swarmed out of their oak castle and took up residence in the English attic. Limbs everywhere. Leaves. Dirt. Debris. And water. "It [the tree] opened up the house so wide the rain blew in."

English remembered the hours spent building the smashed home she stood in and couldn't help but rewind to a few months earlier when she had vacuumed every inch, including the bee-filled attic, to ensure against dirt and dust. Honey heaven. Mud city. A fulfilled dream that took years of planning and designing and building was remade in a matter of hours. Rita utilized a tree as her knife and precisely carved an octagon chunk right down the middle of their house, leaving it open to Mother Nature. Every room in the house was affected.

"On top of that, there was another tree that same size that uprooted over the master bedroom and master bathroom and poked a hole in those rooms," the grief came visiting back in such an emotional way that English trembled. Two oaks, the wooden rocks were aged and experienced. "I counted the rings on one of them," she spoke briefly about not believing how long the trees had lived there before them.

After Cheryl and Mike English saw the destruction via flashlight, their nerves were shot and the same words kept being uttered from room to room: "Oh my God." Later, by the light of day, another hurricane revelation hit hard. "If the wind would've blown in the other direction, all of our neighbors across the street would've had trees in their homes, but on our street, we were the only ones that had trees behind our house so ours was the only one that was damaged." It was reality unshackled from logic. English counted six neighbors with minor damage. Amidst all the devastation on her side of the street, English noticed a small object that looked as if it hadn't been moved by Rita. *Like a tree that's planted by the water, I shall not be moved.*

"A little Playskool plastic toy car was out in the driveway, across the street, still just sitting there." English mentioned, several times, the mysterious ways of God, His power and plan, her faith. "It's funny," she says, "my husband was stronger than I was there because he said 'Well, you know, look at Job, what he went through. God's not going to put us through any more than we can handle.'" Mike reminded her that Job suffered endlessly and never once cursed God. The man who offered his last name in marriage made the following proclamation: "We're not going to curse God either."

Mike English is a good man. He insisted, through the pain and misery of torn down spirits and destroyed physical home that they continue to bless and praise their Maker. They were alive. It would be okay. "Knowing that we had worked so hard on it and did so much of the work ourselves and to have to start all over," water laced her words. Rita was enough to make a person question things. Instead of one single 'why,' the couple moved forward.

"Our neighbor with the tractor left and we stayed in the house that night." Gaping hole and all. There was another bedroom with minor damage, it became post-Rita repair headquarters. Drained, English was faced with another sleepless night. "I did not feel safe at all because we were afraid of looters, we were afraid of the tree, the bees were buzzing around but they did not bother us." She was consumed by the thought that other unwanted guests, looking for food or expensive goods, might use the darkness as cover to intrude and terrify.

No sense of time, watches hard to read, the earth did not move or turn. Except for one unnerving sound. "I was afraid the tree was going to continue falling because it did creak and creak and creak all night." A constant motion, sleep was impossible on every front. English feared the talking tree because it hadn't become unhinged at the root like the twin that banged into the master bedroom. The partially-exited foyer tree wasn't free. It tossed and turned like a human all night, desirous of a place to land. One big drop, she believed, they both did, and a mighty oak would topple the rest of the roof down right on top of them as they pretended to rest.

"That was the first time I'd ever seen Mike cry," English says of the strong shoulder she relied on. "He tried to take the blame but I wouldn't let him. Both nature lovers, they had wanted property with trees and hated the idea of removing God-made trees that were so breathtaking. So they decided to let them stand. Right next to their dream home.

Proud of her electrician-spouse, English again revisited the heady days that defined a labor of love, an excitement produced by building that brought the pair so close their soul and foundation became one. "He wired the whole house and the plumbing, put down the floors, he built the fireplace mantle," then her voice trailed off. English couldn't finish the list, the man had done so much with his own two hands. She right beside him.

"Before Katrina hit, we had been visiting Mike's brother in Louisiana and bought a crystal chandelier, a Schonbek Chandelier, and it was hanging in the foyer." When they returned after Rita, the expensive fixture was still hanging. It was untouched. Perfectly smiling and glittering and greeting guests, along with its wooded companion. "That tree came right across," English demonstrated with her hands, "right near it, but missed the chandelier." *Very expensive?* It had set them back a few thousand dollars.

Like other items in their home, English was relieved that her husband had taken photos of the chandelier for insurance purposes, before they evacuated. "That was very smart," she smiled again, beating the reporter to the punch line, "He's a good man." They stayed in the house a few more nights, but they were sleepless and somber too. It was slightly cooler at night. Dark with eyes open or shut. Eerie because a deafening silence and stillness would creep in after daylight. Occasionally, the couple heard four wheelers.

"Our neighbors would patrol for looters because we kept hearing about that." English lived in a fairly new neighborhood. Looters were aware that new homes meant new stuff. Without power and limited communication, resilient people banded together and devised common sense strategies. Lance and Kim Guidry would buy ice and gasoline, while Don and Linda Bimm were assigned food duty. David Riley, Wynne O'Bannion and Billy Daniels took turns patrolling the subdivision. "Even though neighbors had cut the trees off the road," English says, "at night they would drag them back across the road to keep looters out."

Before Rita, neighbors hadn't really known one another. They weren't close or tight knit. At least three of her neighbors, English had never met. They spoke. They waved. They went on with individual business. Rita changed the surface niceties. "It brought us together. A neighbor behind us came over and said, 'We're all in this together.'"

David Riley shared an unusual tool at his disposal. The tractor man had a bucket truck and used it to climb up to help cut the menacing tree being held by a weak timber thread. The oak, for too many consecutive hours, applied enormous pressure and weight on the English home. "Mike put up supports, some large 2x12s to help hold the beam so it wouldn't come crashing down." That made English feel slightly better.

Sunday after Rita, they ventured out, again, in separate vehicles. While her husband went to hunt down gas, English wanted to check on her son's home and neighborhood. The damage was not extensive. At least there was something good to tell him. She was very surprised at how widespread destruction was, and how Rita hit in sneak attacks, giving a black eye to some and barely punching others. On the drive around, English ran into two men who worked at the Road and Bridge Precinct 3 Barn. She stopped on the parking lot where the employees were removing trees to escape concrete and hit the road to survey damage, help residents. English offered a deal.

"For a cup of coffee and so I can charge my cell phone on your generator," she told the pair, "I'll do some work right now." English got the heavenly brew and kept her end of the bargain. She helped move boards with nails and other debris from the parking lot to make it passable. Her phone recharged while she finished the manual labor. A will-work-for-coffee moment resonated with a caffeine addict. English smiled at her own resourcefulness. Like others, she did what she had to do to make it another day.

"Monday morning I called my insurance, couldn't get through to FEMA, so I called my son in League City and he got on the computer and turned in our claim." Insurance agents responded fairly quickly. FEMA did not. Almost three weeks later, English did receive a packet from the government with money and instructions on how to apply for a loan, if they needed one. They protected what was left of an unrecognizable dream home.

English laughed when asked about the politically correct royal blue tarp issued by the federal government. "As a matter of fact, at one point," she says, "we had an Outback Steakhouse tarp across our house." At least the structure could be used to advertise, English smiled, then added, "Home of the blooming onion." While the steak-dream home reminded anyone traveling an aerial vantage of a familiar eatery known for its "down under" origins, for three weeks the couple stayed with Alan and Perry English. The idea that they would dream again seemed down and under too.

Back in the moment. January 2006. "We're painting now, my husband put in some of the light fixtures last night and we'll be able to put in flooring and trim work soon." English slowed down to gauge the magnitude of that statement. "Then clean up and move in." She projected the end of February or early March as the date they might return. For the months following Rita, after leaving relatives, the couple lived on the other side of town in her former home.

"I was very happy yesterday and for the holiday, [MLK] I went out and bought paint. I cleaned up in the house, all the sheetrock, the mess, the mud. It made me feel very good because I'm finally getting my house back." English rolled simple pleasures around in her brain. She couldn't wait to do yard work for Spring. She couldn't wait to take a bath in her garden tub. Sleep in her own bed. Entertain family and friends. Be still with Mike. "It has definitely brought us closer."

Perhaps for therapeutic reasons, English wrote to Oprah, she says, because Americans haven't yet realized how devastated the area was. "It will never look the same, the trees won't grow back overnight, the lumber is useless. A lot of the mom and pop stores won't be rebuilt. Restaurants won't open again." Far worse, English says, than those things, is the fact that so many people, thousands without insurance, lost their homes and lost a way of life. Many left and may not come back. She reiterated her theme, "The landscape will never be the same."

English received the customary auto generated response, a nice one from the Oprah staff to acknowledge receipt of her letter. Thinking I might listen to her ordinary story, one known to many, English contacted me. "There are communities that were totally wiped out." She mentioned Cameron Parish, then the confession echoed throughout the Piney Woods and coastal areas affected by the storm. "It's like Rita was downplayed compared to Katrina, if they would've had levees that would've held, they [New Orleans] would not have had nearly the destruction." English noted the shocking loss of life that might've been spared for poor people who managed to survive a hurricane, but not levee-induced flooding.

A few minutes later English spoke the three words that more residents have said than not, "The forgotten hurricane." Her spiritual home, Common Ground Community Baptist Church, has been a source of strength during Rita-related trials. Her heart continues to be with victims of Katrina, just as it was when so many first fled Louisiana right into border cities and towns like Orange. She knew an invisible state line was long ago erased by a co-joined history between neighbors. They embraced Katrina evacuees. But worry America will never know that Rita walloped a powerful and lasting blow when those who had helped needed help the most.

"The main thing is," English cried, "is that Rita has opened my eyes and made me more aware of what could happen again this year." She talked about weather watchers and how they had monitored a record 27 systems, "We never had that many." English is anxious about the trend of stronger more devastating storms, a cycle forecasters have predicted may last two more decades.

"If it happens again, we will probably just rebuild again and keep trudging on." While she frowned at all the little inconveniences, like hanging clothes on a line to dry, living out of an ice chest, stripping down to underwear in the heat to work, and living without electricity, English blushed when reflecting on the handy, handsome husband who knew how to rig the shower so it would work with a garden hose. "Like my neighbor said, we're all in this together."

We walked out of the office and into a common area where her co-workers were completing an assortment of tasks. Lisa Roberts, the county floodplain administrator was there, along with secretary Michelle Sonnier. English mentioned Harold Welsh, the former

Inspector and department head who, after 30 years with Orange County, had retired just weeks before. Her new boss, Joel Ardoin, compared notes with a tall man who didn't work there. A white box had been strategically positioned on a table in the center of the room. A lone grease stain tempted us. Something tasty was in the box. The welcome native had brought glazed donuts and pigs-in-blankets. After introductions and a sticky sweet, he agreed to chat.

Jay Hall worked for the University of Texas Medical Branch. His title was longer than his employer. Hall was the Bioterrorism Homeland Security Representative for Orange County. A native of Orange, the 40-year old husband and father, had interesting opinions to go with all that pastry.

"One of the things that struck me the most, even before Rita hit, we were dealing with Katrina, so it's part of my job and Joel's and everybody else here, that we dealt with a mass amount of evacuees from the Louisiana-Mississippi area." For three weeks, they labored non-stop. "We were working on that, trying to get them placed and settled in, and then we had to deal with evacuating the evacuees."

When Rita came along, barely a month after Katrina, Hall remembered the feeling of "a double-hit," and how county resources were taxed to the limit. "That's the thing that struck me most," he repeated, "a lot of people don't realize this area was really hit twice." Hall never heard much reported in the news on Rita outside Southeast Texas. Many likened what happened after Rita to primary caregivers suddenly being viciously sacked by illness with no one to take care of them.

Hall described Orange as "the border city" that was "the first place" hundreds flowed into as they outran Katrina. "We had a site set up, clothes that were donated, churches cooking food and a lot of those people came out of New Orleans and Mississippi with what they had on their backs." The welcome was warm, the food was hot, it was the first real meal many had eaten in days. Some stayed. Others were just passing through on their way to larger cities. Before Rita, countless Katrina evacuees had vowed to stay in Orange, "They said they had been treated better here than where they came from."

Absorbing Katrina people was a fulltime job across Texas. Dozens of states now have a new influx of Gulf Coast residents, but

Texas herself welcomed more than all those states combined. Orange County pulled together, securing housing for many, placing others in jobs, and enrolling their children in the schools. Evacuees constantly stated their gratitude at how well they were treated and how much they wished to stay, but Rita proved too much to bear.

"When we evacuated, for them the second time, a lot of them didn't come back," Hall says. "It was truly a culture shock." Many had lost everything after Katrina and found their way across the border, welcomed but weary, thinking Orange was a potential home. A month later, Rita relocated everybody. For those who wanted to return after Rita, there were other realities more closely related to urban existence.

"A lot of people coming from the New Orleans area were used to mass transit," Hall explained, "and used to being able to walk where they needed to go. You can't do that here." Without transportation in most parts of Texas, life would be limited indeed. Hall had the same kind of compassion for his neighbors in both Louisiana and Mississippi that others have expressed. Yet he understood the frustration of neighbors who hoped people would understand Rita's economic impact and devastation in counties that lined up to help after Katrina.

"I don't harbor the resentment that some people do. Obviously, what happened in New Orleans and Mississippi was a tragedy with the levees breaking and in Mississippi where the hurricane came ashore. They deserve the attention, but by the same token, we got hit by the same size hurricane and were forgotten to some degree." There again, was that word, *forgotten.*

Only once, Hall says, did it come in handy to be 'forgotten.' It meant, initially, not having to deal with the media and squarely focus on difficult jobs. "We set up an Emergency Operations Center at Mauriceville Elementary, that's our secondary site. Our main EOC would be the sheriff's department in Orange." They decided on Plan B because of where the offices were located, "right on the water."

No one downplayed the fears and concerns that prompted a move north to higher ground, away from the sheriff's office. Judging from Rita's path, it was the right call. "The primary Emergency Operations Center suffered extensive damage." Some of the offices, in January 2006, according to Hall, were still closed.

"That hurricane came in at night so we had a big spotlight," he says. "We could see when we were able to get close to a window, which we didn't want to get too close. It was blowing pretty bad." Friday night, September 23, 2005, things heated up outside. Inside the EOC, which doubled as an elementary school, they had no idea the extent of damage until they were able to get out on Saturday afternoon. For hours, they waited. For days, they had been planning and felt ready.

"We were able to, whether it was smart or not, sit and look out a window and it was just amazing. We had a big diesel generated-powered spotlight shining at some trees." Hall told Joel Ardoin, "You just can't imagine that trees would bend that way." In all the snapping and bending and blowing, dozens of first responders knew tough jobs on the other side of daylight would take an emotional toll, wreak psychological havoc on security oaths they had taken. They attempted to remain calm.

When the eye came through, everyone knew, instinctively, it was time to move from positions too near windows. Someone voiced the same shared thought aloud: "We got to get to the center of this building." Hall thought of loved ones, wife, Stacey, and a nine-year old daughter. Then the dash to find the building's interior. Hall thought of home and then put personal in the back of his mind. Hall had a job to do.

"Minute by minute, there were so many different things that happened," he says. "The one thing I took is that we had people from the sheriff's department who were working and some of them had their homes completely destroyed, yet they did what they were supposed to do." Some residents had complained about the order to evacuate. Hall had no such option or he would've gone with his family to Dallas. Others from Orange County went as far as Oklahoma and Kansas. "When we call an evacuation, we want you to go," Hall says it's not to inconvenience anyone. The weapon that moved more people than ever was Katrina. "That prompted a lot of people to evacuate that normally would not."

As the night and storm progressed, Rita finally backed off, but it was touch and go, tense moments. Everyone was eager to see, prepared to help, "We were out there with 250 people in a DPS law enforcement military environment, just a lot of people getting ready to respond for what was going to be the aftermath." Hall thought of his neighbors, coworkers and friends. They had homes and families just like people who had evacuated. They concentrated on faithful promises to "protect and serve."

Hurricane hindsight wasn't something Hall seemed fond of. He knew there were things that needed improvement. "I will tell you this, your local entities, Jefferson County, Orange County, Chambers County, coastal communities, this is everyday for us. We live this every year so we had a good plan in place." Hall refused to fault a particular agency, but added, "There were some mistakes made at every level." Most Texans would agree with Hall that the evacuation plan could use fine tuning.

"Originally, Rita was projected to come into South Texas and it kind of inched up the coast," he remembered. "From Tuesday to Wednesday night, it went from a Victoria, Texas hit to a Galveston hit." Hall wasn't sure that people in Houston had much choice except to leave. The fear factor, Katrina images, and uncertainty about Rita's target gave panic an unseen color-coded elevation.

"We have called for three evacuations in the last 10 years and usually it [a hurricane] has moved east of us and people had become complacent," Hall says. A worse case scenario, "from an emergency management standpoint," would be a direct hit from a Category Five in the New Orleans area. Hall knew neither Rita nor Katrina were Category Five storms when they eventually came ashore, but both ladies may have provided frightening previews of the vicious cycle of future activity predicted to last up to the year 2035.

Preparedness is key. Hall gave kudos to a man named Chuck Frazier, "Our emergency management coordinator did a tremendous job." The 250 troops that stayed behind were inspired to work through tears, heartache and enormous loss. "The amount of people who had some type of damage that were part of the emergency response team just tabled what they had to do for the betterment of everyone else." Despite the torment and destruction and frazzled nerves that Rita left behind, some good came of her arrival and departure.

"One of the things we talked about was—you live in a neighbor-hood—you may know your neighbor or you may not," Hall paused, "after this, [Rita] you knew your neighbor." Hall seemed most proud of the fact that Orange County residents did not sit back and wait for help. They cleaned up. They checked on others. They patrolled. "People were out in their own personal bulldozers clearing land, starting the process so people could at least maneuver."

Stronger evacuation plans are absolutely necessary to make citizens less stressful about leaving next time. "I attended a meeting on Tuesday and we had some representatives from the Nacogdoches area and they were overwhelmed with evacuees. I'd like to see the northern counties and the inland counties and cities in the state of Texas develop a better sheltering plan." The meeting was still fresh in Hall's mind as we chatted about exactly how to do that. Then he asked out loud what he was thinking, "How does Nacogdoches, a town the size of 25,000 people, deal with three million evacuating from Houston?"

In what Hall called a "normal hurricane event," the northern most cities were only designed to house people about three days. And most fleeing people believed they'd return, no more than 72 hours later. "It just didn't happen." Without water, electricity, gas, no stores open, citizens simply couldn't be allowed in. It wasn't safe. His suggestion had been noted at many a meeting since Rita. "Be prepared to house them [evacuees] for 10 days. Be prepared to be overwhelmed, be prepared to ask for help because the state will give you help, but only when you've exhausted your resources."

In 2006, the city of Dallas released its financial hurricane report. Price tag for helping victims of Katrina and Rita: $7 million dollars. Cities that help must be prepared to be overwhelmed and prepared to ask for help.

FOURTEEN

I hit Jasper city limits—population nearly 8,000, on a gorgeous weekday morning, zeroing in on the lunch hour. Destination: Jasper Fire Department.

According to my itinerary, an interview with the chief was supposed to be an ordinary Q&A, take about an hour and be chock full of Rita stories. It was anything but ordinary. Nor was it an hour. Nobody warned me that James Gunter's other job was walking-talking machete. The 37-year old saw me coming. I didn't even get the proverbial coat off before Gunter fired the first comedic shot.

Journalists often regret that some of the best stories never make it to tape, audio or video. I'd never met Gunter and hadn't expected company but he probably wisely decided he might need a witness to help double team the Dallas author. 55-year old George Marvin "Buddy" Rector occupied the chair right next to me, we sat across from the man I instantly took to calling "Jamie." I started the recorder too late to capture our initial conversation.

Gunter had me laughing so hard, tears were streaming down my cheeks. It was 20 straight minutes of nonstop laugher. I needed a timeout to recover and regain control of the runaway interview train Gunter had masterfully hijacked with that one shot. I pushed the record button, uttered the standard refrain about both men spelling first/last names, ages and titles, to which Gunter answered, "I'm not gone give you my name."

After providing handles of two well-known area lawmen for himself and Rector, the chief started in on his longtime colleague. I warned him the tape was rolling, we were officially "on the record." The Chris Rock routine continued and I was not taking a single note. Too busy laughing and crying and playing referee.

When Gunter first started at the Jasper Police Department, he'd heard the stories circulating about Rector being "the biggest prick that walked the face of the earth." Gunter says, after a few encounters, there was little doubt that Rector was holding the title. "It didn't take long before we came up with his real name—Buttocks Rectal."

The mild-mannered police captain sat silent with his right profile to the wall. His expression never changed. It was clear that Rector had heard every joke about himself and learned to take it all in stride. The two men first locked horns after Gunter was a youthful dispatcher who went through the academy before accepting his first assignment as a full-fledged juvenile officer.

"Every day I had to come in and look at Buddy Rector. He treated people like crap. I had never seen anybody with less personality than Buddy Rector." I looked over at Rector, still smiling. That meant it was okay to keep laughing because Gunter was killing me with a succession of comedy arrows. It felt good to laugh after Rita.

During the early days, Gunter thought Rector would eventually loosen up with time and accept him as one of the guys. Didn't happen. Finally, Gunter came in to work one day determined to make Rector enjoy his work but didn't have a clue how to achieve it. Rector was at his desk madder than anything, Gunter says, at him. "He was just staring at me, had that old mean look on his face and I said, 'This is it, I can't stand it no more.'" Gunter flat out asked Rector what was wrong. The curmudgeon growled at him, no words, just a bear-like noise for an answer. While Gunter talked, Rector didn't move or say a word. His expression remained the same.

"I took my arm and I swept everything off his desk, the computer and everything and I turned around and walked off." That did it. Glacier melted. Rector broke out a big grin Gunter had never seen before. Not a laugh, but the young officer had him, "We been fine ever since." These guys make Moe and Curly look tame by comparison.

For all the jokes that Gunter told, he piled on accolades, "Don't let the name 'Buddy' fool you." Rector has a master's peace officer degree, a four-year college degree and countless investigative hours logged under special training. At that point, Rector still hadn't said much. Gunter told more Buddy stories. We laughed so hard the mountainous echo, in broad daylight, shook the Belle-Jim Hotel a block away in the square.

When I expressed surprise that any work gets done with all the potshots and storytelling, Gunter, quick as a flash, "We are too." Then the man of few words spoke, "Oh it was after 4:30 in the afternoon when we got it done." More howling, traded jabs and crime stories. It wasn't an interview at all. Just three Texans around a blazing desk fire, having a conversation about the region we loved, doubly affected by two ladies, hit twice while on her economic knees.

"Words can't even describe the outpouring that the people in this city and county had toward the victims of Katrina." The August Sunday before she made landfall, Gunter was on his way back from New Caney when he noticed traffic was unusually heavy. "I started counting the Louisiana license plates. Between Livingston and Woodville, I counted 500 going west on 190." Something was wrong. Gunter started making calls as he drove and suggested hasty meetings to deal with what he knew would be an inundation of people. By the time Gunter made it to Jasper, there were lines everywhere. For gas, for food, for lodging. The meeting started at 10 p.m.

At that critical juncture, state officials hadn't activated because Katrina was primarily a Louisiana issue. Jasper decision makers were concerned, rightfully so, that panic would set in as scared residents poured into border cities and towns in search of shelter and supplies. First, an identifiable information area to guide Louisianans was constructed using a flashing message board at the intersection of Highways 190 and 96. Mike Lout, a local radio legend, broadcast the information every 15 minutes to get the word out.

"There were just tons of people," Gunter says. There was nowhere to put them, hotels and motels quickly filled up. Jasper was not a designated hurricane stop, but officials had little choice except to find a way to house unexpected visitors. Without waiting or being asked, Community Church, Harvest Way, Hillcrest and Beechgrove Baptist opened their doors. Everything they organized came together in about 60 minutes. Then, for the first time in our conversation, Gunter's expression changed. His tone was suddenly serious.

"These black people pulled up, and they were from New Orleans," he started, "they didn't even know where they were at." Gunter was stationed at the information help site when they asked, "Where are we?" When the vanload of Louisianans were told 'Jasper,' they responded, "Oh hell no, we're not stopping here. We've heard about y'all." A mini scowl mixed with sadness had replaced the laugh lines and ease of moments before.

"During the entire ordeal of evacuating and helping Katrina residents, during this whole ordeal, including Rita, that's as mad as I got," he reluctantly admitted. Gunter was personally involved with the James Byrd case from beginning to end and knew the crime was never "reflective of the people of Jasper, Texas." On that, we agreed. Gunter sighed, "That made me so damned mad."

As did many others, our "interview" veered off track or maybe it was right on course. We tackled stereotypes, hatred, discrimination, snap judgments. Gunter almost fell off his chair when I told him I'd rather be "back off in the woods with Billy" than in some of the upper crust highbrow neighborhoods I'd been pulled over in countless times by overzealous citified folk who questioned my right to get dinner. It was my turn, and Gunter freely acquiesced, letting me borrow the invisible comedy club mike.

Telling jokes, recounting old memories, and even a few stories from the three trials, bonded me with two more white men I'm bound to take some heat for somewhere down the line. I was on a roll when Gunter blurted out, "You been hanging 'round Billy Rowles too much." More laughter, but true. Billy is the one white man I've already been KGB- interrogated about for having the audacity to have a close friendship. I've actually gotten nasty grams over Billy. They made one hell of a bonfire.

Gunter knew many of the same stories I did, but when he mentioned Al Sharpton, it was one I hadn't heard. In 1998, after the dragging, there was a loose plan to march from the sheriff's office to the Byrd family home by one of the uninvited visiting groups. Before the march, participants had a big news conference where heavy hitters camped around the bank of microphones had spoken. Someone announced it was time to leave. Sharpton had patiently waited his turn when suddenly everyone sprinted away. Naturally, reporters followed with camera crews. A few spectators gave chase.

"There were two people left standing—I will never forget this— me and Al Sharpton." Gunter looked over at the New York minister who had the most disappointed expression on his face because he hadn't been given the chance to say anything. "He's big and fat like

I am and he didn't want to run," Gunter laughed, another reason Sharpton wasn't in any hurry to pursue the marchers.

Gunter couldn't resist the moment of solidarity with the black leader, "Well, Rev. Sharpton, what do you think about it?" He glanced at Gunter and threw out four words, "Didn't get my chance." Gunter retorted that he wished things had turned out differently. Again, Sharpton, kept his account down to an economy of words, "Well, I didn't." Gunter darted up Birch Street to help monitor the march.

I also learned that Rector's wife, Linda, was a juror on the third dragging panel for the Shawn Berry trial. And the lawman's daughter, Alice Rector, was the dispatcher on page one of *HATE CRIME,* the same dispatcher who called Sheriff Rowles home after James Byrd, Jr. was found on Huff Creek Road. Our chat went south, west, off the map, and took some unpredictable detours. Gunter veered again without warning when he mentioned the shuttle tragedy in 2003.

North of Jasper. No one knew for sure what had happened until NASA confirmed it. Seven astronauts were feared dead after the Shuttle Columbia broke apart over Texas. "We got up there, we met with Sheriff Tom Maddox who had given directions to where he was," Gunter says. Along with then-police chief Stanley Christopher and Sheriff Billy Rowles, they assured the Sabine County sheriff they would do whatever he asked. "We get to the middle of this cow pasture and I'll never forget it because I thought, 'What the hell is he doing standing out in the middle of a cow pasture?'"

They walked out to meet Maddox. Maneuvered past fire trucks, ambulances, emergency crews and investigators all milling about. They walked right up to Maddox, spoke the law enforcement lingo, again offered their sincere services. Brothers to the bone. At that moment, Gunter says, Maddox leaned toward the scorched earth. "He picked a sheet up off the ground and there was a human leg severed at the hip and burned black and just laying there."

No doubt, Maddox and veteran investigators who thought they'd seen everything were reduced to shaken men required to compartmentalize what they were required to look at. Hard jobs that had to be done. Gunter paused, back in the cow pasture for sure, "Man, that hit me like a freight train."

Gunter has seen plenty. Much of it with the police captain who sometimes doubled as his sidekick, Buddy Rector. Both worked the Byrd case. Both possessed intimate details they'd rather never know on the shuttle tragedy. Both were neck deep in a 17,000 acre fire in Newton County when Gunter worked for the state fire marshal's office. He later returned to the city of Jasper as marshal. As fire chief, Gunter didn't know what to expect. In his never understated fashion, Gunter belted out, "And then the damn hurricane hits." We were instantly back on the laugh rollercoaster and I had to wonder how his wife, Jennifer, or his 13-year old daughter, Emily, ever managed to not smile.

Early in our discussion, Rector mentioned the new police chief was from my neck of the woods—the Dallas suburb of Addison. Todd Hunter had gotten a real baptizing with Katrina, only on the job three months. Prior to Katrina, the police chief had received appendages to the emergency management handbook and wanted to know what to do with them. Rector suggested placing them in the back of the thick volume and advised Hunter not to worry about the book's contents. All he needed to familiarize himself with was the evacuation plan. To that, Hunter asked, "Evacuation for what?"

Two hours after I first laid eyes on Gunter, he and Rector told a Newton County story together. "This was one of those 4:30 trips," Rector says up front. It involved a woman from Houston with a brazen check writing scheme that went all over Texas. "And we chased them *all over Texas.*" The trail went from one place to another, one store to another, with surveillance tape of the woman working her charms in Houston, New Orleans and Dallas. The woman was slick alright. Her downfall may have been the marriage to a fellow in neighboring Newton County.

"About 4:30 one afternoon, Buddy and I are talking and I said, 'Man, just out of the clear blue, let's go see if they're home.'" A shot in the dark, the pair had nothing to lose. Well, Bonnie and Clyde weren't home, no cars, no bandits. It was a quiet dusk. On the highway back to Jasper, the two lawmen passed the husband and wife. "They saw us, we saw them, Rector locked it up and hit the lights and you could see smoke come out of the back of their car. They were gone." Then Gunter had to officially inform the sheriff of Newton County that he and Rector were in hot pursuit.

After specifics like alleged crime, suspects, vehicle make and model, location, etc., Gunter says Sheriff Wayne Powell simply replied, "Jamie, I ain't got nobody available, just act like you're one of my deputies. Do what you need to do." Gunter responded, "<u>No,</u> we're not going to act like one of *your* deputies." The radio went dead. They raced on.

Rector picked up the story from there, Gunter was too tickled. "We chased them so long that night and we were so far back in the woods we had to call somebody to bring us a can of gas." They ran out of fuel in the woods. I assumed that meant the chase was over until Gunter chimed in, "I'm like you going to Billy's hunting camp—I don't know where we're at, we're in the middle of nowhere."

They followed all night, for hours, for miles, and the woods just kept getting thicker and thicker until, finally, a break. "They ditched the car and took off running through the woods." Both men agreed the main thing was to keep going, not to quit. Where the couple bailed, the lawmen put a dog in the hunt. "I couldn't get back if I had to," Gunter laughed, "I was praying my radio worked because cell phones don't and it was dark."

The enthusiastic animal led them straight to a quiet residence. By that time, a Newton County Constable had been tracking with them. His name was Bubba Johnson. I do not say what I'm thinking, but Rector read the arched brow, "Can you imagine *Walking Tall* with a broken foot?" The dog went right to the front door of a trailer. The trio devised a strategy for one person to man the back door and let Gunter have the front. That's when Bubba insisted on knocking. He was overruled. It was a Jasper County collar. Gunter knocked. They waited. "No answer," he confirmed.

Bubba was not satisfied with Gunter's approach or the result. "All of a sudden Bubba said, 'Get out of the way, and bam, just kicked the door in with that damn cast on his foot.'" The door splintered and fell. A woman inside became hysterical, screaming and hollering, "She thought we were breaking in." It was a gone wrong episode of *The Dukes of Newton.* I was practically rolling on the office floor.

They attempted to calm the shrieking woman by telling her they *were* the police. She didn't care. The lady was furious and her door was off. The suspects, if they'd come through, were gone by then. The slippery criminals vanished into the pines. Homeowner allowed officers to search. A crazy chase ended right there and two tired officers went on home. A month later, Sheriff Powell called Gunter with one serious question.

Powell told him that the trailer issue wasn't resolved and the woman was all over him wanting to know who would take care of damages. Powell needed to know exactly what on earth had happened back off in the woods. "I said, 'Sheriff, we were knocking on the door and Bubba told us to get the hell out of the way, he had this.'" Powell went, "Oh boy, that ain't good."

"A day or two later," Gunter shook his head, "Bubba called me and said, 'You gone back me up on this ain't you?'" Gunter told him there wasn't anything to "back up" because he had already given the full account to Powell. That's when Bubba gave Gunter his version of events. "He said, 'Now you know I was justified in kicking that door down,' and I said, 'No, that's why I knocked Bubba.'"

Time went on and the incident was never mentioned again. Maybe the sheriff of Newton County did settle the score with an angry female resident who had her door kicked in by a large man named Bubba with a cast on his foot. *Walking Too Tall.*

A few minutes later, Todd Hunter came in. His ears were probably burning from all the times we'd said his name. For a little while, the three of us were on our best behavior in front of the new police chief. If such a thing can be said of Gunter. Then Rector talked about what it was like waiting for Rita to arrive. Hunter reflected on the standard "72 hours" that all the preparedness books recommend, "I got water, I thought we had plenty of water. I don't know how many cases I got." Rector got cranked up right away, "My dog was thirsty." *I guessed it wasn't enough water.*

Rector applauded Hunter for his plan that allowed officers and staff to house family members inside the department so they wouldn't be worried about loved ones stuck in traffic. "It was like a 60-member family." One of the 18 officers' wives was a hairdresser. She gave everyone haircuts. Another wife was a nurse for the prison system. The state allowed her to stay behind as their health officer. "She took care of us, and of pets that got bit by bigger pets." Everyone got along, used their various talents in a village fashion. Gunter took another swipe at his longtime friend, "Even Rector."

Chief Hunter, a handsome man of 37, who looked 27, had only arrived in May 2005. Hunter and wife, Sherri, were excited about getting acclimated to their new lives when Katrina slammed into the Gulf Coast. Immediately, the Hunters were impressed, "These people came together and helped each other out, had they waited on others, it would've been too late." The community isn't a rich one, but Hunter saw a generous spirit that only crystallized a list of great reasons that led him to move to Jasper.

He fit right into our marathon conversation, as Gunter directed us back to Rita. "We were getting calls every 30 minutes from the National Weather Service saying it's there and it's not moving." Rita sat on top of Jasper for nearly nine hours. Around midnight, the calls started pouring in from residents. They heard things like, "A tree fell on my house," "I can't get out," and the ever popular, "Come get me." Rector manned the phone lines along with every able body. He even heard from a woman who called before Rita, "Do you think I have enough time to finish cooking my brisket?"

Crazy calls were sandwiched in with serious ones. Before they were forced into the house, officers worked at a grueling pace to move nursing home patients. Communication between counties was fine in some areas, lacking in others. At one point, when Highway 96 was opened to free southbound lanes and have all the traffic flowing in a northerly direction, cars poured out of Beaumont and into Jasper. No one had told officials in Sabine and San Augustine Counties about the new lane assignments to help the flow of traffic. So it was down to one lane again and a bottleneck developed just north of Jasper.

"So many people came through," Hunter says, "it was almost like locusts because they ate, they went to all the grocery stores and bought all the supplies and got all the gas." Jasper was left with almost nothing. Hunter was quick to underscore, it wasn't the fault of anyone evacuating. "The problem was the plan," he says. "Nobody had planned on getting freeways that full and running out of gas."

Gunter had recently heard the number one priority on the new TXDOT (Texas Department of Transportation) Agenda was pre-staging areas for gasoline tankers. Officials and citizens alike now know that preparedness means provisions, supplies, and gas for *more* than 72 hours. "Nobody ever thought that when you told Houston to leave that three million people would say 'Okay,'" Gunter jokingly stated. The four of us debated how far north Houston needed to evacuate. We talked flooding, whether people would go again and risk being stranded without food and gas and where to house evacuees. "If you have buildings that will withstand winds, why not have them there?" Rector argued. No one thought clogging the highways all the way up to Dallas was the most swift response to potential surge and pending destruction.

Jasper officials had evacuated elderly citizens on the few air conditioned school buses they had. But after seven hours of torture, police went and escorted them back. They had moved seven miles in seven hours. Gunter summed it up best, "We'd rather have them in their own beds." Rector agreed. He called the gas shortages one of the state's biggest downfalls. Because Houston evacuated first, then the Beaumont area, it meant thousands of people, mostly in rural areas, were stranded once all available fuel had been purchased.

"We need to enforce what we've got on the books right now," Rector was adamant. When fleeing Texans couldn't go north out of Houston and Galveston, many had no choice but to come east or west. "When they did, they actually came into the storm." Rector wasn't thrilled that nursing home patients from other areas were brought to Jasper and "dumped." Once the county got its own evacuation order, it simply meant double or triple the workload to ship sick people to Broken Bow, Oklahoma.

"It was 100 degrees, school buses were overheating, the people nearly died," Rector says. That's when Chief Hunter spotted four sparkling charter buses going down the highway empty. "He commandeered those buses," Rector says. They were contracted by FEMA and on the way to a staging area in Alexandria, Louisiana. After some phone calls, it was agreed if passengers actually sat in comfortable, air conditioned buses, it wouldn't violate red tape agreements and get them out of the heated chaos.

A few weeks before meeting these men, I saw a report on why people were still living in sheds and tents and motel rooms when FEMA had empty travel trailers available. 1400 parked on Arkansas soil. Gunter knew of others right under our noses, "There's a storage facility, a staging area just west of Jasper. There's probably a couple hundred sitting out there." The man to my right had a simple but scathing commentary: "The system is broke." We knew why, we understood the drill. Brand spanking new trailers sit empty until someone or some company the federal government has contracted with can deliver them, one by one, and only after inspectors check out proposed sites and give passing marks. Sometimes payment is an issue. The trailers aren't moved until money changes hands. Did the government have enough warm bodies doing the hauling, inspecting and getting people into empty trailers? Rector was fed up. Not so much for himself, but for folk who had waited and waited for help and housing, "People are living in tarps."

Gunter revisited the two weeks after Rita, "This whole part of Texas was nothing but a black hole." No electricity in pockets. "We were like two bright lights in the middle of the night that everybody could see," a reference to the police and fire buildings that ran on generators. A black man with an incurable pulmonary disorder showed up one night in dire straits. The man simply asked, "What can I do?" He would not survive without breathing treatments.

"We let him start coming down here every evening, 4-5 times a day and plugging in his breathing machine back here so he could get his treatments," Gunter says. His home was damaged. His health was deteriorating. As Tavis Smiley would say, "even Stevie Wonder could see" the man needed help. Finally, a generator was secured for the man and Gunter delivered it. The backup electricity helped. After Rita, and well into the recovery stage, the man returned often seeking a different kind of help. He was battling FEMA, appealing a denied claim. The fire department would fax things for him. "He was just one of many."

Months later, Gunter still can't figure how some people with similar damage to those who received money ended up with nothing. No rhyme or reason he says. "One of the most serious issues we had to face—Jasper is more than just the Timber King of East Texas, there are also recreational opportunities here not afforded elsewhere." There were beautiful lake homes and many evacuated to their serene getaways believing they'd be okay. "We had winds of 120 mph, so this was *not* far enough inland."

Gunter offered a rough estimate of how many evacuated Jasper County. Probably half. But a greater percentage of people came in to ride it out, believing Rita wouldn't dare follow. After she started trotting down her unpredictable course, no one near the eye was untouchable. All of Neal Street was hemmed in and frantically calling for help. "We jumped in my truck because it's a dually and I'm thinking 'six wheels on the ground are better than four.'" It was the first opportunity to see trees down, poles everywhere and no way to even get to Neal Street. The Ford F350 with its dual rear wheels on each side barely stayed put, coming up onto one side, the wind pushing it around pretty good. They weren't supposed to be out. The men knew it. But people were desperate for help. Gunter laughed again, "Rector was screaming, 'Let's go back, let's go back.'" They did.

"We literally thought the roof was going to come off," Gunter looked around his office at the fire department, seemingly still amazed that he was indeed seated there for Sleepless in September. He recalled an interview with a Houston TV station about 5:30 the morning Rita hit. Even with windows completely boarded up, just to be heard, Gunter had to scream because of the noise. "The wind was that loud." The fire chief was doing another phone interview when Rita demanded her presence be recognized. A news anchor asked Gunter what the great racket was. He told her "the storm." She encouraged him to go inside. After all, the phone interview wasn't so important he needed to be out in it. Gunter replied, "I am inside lady." She asked, "And we can still hear that?" Ever the cutup, he told the Houston interviewer, "You ought to be on this end."

Hour after hour, Jasper was on the receiving end of a wind-aided nightmare. Trees snapped off at the heavenly end, it had taken years to reach such heights. Others were mercilessly maimed at the base. Many more uprooted whole and rested on timbered sides. Those that won stays of execution were punished nonetheless with brutal bending and lashing. They stood up to Rita and she made all say Auntie. And then the dawn.

"One of the state agencies that helped us the most was game wardens," Rector says. It was a statement that I heard from one end of Texas to the other, community after community. Captain Rector reiterated the fact that game wardens have never received the recognition they deserve, not with Rita, or for Katrina, the dragging case, the shuttle tragedy, and a number of situations. 10 regions in Texas are headed by captains. 500 wardens in law enforcement alone. No one ever credits their director, Col. Peter Flores.

"They went up here to the lake and set up a tent city and they would come in their own pickups or whatever and load up food, ice, and water. They'd go out in the county to the people who could not get to town," Rector says. He recalled putting in a long day and evening shift in the initial hours after Rita and running into three captains, all game wardens, just standing in the hall like they were reporting for duty. Rector thought they had come to the station for a bite to eat or a shower. The men flatly stated their mission was to patrol with Jasper police officers. Rector factiously asked, "Who would send captains to patrol?" And they answered, serious as a heart attack, "The Major."

Chief Hunter agreed that game wardens were rarely mentioned when people talk about the efforts of first responders and support. "They are a can-do agency," he added. Just about the time he uttered the compliment, a cowboy stuck his head through the door and announced they were tired of waiting, "We're going to the Lone Star." I've eaten there once before, had a steak the size of a plate and a mutant baked potato on a separate plate. Abnormally huge. Can't say I recall any vegetables. If they came with the meal, they too were on a separate plate. Large Texas vittles. Our conversation lasted through lunch, into late afternoon and beyond.

"We had been sent a team from a company called Rural Metro out of Yuma, Arizona," Gunter started. "They were contracted by FEMA, an EMS provider." Jasper got about 15 ambulances and 25 paramedics. "We went to the Community Church and set up a triage center, a MASH, if you will." It was the only medical facility they had that could treat the walking wounded and provide care for critical patients left behind. They saw 1,000 people in 10 days. Conditions ranged from childbirth to cardiac issues. Frail folk need-ed transporting out, a break from the stifling heat. Officials in Jasper begged for a C-130 but were sent smaller helicopters. "The state had already committed so many resources to Katrina, and then Rita hit, there wasn't anything left."

Thankfully, owners of area medical supply companies gave permis-sion to break into their stores. It kept Jasper going. Some higher up had suggested Jasper use the 15 ambulances to take patients out, one at a time. Gunter had a struck match response: "The paramedics that came with those ambulances were running the triage. If they leave, who's left?" Gunter couldn't fathom hauling one patient at a time. To Dallas from Jasper and back is a minimum 10-hour excursion.

Five days after Rita hit, powerless and hanging on in the heat, Gunter was sitting with Rod Carroll, president and CEO of Stat Care EMS, and overheard a phone conversation he was having with SOC (State Operations Center) housed at the Texas Department of Public Safety in Austin. Carroll finally just sat back in his chair and said, "Thank you, thank you, thank you." Gunter was sure, after hearing this, they'd finally get the supplies necessary to forge ahead. Carroll hung up and Gunter asked if they were going to get help. Carroll very emphatically stated, "No, they told me no." This surprised Gunter who asked why the medical director had been so excited in thanking them. "Carroll said, 'Jamie, you don't understand, it's taken them five days to tell me no, we're on our own.'"

There were basic things Jasper needed to survive. A large generator to run the water treatment plant would've meant clean water much sooner. Rector says they asked everybody, all the way to Washington and U. S. Senator Kay Bailey Hutchison. They got no response and no generator. "You know who we finally got the generator from?" After a couple seconds of silence, Rector answered, "Wal-Mart."

It didn't take days of red tape for Wal-Mart to send an 18-wheeler that Rector warmly greeted with an offer to help unload the mammoth generator. That's when the driver turned to the officer and said, "The 18-wheeler *is* the generator." Jasper officials found creative ways to keep sick and overheated people alive. Citizens checked on each other. People with important positions did grunt work without a single complaint. Neighbors volunteered to help. In the midst of all the recovery efforts, Chief Hunter called Rector into his office to help judge a strange phone call real or joke.

"He turns on the speaker phone and it was this little whiny voice, 'What can I do for you today?'" Rector says some unknown person asked. Since he didn't recognize the voice and was too exhausted for guessing games, Rector asked Hunter who the high pitched set of pipes belonged to. Hunter answered, but wasn't sure, "H. Ross Perot."

The Dallas billionaire and one-time presidential candidate offered whatever they needed, including his helicopter to do an aerial assessment. "We thought it was a joke," Rector says. The would-be prankster was persistent, calling every day to offer help.

Finally, Hunter told the phone voice the sewer station wasn't working and potential for a backup nightmare seemed imminent. The man countered that he had vacuum trucks next door in Louisiana and would get right on it. Believing they had sent the telephone impersonator on a fool's hurricane errand, the trucks arrived the very next day. Rector had just one footnote to the story, "It was H. Ross Perot alright."

The stories kept coming. Bravery. Courage. Fortitude. Heartbreak. Weariness. "We were trying to cover the northern end of the county, go down every county road and knock on every county door and check on everybody," Gunter says. This was a slow process repeated again and again. They kept assessing situations. They kept delivering the ready to eat meals good enough for American soldiers and good enough for citizens who were beyond grateful to get them. Rector kept returning to the 60 people holed up in the Jasper police building, "I slept on my office floor 17 nights, and the first week with my dog." Even I realized Gunter would never let an opening like that one pass. He ribbed his friend again, "Unlike the Red Cross, y'all took pets?"

Rector was so accustomed to Gunter's swipes that he ignored him and turned to me, "I had a little Schnauzer, bet you thought I had a bulldog," to which Gunter again laughed, "It would fit your personality." If I'd stayed much longer, I might've ended up on one of their famous "after 4:30" chases into Newton County. I was fairly sure I didn't want to be back off in the woods with Bubba and his Kung Fu Foot trying to explain my friendships with half the lawmen in Texas. It's the other half, *I'm a still fearing.*

Rector and his rhetorical comments have been well documented, and not reserved for close friends and writers from Dallas. In a post-Rita city staff meeting, Rector began to sense a few employees were upset that the police department wasn't sharing goodies they had brought from home to cook in case stores, as they certainly did, shut down or were destroyed or ran out of food. So Rector asked, "Why didn't y'all plan?" It's not so much what he said as to where he was sitting when he said it. Next to the mayor. An awkward feeling hung for about a nanosecond. "He kicked me out of the city staff meeting." Never one to be outdone, Rector had parting comments for all in attendance. "I said, 'That's alright, I think my rib eye's ready.'"

The floor was soaked that day from all the water our wet eyes loaned it. Robust laughter was the healing medicine for hurricane heartache. Before Hunter arrived, all that was missing was cigarette smoke and Tequila shots. We were as loud as any barroom brawlers. Other times we felt a heavy sadness encompass our hearts as we took turns at the microphone. Almost to support one another. Gunter did it again when, out of nowhere came, "It's just by the grace of God that there weren't dead people stacked everywhere." Silence. One man, an elderly gentleman, shot himself, the only recorded suicide in the county. We respectfully paused.

"New Orleans had water," Gunter says, "we had trees, that's the difference." Gunter had so many stories, Rector had a ton of true tales, there would be no way to cram them all into a single chapter. As soon as Gunter listed Rodney Pearson as one of many volunteers who logged countless hours helping Jasper, I knew him instantly by reputation. The DPS trooper had a brother named Earl who was a captain with the Texas Rangers. His son, Ronnie, was a firefighter and volunteered right beside him. They are a law enforcement family. These fine men are black. They are hard workers, certainly what peace officers and protectors ought to be.

Pearson was already working a 12-hour shift everyday for the Department of Public Safety, then coming into Jasper at night to work until the wee hours. One evening, Gunter sent a reporter from *The Houston Chronicle* to ride along with Pearson. Steve McVicker had come down to write a story about the aftermath. He ended up on patrol with the father and son Pearson team, and David Shultz, a local funeral home operator.

After a night of saving lives, delivering ice and checking on shut-ins, the next day McVicker came to Gunter in appreciation. Once the reporter saw how dark the "Jewel of the Forest" was minus her well-lit crown and power throne, McVicker was probably more grateful to be in the company of such well-trained men. Rodney Pearson is professional with a capital P.

Deep into the East Texas thicket McVicker had an epiphany, "He says, 'I'm in Jasper, Texas and there's two black men in the front seat and two white guys in the back seat and that ain't supposed to happen." McVicker confessed to instantly thinking of James Byrd, Jr. and the dragging that had riveted a nation. It was too bad that Americans couldn't see black and white working together, many do so every single day, in a branded Texas county millions of others only associate with a brutal hate crime.

Buddy Rector then recalled an article he read some weeks after the storm, "Rita: The Hurricane That Never Was." Gunter sadly shook his head in agreement. Jasper is not a rich county by any means. In the end, for the hurricane that never was, officials spent more than $7 million on aid. Like other counties, they're fighting to recover funding from the federal level. No one is sure when or if the money will come. They worked and continue to do so.

Gunter tallied 309 overtime hours, not counting regular work time, just OT alone. All Rita. He logged a similar number for Katrina. Toward the end of our visit, Gunter was philosophical in his political musings, finally landing on something none of us wanted to dissect. "We've got the military presence and the power to go into any country in this world and take it over, but we can't feed and clothe and water and bed our own people after a natural disaster?"

If the federal government would like to answer that one, I know a few boys in Jasper County who'd be glad to throw some steaks on the grill and beers in the cooler, say, some time after 4:30 in the afternoon?

FIFTEEN

Rosemary Miller had a sweet life. A sweet husband named Fred. And a 14-year old Schnauzer named Heide. Life was good. So good, the Millers decided to take a dream vacation to Branson, Missouri, one they had put off for years.

What is striking about Miller's story is the ordinariness personified. An ordinary life with extraordinary circumstances. She was thrust, along with thousands, into a storm that required going ahead, no matter what, and making do, then doing without, survival of the southern fittest without complaint.

Her Nederland home was uninhabitable thanks to Rita. She pined for it every day from the nearby perch inside a comfortable recreational vehicle in the driveway. It was a windy day with gusts so strong weathercasters had issued an advisory. Miller, another stranger to me, emerged from the motorized home. We smiled as nature rushed us inside with our blinding sideways hair.

"Was it therapeutic when you were writing?" I asked Miller about the five-page, single-spaced letter from a few weeks earlier. Dozens of residents sent email, like Miller, after seeing me on KFDM-TV in a live interview about research I was doing for this book. Response was overwhelming. I was only able to select a few. One vital thing connected me to every single person that wrote— our very ordinary lives and the values held so dear.

"It was just pouring out and I probably ought to thank you because all of this was bottled up inside," Miller kindly answered. She lost track of time when she first sat down to pen her emotional account of the impact Hurricane Rita visited on the life she loved, with the man who loved her. "It began to spill out, once it started it was like a faucet."

For close to five years, the 62-year old woman and her husband,

Ulyss "Fred" Miller, Sr., 68, had been remodeling their home. An upstairs bathroom had only been completed six weeks prior to Rita. The colors were vibrant and added something fresh for the end of spring, beginning of summer. Miller was drained from all the extra work of looking at swatches, matching wallpaper, picking new towels and accessories. She also found life particularly busy with a labor of love—taking care of the 93-year old woman who raised her right.

Miller's mother, Margaret Crawford, had come to stay in 2000 and was always notoriously independent. It was clear she looked up to her mother, "Oh yes, she was quite the pistol, the original woman's libber." Sadly, the firebrand passed away in 2004 after a long and fruitful life. Miller's voice choked back fondest memories of the mother-daughter eternal bond. She pushed herself ahead to 2005.

"We just decided we'd been wanting to go to Branson, we were going to take a well-earned vacation," Miller says. The couple drove from Texas to Missouri, and had all kinds of fun along the way, leisurely cruising and enjoying each other's company. They arrived. Settled in. First on the agenda was a visit to Silver Dollar Amusement Park. More fun. The Dollar isn't a ride-themed cotton candy place but more arts-crafts and family oriented with heavy emphasis on the entertainment side of amusement. Miller's voice was gay and light, good smells of fattening food and adult adventure surrounded the Millers. They were caught in the pores of a huge funnel cake. The trip started out with every topping they had imagined—whipped cream happiness and chocolate satisfaction. Their first vacation in three years was off to a delicious start.

On Tuesday morning, September 20, 2005, Fred and Rosemary Miller slept a little later than usual, enjoying the fancy hotel and complimentary room coffee. They read the paper, talked about pending events for another day of sightseeing. For some reason, perhaps habit, they switched on Fox News and quickly discovered Rita had her sights set on Beaumont/Port Arthur. Or somewhere in there. They glanced at each other and had the same finish-each-other's-sentences-thought. *Nederland was between Beaumont and Port Arthur.* "I just looked at Fred and said, 'We've got to go home.'"

Not a mad scramble, but a disappointingly sad one began. The Millers had nothing but great things to say about Branson. They first called the tourism center, which graciously canceled their reservation, refunded their money and sent them on their way with God speed blessings and prayers. Many places would've left the total amount in place, on the credit card and let weary travelers duke it out themselves with the bank.

"We drove straight on through and got in about 8:30 that Tuesday evening before the storm," Miller says. Next they contacted the man who had their RV. Daniel Travis met them to return the rolling vehicle that would soon become a permanent home. Uncertain about what might happen, they left nothing to chance and remembered earlier hurricane procedure. "The next morning Fred went down and gassed up the Jeep and he went to Miller Electric and began to board up the business and secure things there."

She packed. Pictures. Papers. Irreplaceable items. "We had done this so many times before," Miller knew the drill blindfolded. They'd evacuate. They would run up to Dam B, a campsite near Jasper, more commonly known as Hen House Ridge at Martin Dies, Jr. State Park. The storm, as was typical, would take a last-minute turn and the biggest headache would be interrupted lives, inconvenience. "It would go up or down the coast and we were always spared the bullet."

Miller checked on their adult children, six in all, four hers from a previous marriage. Between them, there were 14 grandchildren who ranged from age two to 15. They had all made plans. Her mind felt some relieved to know where everyone was headed. Fred's brother and business partner, Jackie Miller, thought Dam B was a safe location. "He went up to Hen House Ridge and had three nights up there and we pulled in." Situated too near a mammoth pine tree beside the RV's rear bedroom window, her husband wasn't fond of their new parking arrangement. The tree hovered over like a menacing wooden puppet that might come to life in the dark of night beating down on them with arms pulled by Rita's unpredictably violent strings.

Soon where the Millers were parked and how many trees were at the campsite became a moot point. A park ranger pulled in Thursday morning and ordered everyone out by 5:00 p.m. Officials had received word that high winds were possible. It would be too dangerous for folk stationed in motor homes nestled cozily in thick

Piney Woods. "We pulled the slides in on the motor home, let the jacks up and we headed up 96 not really knowing where we were going," Miller shrugged. Her twinkling eyes and laidback personality spoke to the faith in her nomadic situation.

Rosemary Miller knew her husband was searching his brain for a firm destination. They didn't have one but drove away from the RV site. Just tooling down the highway. "I wasn't too bothered, I had just enough gypsy in me to be okay." The Branson adventurer kept coming out to monitor the level of intensity. "We'll do whatever," Miller told herself, confident that the protective husband would find a spot. Both were grateful that they didn't have to dwell on things like finding bathrooms or water as Rita's hour of arrival neared. "We're fully self-contained, so we just slip on the generators and can run the air or whatever." Branson wasn't a place they had been laughing in only 48 hours earlier. It felt like eons before. Technically, they kept reminding themselves they were, in fact, still on vacation. Just not the one they had dreamed of and driven to.

"Finally, we got to Carthage, up around Marshall, and found an RV park there." There was only one place left with hookup capabilities. Unfortunately, it was located on sandy ground, "All the paved surfaces were taken." They were exhausted. There were no other ready alternatives, so they got in, hooked up, set everything up again. Her sister-in-law, Betty Ann Miller, had also evacuated to the same area and was staying with a friend. They were glad to chat with her. It was time to rest and wait.

"We turned on the TV that evening and the weatherman said, in fact it was emergency management for Harrison County that came on and said, 'We're expecting 100 mph wind gusts and 30 inches of rain.'" Again, the marital partners who could read the other's next words stared into matching faces of concern. "Fred looked at me and said 'This is not where we need to be.'" Miller laughed then, but it wasn't funny that night.

They uneasily stayed parked on the loamy tract, half sleeping, half wondering where to go next. Early the next morning, the smell of coffee and birds singing in the pines, they got up with no fixed destination and certainly no ETA (estimated time of arrival). "We pull in the slides, pull up the jacks and get on the road Thursday. Down Interstate 20 we go." The Millers were running from Rita with one thought: How many miles would it take to be safely out of her wrath? They made it to Terrell, the place her son, Michael Scott Grumbles, had gone to evacuate with his wife, Tamara, and their children. They met at the Tanger Outlet Mall to compare storm stories. It was refreshing for Miller to see grandbabies, Jenna, Hannah and little Michael. But the journey did not end there.

"We went on down the road to Rockwall. That's where I was born and raised." Beautiful sentiment with an unspoken reverence for Dorothy, the gal from Kansas, who knew there's no place like home. Multiple times, people compared Rita to the feeling of being in *Oz* and having homes lifted or flying but there was also something about home. Warm. Welcoming. Mom's good cooking. And Toto too.

A cousin met the Millers at Wal-Mart and had found them lodging at Lake Tawakoni. Miller was certain she didn't plan on returning to the same part of East Texas they had just left. So Jo Nell and Carl Leonard, Jr. offered parking space for the RV on a "nice tree-shaded lot" that was next door to their home. They lived in Fate. Given the details and circumstances, the name seemed almost too perfect, the same place Miller's father, B. F. Crawford, was born.

Something, call it instinct, told the couple to stay in Rockwall where they were and not take the road to Fate. They chatted with cousin Pat Hairston, who also lived in Rockwall. The Millers found good parking and stopped. When Rosemary Miller called again to thank her other cousin in Fate, the weather news was bizarre and not related to the hurricane winds they were trying to escape.

"She said, 'Oh I'm so glad you're there. We've had a storm blow through and have no electricity and one of the trees has been uprooted and we have limbs everywhere.'" Miller's heart skipped a beat when she heard the dramatic news. The same intuitive voice that advised them to stay in Rockwall came out, "If we had just gone five more miles into Fate, we probably would've had a tree on top of the motor home."

The Millers were in the eye of a traveling storm that gave a precursor, a mini preview of what was headed, miles away, to Southeast Texas, a shadow of the monster that had been stalking them. "We were real fortunate that we stayed behind in Rockwall." By then, it was Thursday evening. Whatever company Rita planned to bring and the devastation she was intent on leaving, Rosemary and Fred Miller would need their rest.

On Friday tension woke them. They got some of the bugs that resembled horseflies off the giant windshield. Both attempted to stay calm and composed, there was no reason to panic. Like millions of others around the state, they started to monitor the storm again. "I was real antsy." After hiking back to Wal-Mart for more supplies and gas, Miller watched the news, which wasn't a comfort but confirmation of "a dead eye hit on us." It was the first time Miller and her husband began to wonder what they would find when they returned home.

"I knew everybody was safe, knew all of my children were safe and out. My second daughter, Shannon, was in Waxahachie, my son in Terrell and my youngest daughter, Georgiana, in Dallas." Another daughter, Terrie, moved her horses and goats to a friend's farm in Hardin County to ride out the storm. Terrie "Shawn" Looney is the Agricultural Extension Agent for Chambers and Jefferson Counties, overseeing the wetlands. Miller's two stepchildren, Ulyss Miller, Jr. and Terri Annette Miller, lived in Kansas and Tomball, Texas. Both were fine and waiting to hear something.

"That Saturday morning, we got up and we knew the storm had gone through." Neither of them had experienced that good, deep sound sleep people crave. Instead both kept an eye on storm reports for any word on damage or loss of life in the Nederland area. "I can remember seeing one man at the Elegante' Hotel [Beaumont] sitting there with this silly little tree," Miller smiled. The reporter was excitedly going on about a shrunken tree that was only five feet tall. She was talking back to the TV and telling the man to just take a look behind him at giant pine trees that had been uprooted or snapped. But he went on and on about the small tree, that was priceless to Miller.

Wal-Mart, despite its many critics, was a retail savior for faithful fans who shop nowhere else and others who learned to shop there for things like generators and kerosene lamps and flashlights and water and snacks around the clock. By 8:30 a.m. Saturday, the Millers were back at Wal-Mart on Interstate 30 in Rockwall to buy all the gas containers they could find and prepare for the journey home. They filled them up and decided to try a different route for the ride back. Their odyssey began.

"When we got to Palestine, I told Fred, I said, 'We'd better stop and gas up.'" Not only did it prove sound advice, Miller went beyond simply 'gassing up.' She looked at the home on wheels that had provided them sanctuary and knew it had to make one last long haul. She put the pump inside and heard it loudly shut off at 20 gallons. Miller did the unthinkable. She squeezed the handle and ran off an additional seven gallons to give the motor home extra gasoline security.

They drove on. Wondering. Hoping. Anticipating. Not knowing. When the fuel needle didn't budge for miles, her usually calm husband was slightly concerned but only in the most humorous way. "Fred said, 'You've broken the gas gauge.'" The soft spoken woman wasn't sure why she chose to go past the automatic full click. All she could think of was not having anymore gas until, whenever. The water tanks on the RV were filled to capacity, they had gasoline and plenty of food. Miller had never before risked filling up their motor home with gas. "Something inside me kept saying just fill it up, fill it and keep going on."

Miles later, they hit Crockett. Seven turned out to be like Fate, their lucky number in more ways than one. The husband who had teased her about the broken gas needle was impressed and they were both relieved Miller had topped off back in Palestine, to the tune of $75 dollars. All they saw for the rest of the trip were lines and lines of tired, frustrated motorists and signs with two words: "NO GAS."

"As we got into Woodville, it began to really hit, you know, the devastation," Miller says. Her voice suddenly turned more somber and reflective as she slowed down to harness in emotions that wanted to run free. Produce tears. There were no lights. Police were directing traffic best they could. "Everybody was courteous, everybody was taking their turn." Sitting in the long line waiting for their chance to get the nod of approval, they decided to make a turn and head back toward Dam B to check on her brother-in-law. They weren't able to get him by cell phone or handy Nextel Walkie Talkie the brother-electricians were fond of carrying.

"There we saw trees that were down, roofs that were off, power lines that were hanging. It was just almost surreal," Miller quivered. Real estate resembled the aftermath of a tornado, nothing was where it was supposed to be. "Then we got up to Dam B, and headed back towards Jasper and we stopped on the road going into the camp." The

RV was too big to get back inside the campsite so they pulled off the side of the road. Her husband ventured in. He didn't get far. "When he got in there, the camp had flooded. It had four feet of water."

The Millers later learned that Jackie and Virginia Miller had gotten out at 2 a.m. by using a chainsaw. The water was coming in so rapidly they had to scramble to not find themselves stuck. Their relatives spent three nights in an old bar that had nothing but a cement floor and a couple of musty mattresses. Her sister-in-law, when they met them again, was covered from head-to-toe, in mosquito bites. "As we were going down the road to leave, we saw more trees down everywhere, we saw houses with trees *through* them and houses, again, with roofs off."

A few miles later Miller let out the most awful screech, "My God, Fred, there's a line!" A power line was across the road. Dipping and dangling. Not in the road, but hanging like a thick black clothesline. He slammed on brakes. "And this motor home is pretty tall," Miller says. Neither were sure if there was leftover electricity. That was the first thing. The couple was also concerned about getting tangled up in the strong line or having to fight through it. With no room to spare, they finagled around it, inch by inch. For the rest of the trip, thankfully, people had hung colored ribbons to alert drivers of low hanging power lines or live/dead wires. Slow. Tedious. Deep dark. And more roadblocks.

"As we got up closer, people would get out of their cars and argue with officers." The couple's vantage in the motor home with extra high seats allowed them to see an impressive distance past smaller vehicles in the lines ahead of them. When it was finally their turn to speak to an officer, after seeing countless cars and trucks ordered back, Miller's husband was quick on his feet, or quick in his seat. He thoughtfully explained his profession as an electrical contractor, how much his services were needed at home. The second generation electrician whipped out his contractor's license and gave troopers the handy plastic that confirmed his skills.

"They gave it back to him and the officer just looked at Fred and said, 'Man, you got your work cut out for you. Good Luck.'" Amazingly, they waved the Millers through. So many others were turned away, frustrated, cursing, crying, begging to be let through, and coming up with some incredible stories trying. When I first arrived, Miller told me to sit anywhere in the motor home, pointing to a big comfy chair. I declined the offer knowing it looked like a favorite resting chair for this man with the credit card license. On the sofa we shared, we had to finally take a break, change positions, and let the blood circulate in stiff legs. Our conversation resumed. Hundreds of neighbors could relate.

Once the Millers got on the other side of that roadblock, they were inside Jasper city limits and witnessed the same kind of devastation they had seen before. "You just kind of had this sick feeling in your stomach." Miller wasn't sure what to expect for the whole ride home. Somewhere along the way they received word from daughter-in-law, Tamara, that their house was still standing. Tamara's Aunt Michelle, was married to a Beaumont police officer, Ken Hobbs. His brother was a sheriff's deputy named Ron Hobbs. I knew *Chief* Hobbs. "He [Ken] had gone by and checked their house and our house." The Beaumont officer did send a one-sentence assessment to be delivered via cell phone: "You're gonna have a mess to clean up."

The dark drive continued. It was almost indescribable, something kin to a third world nightmare. "Huge trees looked like toothpicks knocked over," Miller found lost words. They were approaching Lumberton and got stopped again. People were being ordered back at a frenzied rate, no one was getting through no matter what their story was. "It was u-turn city." The Millers wondered if the credit card would work its magic in Lumberton. "Once again, Fred went through his spiel, he's an electrical contractor and was needed at home," she says. Like before, her husband forked over his contractor's license. They examined it closely and let them through. Miller had one thought—"We're going home."

Miller's daughter and son-in-law, Shannon and Bobby Flanagan, also returned the weekend of the hurricane. They had his mother and their twins, Austin and Justin, with them and needed to get back to their 15 acres in Lumberton. The Flanagan family feared what was waiting because of dense acreage where their home was located. Sure enough, they had to fight their way in, "They had about 70 trees down, they just had to cut into the property." Miller thought of her child as she bid Hardin County farewell.

The door to the RV suddenly opened. Wind gusts bent it all the way back to an outside wall as a man grappled with the blustery dilemma of closure. Miller perked up and a big smile decorated her happy face, "There's my husband." Her voice was so sincere, its tone unrehearsed and loving, so satisfied at the sight of her hardworking man, the one trying to tame a misbehaving door. Miller greeted him, "Hey Sweetheart" and made introductions. Fred Miller looked like a sweetheart. He stopped by to pick up something, but his wife confessed, "I wanted him to meet you."

The man of the RV sat in that same masculine chair I was relieved to not be occupying at that moment. I had learned, as a child, to never sit in a big recliner or chair so inviting. It almost always belonged to a man, a single owner, usually a man, whose wife or fiancée or girlfriend simply tolerated furniture that didn't go with anything else in the room. Fred Miller looked perfect in that chair. It was like the joke Chris Rock told about his mother warning the children not to eat dad's "big piece of chicken."

Miller asked her sweetheart if there was anything that stood out about the return trip home after Rita. "All the landmarks were gone, you could get lost easily," he says, and added, "When we saw them turning people away, I knew I'd have to use my license." It worked on Department of Public Safety troopers and local Lumberton Police. Would the contractor's license work a third time on Interstate 10, where every exit was manned by law enforcement from different agencies in Beaumont?

A quiet deserted interstate was more eerie than anything. Exits closed and guarded. Red lights danced in the dark. Blackness enveloped evening. Torn up buildings could still be seen, misshapen and roofless. Signs gone. Blown up the block to mark wrong locale. It was so destitute of life and people, Miller says, "Everyone was gone to a party and they forgot to tell you." Home was close. They were becoming more anxious and afraid of the big surprise waiting on them.

As they passed the Elegante' Hotel, Miller and her husband laughed thinking about the reporter who could only find such a small tree to share with viewers when they easily located taller pines strewn like a game of pick-up sticks. Windows were blown out of the fancy hotel. Drapes blew in the wind, suite colors protruded from all nine floors. "We came around on 69 coming home and you could see more buildings torn up along the way." They took the Twin City exit. There was no waiting on Highway 347. No lines and no people, except for faithful law enforcement protection.

They drove, and were just blocks from reality's front door, more practiced in the only truth that would get them there. The exit was blocked. Theirs was the only car that pulled up to officers waiting and patrolling. Authorities were curious about the electrical license, it wasn't enough to work by itself. They needed more. Miller's husband was asked, for the first time on the journey, to produce his driver's license, something to show his home address and official identification. He did. They were allowed to *carefully* proceed.

Coming down Twin City, two pair of eyes darted from one side of the street to the other. Miller used the word 'devastation' again and again. "Your heart just begins to pound a little bit more." They were almost home. Nederland High School was the same parking lot they always stopped to disconnect their 1995 Grand Jeep Cherokee. They surveyed an abandoned campus, "Roofs were stripped bare of shingles, power lines crumpled." Not many words passed between them. Both desperately wanted to get home, but then again, they didn't.

"It was the longest time, from the time we left there, [Nederland High] Fred took the RV, I took the Jeep and I went out ahead of him." When Miller turned onto Canal Street, there were bent up carports, missing chunks of houses bitten out by vampire Rita, a night attack that left trees on trunk bellies in ditches. "To be a small street," Miller says, "Canal is really busy." Not that night. It was sleepy pavement, quiet and in shock, its traffic and busyness silenced by a girl storm.

When they hit their street, Miller's husband carefully backed the 2001 Damon RV into their driveway. It was hard to see how to maneuver the white body with its flash of desert gold. Finally, they parked. "We got out and I had my little camera and he had his camera—and we opened the door to the breezeway." Miller paused, "What we saw was just unreal." Their carpet was a bed of white snow. Plants had transformed from leafy green to soapy silver. It was a field of white heat, a creation made possible by some freak act. "All of the sheetrock texture had been blown off, it just covered everything." It may seem farfetched, but Rita was responsible for snow in Nederland, Texas.

Miller forged ahead and opened the door to the backyard. "I was not prepared for what I saw." A major brush pile stacked high and waiting to be burned. Three big oaks, one was 12 feet, had fallen like dominoes, one on top of the other. The scene, if given a physics perspective, was unnatural and impossible. If it hadn't been right in front of them, neither would've believed the oak card game. But there was another player with a slim bluff. A lone pine tree had broken the fall of the oaks, miraculously, it stood between them and more devastation to the house. The pine had been pushed over, but it was still strong enough to hold the oaks at bay. It didn't sound logical, and indeed, to Rosemary and Fred Miller, the sight was too incredulous to believe or deny.

"Apparently, the pine trees have very deep taproots and the oak trees just all blew over. They did punch holes in the house." They were grateful that all the oaks hadn't ripped completely through the structure. Miller handed me photographs like exhibits from an unbelievably brutal crime. She knew no one would fathom her description without the proof to support it. We marveled, me for the first time, and she for the hundredth, at the strange direction and route taken by the fallen oaks, right at her back door, just over a well tended flower bed that had been much admired by everyone who entered that door. Now the area resembled a wooded cave, where women and children dare not venture into so scary it looked from the edges. Photos of the Millers in their backyard after Rita made them human Lego people, tiny by comparison standing in a giant remade forest. Miller was barely visible peeking out from next to one of the tree trunks. In another photo, her husband posed by the roots of a different tree. A backyard swing had been slung across the yard from its original position.

"We had nine inches of rain, according to weathercasters," Miller says. Water was gushing all around, she added tears to the mixture of flooded debris. Maintaining his sense of humor, Miller's husband saw the shock and heartbreak on her face, looking at his pretty wife, "Well, you've always wanted a pond." She agreed, but not at the expense of her oaks and backyard, and more importantly, her home. A weeping willow on the other side of the property was ruined, depressed at its own condition perhaps. "It just wrung the limbs all into my house, there were spots everywhere, on light fixtures, smoke detectors, everywhere. The stairs were soppy wet."

Standing water meant sheetrock upstairs had to come out. Dirt and mud poured from the wood walls, stuck thick like maple syrup dripping from sticky bark. "It was just a mess." The 60-year old house would require more than TLC to find its way back to anything remotely close to before. It took about 10 days before the Millers could even get someone over to look. They were frantic to remove waterlogged carpet before any permanent damage set in. Damage like mold. They were well aware that some insurance adjusters had been denying claims if they saw mold, even if it was caused by water Rita left behind. No matter where Miller looked, outside and inside, there was damage. Her unrecognizable yard would take an army to wade through and clean up. All the limbs from one solitary tree had come off in a separate pile of debris, leaving the tree clean shaven, almost naked.

"One good thing I have to say about all this was we met neighbors we didn't know we had." People came out of their shells, Miller says, to help, to comfort, including one good Samaritan on a tractor. Dallas Higgins rode around offering help to anyone who needed it. He lifted stuff. He moved stuff. Higgins drove people to blocked properties that were otherwise inaccessible by cars. The good neighbor had plenty of company.

After finding out all their home insulation had to be removed, and a laid to rest fence replaced, as well as other grueling manual labor, the Millers knew they were fortunate. They were blessed. Miller went to Triumph Church where a relief distribution center had been set up. Her husband knew the best way to help was the very thing he had used to get in—his being an experienced electrician. While he checked on commercial customers and friends, Miller spent the next two weeks volunteering at the church. Helping others took her mind off some of the woes of future repairs.

Church coordinators assigned Miller the role of greeter. She would say hello to people who waited in their cars for help. While welcoming them, her goal was to assess basic needs from car to car. "There was one man who really touched my heart, he began to cry." The older gentleman cracked from the pressure. He had never had to ask anyone for anything in his life. It just seemed to break him that he needed a hand. The stranger only had to look around to understand Rita didn't discriminate or just affect any one group. "It crossed all races, all gender, it didn't matter how much money you had."

When Miller wasn't at Triumph, she rode around to see Southeast Texas firsthand. "I went to Sabine Pass and it was just the most heartbreaking thing to see." Boats flattened. Buildings gone. Power lines down and accentuated with clumps of grass. All of Sabine Pass got hit hard, except the new school and a couple of other buildings. Miller saw too many people to count who lived in nothing but tents and tarps. "There were so many they had to set up public showers and find ways to wash clothes." Miller cried that places like Sabine Pass and Cameron, Louisiana were chosen to reinforce important lessons. "What do I have to complain about?" she mused, "I have been so blessed."

Triumph Church was like so many houses of worship after the storm. They worked to help people. They prayed with some. Members provided comfort to people, as Miller says, whether they drove up in Lincolns or Escorts. The church served two meals a day, along with water and ice for anyone who needed it. During the day, Miller was glad to be doing something useful. It was steamy. The heat was relentless. They turned off motor home generators to save fuel. "You could sit here and be miserable and hot or you could get out and do something constructive." She chose the latter, meeting neighbors and making new friends. Random acts of kindness weren't so random, they were "what anybody else would do."

Modern day pioneers were forced to pull together. "I see the goodness that came out of this." Family and friends, community meant the world to Miller. She blushed when talking about the knight in shining electrical armor, "Fred's a very giving person, very warm and he was also very concerned about our customers." He often ventured out at night to help people who called them. Miller met her second husband in 1996 at a Beaumont square dance being hosted by the Swinging Singles Square Dance Club.

She was there with her date, a nice dentist who suggested they make the new guy feel welcome by inviting him into the square for a dance. Fred took her arm and the rest is history. When Rita scratched at such love, it only made a close couple, closer. "It's almost like our minds run on the same track, sometimes it's kind of scary." Love sustained them after Rita. They knew things would be alright.

"There was a curfew, it was dangerous," Miller admits it was crazy for awhile because people were trickling back in at a pretty good clip and eager to drive at the same time without traffic lights. "For the most part, people were courteous." One morning, a neighbor across the street, went out at 4 a.m. to go back to his job when he noticed flashlights flickering in one of the houses. He called police. Because a few looters tried to take advantage of the post-Rita situation, an element came out with the darkness that residents had to be aware of.

"Two squad cars with eight policemen wearing vests and carrying guns literally surrounded the house. A fellow inside was going, 'Hey man, wait, I live here, don't shoot.'" This was just one example of how vigilant authorities were, working around the clock to protect people and property. The other neighbor had no regrets about calling police. He was relieved it turned out to be the homeowner lurking around in the wee hours of the morning.

Miller and thousands of others, in January 2006, were still waiting for insurance to approve bids. Hers was for a foundation estimate. "We're still in the process of talking with the contractor because trees hit the house, he wants the house to be leveled." Loose pilings meant the two-story structure needed to be "straightened." First, workers will jack up the house and tighten the pilings. Before a new roof can be put on, the house must be securely in place. A heavy rainfall from 12 hours earlier was able to find an opening in the blue FEMA tarp. Little insults added to the hours and days and months to move back into their sweet life.

"We'll just have to wait and see, this [Miller looked around the RV] has just sort of become home."

NOTE: While writing this chapter, an email arrived from Miller. She wrote, "The holes and broken rafters in our roof have been repaired and we now have brand new shingles gracing our house! I never in my life thought I'd be so excited abut having a new roof!"

SIXTEEN

Down the main thoroughfare. Newton is small. A two block quiet town. The square. A stoplight. Courthouse. A handful of business-es. Parked cars, almost no movement. Signs of town life breezed by like nearby whispering pines in surround sound.

A woman emerged from behind the sheriff's door. A deputy maybe. No uniform. She might've been a constable-receptionist-Jackie-of-all-trades. "Where's the high school?" I yelled across the lawn to the county employee. My car was stopped in the middle of Main Street. Door ajar, motor running, lost writer. A highpoint in Newton for an otherwise ordinary weekday in January 2006.

No rush to answer. The woman took another drag on a ciga-rette, the 10-minute break to clear her head of monotony associated with a stream of similar calls. *Help.* Calls from Bon Wier, Sycamore, Toledo, Mayflower, Jamestown, Indian Hill, Call, Sycamore and Trout Creek poured in after Rita. "Stay on this road and keep straight on down," she pointed. "You can't miss it." I waved my thanks. A stranger couldn't compete with the soothing cigarette break. The woman blew out a link of disappearing smoke, which I soon joined down a winding road that led to Newton High School.

The pretty school was deposited in a wooded academic sanctu-ary, peaceful and inviting. Two days earlier, I had phoned a man named Curtis Barbay to see if I could come chat about Hurricane Rita and teamwork. It was a subject he was familiar with, being head coach for the Newton Eagles a sporting eternity.

"May I help you?" a woman asked in the school office. She gave directions to the gym where Barbay was. With classes changing, the principal, Johnny Metz, stepped out of his office and decided to per-sonally escort me. We exchanged pleasantries on the short walk and were examined by curious stares from students of all shapes, sizes and grades. We sifted through the youthful nearly adult pack.

Barbay saw the principal coming. He eyed me without letting on that he eyed me, up and down. I eyed him back. T-shirt, coach's hat, muscular calves, shorts and a Brian Dennehy build. Barbay was a tad rounder, and if I had to guess, a whole lot tougher than the Hollywood actor. We gave hellos and firm grips. Principal vanished.

In Barbay's office, athletic headquarters for Newton High, we got off to a rough start. Usually, microphones, tapes, almost any kind of electronic gadget will do that to a person. No matter how much they are assured it's no big deal, just relax and be natural. One of the most unnatural things in the world is to answer questions from a total stranger with a red light between the two of you. *Red means stop talking*. The light on recording devices should be green and not red.

"I've been here," the Port Arthur native paused, "this is 37 years." Barbay did more head math. Total time in coaching: 40 years. I looked at him incredulously, perhaps misunderstanding and in need of clarification, "37 years at one school?"

Barbay looked at me like I wasn't wrapped too tight, "Yes, at this *one* school." It took a few minutes to find our icebreaker. Finally, the coach's voice let its verbal guard down, "We just had a special group of seniors this year." He sounded half-father, half-teacher when expressing an opinion shared by many. "They've always worked as hard as they could and last year [2004] we got to the state finals and got beat out in that game." That loss fueled the motivation for the 2005 team to rededicate itself to winning. They were intent on a return trip to finals.

"It's a lot easier to talk about it than to do it," Barbay testified for the ethic and efforts that have made him "extremely proud." These are kids who don't have a lot in the way of worldly wealth and material possessions. But they are the owners of qualities that afford a different kind of richness. "We're real strong on discipline. We don't allow them to stay if they're not going to behave themselves."

Barbay inched his chair slightly closer to mine. Newton didn't have the luxury of being a big school with a "tremendous amount" of students on the team, but proud papa stressed their players were "all good kids." As we chatted, the gym was quiet, an adjoining weight room dark. All his athletes were in a special assembly and he hoped I'd get to meet a few.

"You can depend on them and we always get compliments on them whenever we go out. People just can't believe they way they behave." The coach forgot about the microphones and reporter's notebook. He relaxed. Then Barbay used the word "behavior" for the third time in five minutes, when he praised the *behavior* aspect in the athletic program as something not limited to sports. "System wide" was his description of how important behavior was, again, utterly convincing when he smiled, "because of the discipline." It did not escape the writer that the coach had used "discipline" more times than behavior. Being part of the program meant more to the coach than touchdowns and flashes-in-the-pan. He sought substance in each individual kid.

"We try to push them hard as freshmen to make them realize if they're going to college, no matter what kind of football player you are, you still have to have good grades." Of the 80 athletes in the program, a handful are weeded out along the way. During off seasons, a physical push usually got tougher to help determine which players would be in it for the long haul.

After the graduating class of May 2006, Barbay expected to lose 19 seniors. He shook his head, "We lost a good group, but we have a good group coming in." Barbay likened the situation to a double-whammy—"The school and staff expect a lot from these young men, as do the community, but they also expect a lot out of themselves too." Supportive community and high expectations are two of the ingredients that propelled Newton High School to win.

Over and over, people in the eye, aftermath and recovery of a storm repeated the southern mantra for living, a bible for success—the two H's, not heaven and hell, but honesty and hard work. "We don't have much here at all," Barbay waved his hand in the direction of the two-block town up the road. "I don't know how we keep the enrollment that we have." Newton High, grades 9-12, has about 355 students. "Whenever the biggest thing you have for a restaurant is a Dairy Queen," he pointed out an economic reality that has plagued Newton for years, "you're in trouble." Not much had changed over the years, a fact that can make a young heart restless, cooped up, hemmed in, and living with few alternatives. Sports in rural Texas is an outlet for calming trouble and testosterone.

"We've lost a lot of things. We used to have two mills here, a plywood plant, a phone company had their offices here and we've lost all of that." Barbay concluded, as a result, Newton High had suffered too. Enrollment dipped slightly. "There's not a whole lot for them [the kids] to do. If they don't teach, work at the bank, or have a little business downtown, or log, that's it, there's nothing else."

People don't move to Newton, a community one must be born to or headed to for a specific purpose. County population dropped in 2004 to 14,345. The county seat, Newton, has a little more than 3,000. People aren't in a rush to make Newton a permanent destination, "It's kind of out of the way too." Newton is more than 70 miles northeast of Beaumont and rests on the Louisiana border. Because of its close proximity to the state line, Newton County had plenty of Katrina company and the subject of New Orleans brought mixed emotions.

On the one hand, Barbay was delighted that the county did a good job of helping everyone they could. But he mused how some of the evacuees they welcomed "weren't very good people." It was an odd statement, one he struggled to explain, "We tried to help them a lot, they came out and tried to play football, take advantage of the situation." To be fair, Barbay's comment was related to the few students he had contact with, not all of the evacuees. His guess was up to 25 students came to Newton. It was not in the coach's nature to focus long on anything negative. He fidgeted around in the chair.

"These kids here," Barbay gestured toward the weight room, where we could hear faint grunts, "I'm talking about the athletes, the biggest asset they have, they can have a stranger come into the program and I've never seen them not welcome that person." A beam the size of a Texas moon graced his face. Coaching four decades has taught Barbay there were places a kid would have to prove himself, maybe even have a few fights before "you're one of the guys."

"Over here [Newton H. S.] it was just like they [student-evacuees] had been here the whole time." The welcome mat and sporting kindness spoke to the backbone of his players, good boys who have never been a problem. He didn't use the word 'discipline,' but it hung in the office air like one of his signs on being prepared and ready to face the next opponent. *Dare to Be Disciplined.*

The Louisiana visitors didn't stay long. They played and moved on, it wasn't the same kind of turf that many were accustomed to. Newton County hadn't even readjusted from Katrina when Rita came knocking. "We were all pretty lucky, but we did have a lot of damage all over the place." Damage but no deaths. Lucky in the sense that most folk had a roof over their heads and would help those less fortunate.

"With all the kids I talked to, Josh was the only one that had damage to his home," Barbay says. *Josh* was the kid I'd come to meet. He was among dozens of residents who had trees flatten their rooftops. Many more saw limbs and debris force power tool usage for new carved entries. Even with a hard lick like the one Newton County took, they were "still kind of blessed."

Late in the interview-game, Barbay got back to the same winning strategy that crowned him a legend. "That's the one thing [about sports], you can keep 'em busy and keep 'em out of trouble." The coach was uncomfortable discussing the aftermath of Katrina, Rita, and a lackluster economy made worse by both. He seemed to hit his stride whenever the subject was football, goals, the team he loved, the young men he disciplined and guided.

"That's the main thing we try to do," Barbay motioned with his free hand. "Winning is kind of a secondary thing, you like to win, everybody likes to win. But in this business, you can help a whole lot of kids just by keeping them in the program." Barbay held the microphone like an old pro.

"Toughest opponent?" I asked. Last game. Coach didn't hesitate, clearly a night stamped in his brain. "We got ahead of them, 28-to-nothing, and then I kind of got in a different mode as far as calling plays, wasn't as aggressive as I was for the second half." Barbay took responsibility, the same lesson he trains young men ages 15-19 to do. The burnt orange and royal blue held on. Final score: 28-to-21.

Football is a fulltime family affair. "Both of my boys coach, one coaches over at Kirbyville, and the other is head coach over at Hull-Daisetta." Bryan and Darrell Barbay have an impressive act to follow, it's fun on Friday nights trying. His oldest, 39-year old Kelly, lives in The Woodlands near Houston. "Very seldom does she miss a game and she ain't gone miss a playoff game no matter where it's at." Barbay called his daughter "one of Newton's biggest fans." But Barbay's most faithful supporter is the wife at his side 41 years.

Mona Barbay, an elementary school secretary, has a different perspective of the coach. She knew what shaped the former quarterback from his days at a small Catholic school in Port Arthur. Bishop Byrne closed years ago. Curtis Barbay is still going strong. What he liked best about his wife's sports knowledge had little to do with championships and final scores—"She kept me in line."

We heard more activity coming from the weight room. Barbay again promised to produce players who could chat about the teammate who lost everything. In his tenure, Barbay has mentored hundreds of boys to men, just like Josh. Newton High had been state champions in their division in 1974, in 1998, and for the 2005-06 season. They were undefeated. 13-0. Class 2-A, Division II Champions in Texas. The score was Newton 28, Argyle 21.

"Every year," Barbay says, "it's the same thing, it [football] brings out people in the community that don't even talk to one another sometimes. It seems an occasion like that, the town has a lot of pride in football." Texas-shaped monuments around town silently proclaimed as much. "I've never seen anything here in Newton do that." Sports. High school football in Texas. Friday nights. People coming together for a common goal—to cheer for their favorite team. After Rita, Barbay was relieved that Newton County had the distraction of sports to fuel the shaken pride back to something normal.

"I'm more proud when it helps a kid along the way and he becomes a better person. To me, that's winning." Not all of them are football players, per se, but Barbay called the importance of participation the foundation for a good life. "They are a part of something and it may be the only time they're ever a part of a team in their whole lives. They learn something, they get that feeling of being successful though they might not have made a single tackle or made a block."

Players that have passed through the Barbay Program have been scattered all over, excelling on and off the field at schools like Texas, Oklahoma and Baylor. But Barbay hasn't done it alone. He paid kudos to staff members, W. T. Johnston, Robbie Hatton, James May, Randall Reich, Jason Hicks, Clayton Halbrook, Kent Craig, Gene Walkoviak, and Lidney Thompson, who wasn't even on the payroll. "He's got Newton in his blood." Barbay laughed. All Thompson does is coach football, and more importantly, they couldn't "run him off," so decided it was nice to have him around.

Barbay has tried to retire, but can't stay off the sidelines. "Coach, you'll never retire," I told him. "No, I don't think so either. My health would be the only thing to retire me. I have the same love for the kids and care for them the same as when I started." He got up and headed toward to weight room. I waited for the young men who would talk with me about their winning championship season.

It might as well have been their first co-ed party the way tough athletes shuffled in and lined the wall, nobody desirous of being my first dance at the boy-girl affair. Manly shoulders shrugged. Baby faces, adorned with traces of hair, monitored, with suspicion, my presence. Exhibiting the same level of intensity they played their last game with. "Don't make me choose," I teased.

19-year old Terrance Freeman couldn't believe it when he was drafted in the first round. The Jasper native, under any other circumstance, might've been hard to handle, but I had Barbay's discipline on my side. Thank goodness for my own training with five brothers, an athlete-husband who had, himself, years before, been inducted in the Texas A&M Sports Hall of Fame in College Station. I also had more recent training with our two sons, both of whom played sports. One was captain of his high school football team.

"It made me feel real good. Not too many in Texas can say they went 13-and-0 and won a state championship," Freeman tried to conceal his nervousness. That was the one of the longer answers he gave. Mostly it was, "yes," "no," and "that's about it." Freeman was a typical student-athlete. Hobbies were football, movies and driving around in his Caprice Classic, which had just been sold, something he pondered with slight regret.

Handsome and a little shy, his body seemed fully developed. I doubt Freeman was finished bulking up. His physical self had gone ahead of the maturity counterpart he will catch in young manhood. The dual tight end-defensive end measured 6'4 and weighed 225 pounds. When he sat down, his long legs swallowed up the regulation size chair.

How had a hurricane nearly prevented this admirable bunch of young men at a tiny school named Newton from winning their state championship crown? "When Rita hit, I thought I would have to move to another school. I didn't think I'd be playing for a state championship or have an opportunity to play football anymore." Evacuated, gone, uncertain about a return, Freeman felt despair, for the first time, as it related to senior year and sports. Then he discovered teammate Josh Alfred was having a harder time than any of them could imagine.

"Josh's home was destroyed by Hurricane Rita and so a group of us got together and helped rebuild it." With the devastation left behind, just being able to return and be useful inspired Freeman and lifted him to another tier. He was desperate to come back and play football for senior year. Helping Josh was a big part of the healing process. They were building more than a home or a state title.

Players put on shingles and moved heavy equipment, summoning a familiar discipline and work ethic that bonded them as Barbay Men. "Whatever they needed done, we were there helping." The work had been started and organized by a Habitat for Humanity affiliate from South Bend, Indiana. Backup received from Newton County residents, those who knew Josh and many who did not, impressed the out-of-town visitors who came armed with tools and determination. About 10 players from Newton High School joined the rest of the community. "Josh is a good friend of mine. When you see a friend in need, you help 'em, right?"

We joked some about the last movie Freeman had seen, *Crash,* and talked about future plans. He hoped to play college ball. His major was undecided, but he had narrowed the list of choices—McNeese, Louisiana Tech and Sam Houston. A million dollar smile won't let Freeman down in the personality department. He conceded the interview wasn't as painful as predicted. Still, a relieved football player was happy to relinquish the hot seat for teammate Drew Johnston.

"It's made it [senior year] great, you really can't ask for anything else," the 18-year old senior started. "Winning has helped me make a lot of friends, it's a high achievement." Johnston was born in Hot Springs, Arkansas, charming and very polite. Like many Southerners, he instantly took to calling me "ma'am."

Johnston hoped to play college ball as a linebacker and had an eye on Nicholls State or Sam Houston State University. At 6'0 and 215 pounds, he was a lean machine not finished with muscle development, a beautiful man-baby like Freeman. Still growing.

"We just play the game [football], ride around, that's about it here," Johnston humbly offered when dissecting his hobbies of sports, hanging out with friends and his favorite pastime—making money. He loved to work. About the only time Johnston changed his tone was when I blurted out, "Do you have a girlfriend?" He was a little too quick with, "No I don't," to which I shot back, "And you don't want to broadcast it if you do, right?" We all laughed.

Sports run in the Johnston family. His parents were especially proud of their son and the team's accomplishments. "My dad is a coach, so it's kind of like both of us getting to win." Johnston had never seen anything like Hurricane Rita and hoped he never would again in his lifetime. When it came to Josh, players with free time, Johnston says, were more than willing to volunteer because of a kinship—"they knew the same would've been done for them." Newton County may be poor, but is rich in the shirt-off-your-back concept of sharing.

"We're such a small school, we're all friends and we all know each other. Josh is a good friend who just needed help," Johnston explained his reason for pitching in on the rebuilding effort. That desire to be of service, not wait for someone to ask for help, was a message these young adults have heard their entire lives, from parents, from preachers and teachers, and from a man named Barbay.

"Coach is great, he's a good coach, a Hall of Fame coach. He's honest, a good guy and he's pretty tough." Johnston made his retreat to the weight room. It felt like another son had been added to my roster of male children. As each interview concluded, the level of confidence scaled higher for subsequent players. 18-year old Paul Roseman was so sure of himself, it was time for the interviewer to answer some questions before he'd fork over another piece of Newton County information.

"Just who are you and why are you doing this?" he wanted to know. The room got dead quiet like a hot stock tip was about to be uttered. Sometimes, my website answered the question of 'who' much better and Barbay had left his computer on. When it was suggested that punching in my web address would bring up the mission statement, photos and more, the young men in the room looked at me like I was psychotic. Finally a voice chimed in, "Ah, Coach Barbay doesn't like for anybody to mess with his computer." Oh. Minus the website, they listened carefully. Roseman decided it would be cool to fill in the blanks and talk.

The offensive/defensive tackle was 5'11 and 215 pounds, a near match to my own football player son. Roseman first described his senior year as others before him, "just great," but made clear, "Newton's already been on the map for awhile." He was humble in acknowledging past championships, winning seasons and how much they were simply following tradition. "It's a small town and the biggest thing around here in this part of Texas is football."

After every question, Roseman mentally studied his answers before blurting each one out, always, always followed by "ma'am." When asked why he helped rebuild the home Josh Alfred's family had lost, Roseman again paused, "That's just what we do." The handsome young man called it "a privilege" to help and doubted the service meant he was anymore special than the next fellow. At the same time, Roseman allowed his investment of time might've been different from other teammates.

"I was just helping family," he offered. "Josh is my second cousin." Roseman had seen the long line of Habitat trucks when they first drove into town. "Coach Halbrook called and told me they're building Josh's house up the road and that they need help." Roseman only required 60 seconds to hightail it up that road.

To those still in the room waiting to be interviewed or finished, it seemed like the Dallas lady was asking the same questions. I had to make some new moves on Roseman.

"Favorite NFL team?" At first he looked like I hit him with a late block, the offensive tackle didn't see the question coming. "Ah, Pittsburg Steelers." When asked about a favorite player, once again, Roseman looked like he shouldn't have to answer a novice who probably couldn't point out which conference his team played in and had probably never heard of the man he was about to name. "Jerome Bettis," good manners graced the answer. The kid decided to humor the interviewer.

I applauded both as solid choices. A tiny chuckle went through the room, like, yeah, right, she ought to know. Early in my news career, a station event had put me in the same room with an "old school" Pittsburg team. Roseman listened, tried to act like what I was saying was no big deal…until I started to rattle off some of the names of big men I have never forgotten up close and personal.

"Terry Bradshaw, Lynn Swann, Mean Joe Greene, Franco Harris…" he interrupted me with wide-eyed sparkle, "*You* met Franco Harris?" Touchdown. The Newton High 2005 championship squad let an old pro from Dallas run one all the way back. Roseman was impressed that I had met Harris and too many other football players along the way to name. I didn't suppose it was the right moment to mention that my son had once gone riding with a *Playmaker* named Michael Irvin in his top-down black Mercedes or the interview with Roger Staubach before he boarded a plane to Canton one morning. Not the Canton in Texas either.

The last good movie Roseman had seen was *Friday Night Lights,* and he planned to see *Glory Road.* "Watching *Lights* reminded me of what our season was like, the games and the escalation to state championship." He lowered his voice to admit an "emotional feeling" viewing the movie, one that rewound its way back to how an opponent had run out onto the field. I liked Roseman for painting his own personal movie.

We regrouped once more. And he knew the joke that was about to hit like a brick wall defender, "Do you have a girlfriend?" I was surprised at, "Yes Ma'am," so I gently pushed again. "What's her name?" Roseman answered before he could think about it, "Stacy." There was a mini gasp behind him from the chorus of listeners. Roseman threw his hands up realizing he had only meant to say yes he had a girlfriend, not reveal to his buddies the guarded secret of her name. "Ah man, I didn't want him to hear that," the chiseled frame spun around and noted one laugh that couldn't wait to spread the word. We both had to vow the town crier not to tell as they made some kind of deal.

The next player to occupy the chair immediately knew the first question would be about his attire. "It says 'Graduation '06: The End of a 12-year Depression, Newton High School.'" The senior class had ordered shirts and wanted something unique. The back featured autographs from the championship team. Brandon Ray's name was among them.

The comedian in the group enjoyed a good laugh and a good time. His 18th birthday was only seven days away. He did have a girlfriend. He was quick to state the fact and her name, Candria Mitchell. "She goes to Kirbyville High." I asked if she were nice and Ray gushed, "Yes ma'am, lovely, lovely."

He agreed with teammates. None of them could ask for a better senior year than to have the cake's icing be a state championship win. For Ray, it was made even sweeter by storms he survived that had nothing to do with Rita. "Last year, [2004 season] I didn't get to play because of some health problems." Looking at Ray, there was no way to guess he had struggled with an enlarged heart.

"I had been trying to work through it, but during my junior year, it really got a hold of me," the smile faded. It was difficult to comprehend something of that magnitude without familial indicators or any warnings. He had none. Ray found out about the condition his sophomore year. "My doctor's exact words were 'If you're going to play,' [he told my mother] 'go ahead and make funeral arrangements.'" His mom was torn, first refusing pleas to play, then relenting some and allowing him limited play time. "She gave me a good blessing about it and I kept the argument going with her."

Ray realized the entire situation was out of his hands, so he approached his mother one day with a blunt truth, "The Lord will make a way somehow." Suddenly, the young man identified as 'Josh' ducked in and darted out. It was the third time. Josh Alfred had no plans of being caught next to a microphone. A player was on his heels determined to lasso the slippery teammate. Then Paul Roseman went to help, "He's kind of funny, I'll get him."

Brandon Ray continued his testimony about the dilemma that tested his faith. He had the same kind of infectious smile women recognize in a Taye Diggs or Tom Cruise, toothy and genuine. It almost didn't belong with the serious discussion. "After he [the doctor] told me it was going to be a life or death situation, I went home and talked it over with the Lord." Ray remembered the exact moment his answer came. "I was lifting weights and my heart started hurting. When I stopped, it was a pain I hadn't felt before and I kept trying to work out. The more I worked, the worse it got." Ray stumbled out of the weight room, lightheaded and confused.

Football practice started. He made the wrong decision by attempting to tough it out. Ray collapsed. His blood pressure dropped. It was right back to the same surprised doctor where Ray was handed more distressing news: "If you don't quit, you'll be in your grave soon." A child's eyes looked right through me, Ray spoke no more for a moment. Just repeating the words of a pull-no-punches physician reminded him of how fleeting life is. Ray walked away from the game, but not the team. For a year, he let his heart rest. A big chuckle accompanied his next statement, "I was the water boy."

Silent again, Ray reflected on the learned humility. "They called me the strongest water boy in Southeast Texas." Ray nursed other players. He handed towels. He gave Gatorade. He loaded equipment. Anything to stay with the team.

After junior year, the doctor thought all that water toting had made Ray strong enough and his heart able enough to focus on power lifting. Before being disqualified on a technicality, Ray finished in second place at a state meet. A judge declared his belt two inches larger than regulation. Frustrated, Ray couldn't catch a healthy break. The Newton High water boy with a medical crisis was disqualified because his belt, like his heart, was too big. Life wasn't fair.

"This year [2005-06] we won state in football, that's a season you can't ask for, I mean, God, He brought me through my heart problems." Even though he still deals with health concerns, winning state championship and being a part of the team rallied Ray to commit to what he wanted. Ray struck a deal with his Maker bargaining that if he were allowed to do "this one thing," which was play with the team, he'd follow wherever God led and do His will. That's when Ray became an ordained deacon at Fredonia Baptist and saw all manner of incredible doors open.

"I went back to the doctor and he told me my heart was no longer enlarged," Ray says. His blood pressure was stable. He was in pretty good shape from power lifting. Ray floated out on a natural high after being given the green light to play the more physical sport. "In the doctor's office, I looked toward heaven and said, 'Lord, I thank you.'" Ray never reneged on his 11th hour promise to do God's will. His dedication grew stronger.

Only those closest to the 5'8, 195 pound offensive lineman knew that his heart fluctuated between strong and stronger with an indescribable love for life. When he was healthy enough to line up with teammates, it turned out to be as a defensive tackle. A slow start meant Ray had to take it easy. "Brice Coker, the left guard, he's a junior, he took my place." Ray is now on another mission, "I'm trying to do the Lord's will."

Ray had already preached "a few times" but proclaimed he really loved serving God with his vocal chords another way.

"Can you sing?"

He hesitated, "I can do a little bit."

Roseman was back at our side, unsuccessful in convincing Alfred to sit in on the discussion. Ray had been "working on Paul" and was trying to get him to become a deacon too. His friend wasn't ready. I asked Roseman if the singing football player could "get his praise on" and he smiled, "Oh yeah, he can sing, I'm in the choir with him." I turned back to Ray, "Sing something."

A football coach's office with equipment, films, towels and a hands-off computer, probably seemed an odd place to talk about God. But Christians are supposed to spread the word wherever and whenever the Spirit moved them. Ray looked around, held the news microphone closer, "The first song that I was taught by my mother was *Use Me Lord*." He softly cleared his throat and looked up at his bit of heaven, the enlarged heart on his sleeve. A 17-year old deacon started to put us in church.

"Use me Lord in thy service. Draw me nearer each and every day. Lord, I'm willing, willing to run all, all the way." Ray stopped, looked at me and smiled. I let a tear drop. He had a beautiful baritone voice to match robust determination.

"When Rita hit us, I had a better picture of what they [Katrina evacuees] went through and I wouldn't wish this on no one else," Ray summed up his flight ordeal. He briefly put in some playing time after evacuating to Dallas and South Oak Cliff High. Then Ray talked about rebuilding a teammate's home, three days of hammering, pulling, and praising God. "It's all about helping."

Suddenly, I was alone in Barbay's office and knew with all the attention on how his new home was built, by a caring community, that Josh Alfred was suffering from more than a case of shyness. He didn't need unsolicited attention. Or want something on its surface that resembled pity.

Just as I rounded a corner to find Barbay, I stumbled onto a semiprivate chat, "Now you get in there." Barbay playfully whacked Alfred on his backside with a thick wooden paddle. It was my turn to duck behind a door, too late, the kid caught a glance of my profile. Rubbing his buns, he mumbled something to the man who extended the discipline. Alfred didn't want to be "interviewed." I doubt many young men have said no to the rotund coach and lived to joke on the matter. He frowned at me and took a seat.

Alfred was mysterious. Quiet. 17. Moody in a mischievous kind of way. There was a flash of bravado in his eyes, a restlessness, a bit of the wild and untamable. "I play wide receiver and cornerback," he started. At 5'9, 170 pounds, I didn't need to ask about speed and agility. Based on his elusive behavior, earlier Josh sightings, and his ability to dodge blocks meant to snare and deliver him to the interview chair, I knew Alfred was quick and light on his feet.

While he gave a string of one-word answers, I thought of the man I was once married to. A pretty chocolate bar with dark skin like Alfred who had also lived a hard knock, tough luck life. My husband was quiet, shy, reserved, 5'9, just under 170 pounds of pure muscle, a young man who later went on to become one of the fastest men in the world. "Rocket Rod" was his nickname at Texas A&M University. His remains one of the fastest times in the 60 at 6.07 seconds. I looked at Alfred, stared hard into my past and almost cried while Alfred squirmed uncomfortably in his seat like the boy I used to date. Often, the divorce hurricane selected the oddest times to hijack my concentration.

Rod and I had met after one of his track meets. He was so nervous when I talked he nearly fell off his chair, later telling me the sound of my voice was mesmerizing and had completely captured his heart. That same voice, funny how things turned out, probably later sounded like chalk being scraped on a blackboard. Divorce is hell.

"It made me feel just wonderful, really good," Alfred was trying to link more words together about being a state champion. Of Barbay, the young man chose his vowels carefully, his face announced there was plenty of leftover sting from a paddling I wish I hadn't witnessed. "He's pretty tough on us, in a good way."

Alfred didn't talk as definitively about college as the others. He "really didn't know" where he might go or what would happen next. My *ex-husband*, I must condition myself to the X-factor, was in that athletic department with us at Newton. Rod also wasn't certain where life would deposit him after high school. After carrying his high school to state championships as a wide receiver, one of the most painful things ever printed in a long list of newspaper stories was the description of him as "an orphan." I regret never knowing my in-laws, which meant our sons had no paternal grandparents. Rod's mother died when he was a baby, his father died of a broken heart. Many years later the death was officially ruled heart attack.

Alfred's favorite NFL team: Philadelphia Eagles. His player was Michael Vick, he didn't like hip hop or movies. That was odd. We hit a block until, "What about girls?" Alfred gave the first free smile of the interview, "Ah, yes ma'am." There was no one in particular, just "associates," which produced another restless sigh and runaway train look. There was an older girl in Alfred's world that he loved unconditionally.

"When I returned home and I saw my house was damaged," he started, "I was depressed and everything." His family evacuated before Rita and no one was sure what they'd come back to. "I really felt bad for my mom and I had to be there for my mom because she was very down and sad." It was the most telling statement Alfred made in the entire conversation. He begged his mother not to worry, adding he had nothing specific to reassure her with but always believed things would work out.

"Now we got a brand new house and God will *keep* making a way." Alfred, with his five younger brothers, has missed a father he was close to. He died when Alfred was in middle school. He and his mother were tight before Rita, much so after, and there was also a strong grandmother who helped keep the speedster on the straight and narrow. His eyes reminded me of another poor boy who knew intimately the Langston Hughes poetry about life not being 'no crystal stair.'

Alfred was grateful teammates came through when volunteers were needed to help rebuild his home. He felt like "someone cared." Suddenly, Alfred jumped up like a school bell to change classes had rung. He was finished. Looking around the coach's office, he made one last statement.

"Rita destroyed a lot of stuff," he paused, "I put my hands to God that He never let us go through nothing like that again."

Josh Alfred shot out of the room like a world class sprinter I used to know.

NOTE: Jerry and Sandra Freeman's son, Terrance, signed with Louisiana Tech. I wish him and all my dance partners the best that life has to offer.

SEVENTEEN

Back in my Beaumont hotel room, I reminded Angel San Juan of the agenda, "I've got to hit the road for Victoria tomorrow." That Friday he kept me company by cell phone, always starting each conversation with, "Where are you now?"

We talked so many miles for one stretch, the battery on his phone died. The next time we hooked up, I was sitting just outside the Victoria County Sheriff's Office waiting for T. Michael O'Connor.

Four men seated themselves at a long cafeteria-like table with me in the center, on the opposite side, facing them. Two others took up positions at the end of the table. After we started, a seventh man, a number and fact that seasoned my impression of him, entered the interrogation. His quiet intensity filled the room when he scooted a chair right into the crook of the table. A vantage that allowed him to view the door, his colleagues, and the female writer. I had the sheriff on my side, the man everybody calls "T Michael" sat closest to me, as if to suggest to his men, their total cooperation and nothing less. The seven men came in a variety of flavors and sizes and experience levels.

Patrolman Mark Zimmer drew the short straw. I wondered aloud what the 32-year old deputy thought about being dispatched to help in New Orleans. A few days after Katrina, the native Victorian, who had only been through hurricanes like the milder mannered Claudette, had never seen anything like it. The man next to him nodded full agreement.

Lt. Philip Dennis, a SWAT Team leader, saw a mountain of destruction in 1991 when he served in the Gulf War, but it didn't compare to "the total devastation" he witnessed in the Crescent City. The 42-year old Air Force brat was from "all over" and still spoke a disciplined military lingo perfected by dad and travel. "We went to offer assistance to the people there and also to law enforcement, it seemed like they needed a lot of help."

When Zimmer and Dennis arrived, they found pluralistic company, brothers in blue from a long list of states. Much of the looting was under control. The military was in place. They worked search and rescue. "For the main part, we would go around with a certain task force, little groups from the New Orleans Police Department, to check on houses and apartments that had not been checked," Zimmer says. When asked if the door-to-door operation was tedious, both men answered in unison, "Yes ma'am."

Training meant the pair knew what to expect. They dealt with death on a regular basis. Mostly, they discovered abandoned animals trapped or left behind. Other times they found mini retail operations. "Quite a few had participated in looting," Zimmer noted. Both remembered seeing Wal-Mart items, "things that nature didn't require." Dennis agreed, "Lot of things still had tags on them." A few kept popping up in house after house. TV's, computers and toys. Someone had even taken one item in such bulk, we stopped the interview for comic relief and jokes on hair extensions.

"You'd find 500-600 packages of these kind of items in one place," Zimmer shook his head. As he mentioned the ease at which electronics like cell phones could be sold, one rang out in the room. Hair jokes were finished.

"We were assigned, along with state police and NOPD, to do search and rescue, that was our main intent," Dennis got the discussion back on track. Their primary objective was to get into those areas where floodwaters had receded enough to allow searches, including the Lower 9th Ward. It was an "eye-opening assignment" for the pair. They praised the people of New Orleans, who, for the most part, were law-abiding citizens. They had similar praise for officers who never left their posts and remained on duty despite not being able to get to loved ones for weeks.

"We worked out of the Wal-Mart that was affectionately called 'Fort Apache,' the one that had been looted," Zimmer started. "The police department was actually using it as a makeshift department." NOPD officers only had the fleeting comfort their families were on drier ground in Houston. "A lot of the gentlemen we talked to weren't even getting paid and didn't know if they were going to get paid because the city was broke," Dennis says. It wasn't an issue for officers who stayed behind in droves and did their best. "Their biggest concern was bulletproof vests, shoes on their feet, and where they were going to sleep at night."

Officers were using their own PV's (personal vehicles) "just to patrol" and other cars were borrowed from area businesses. "No uniforms, patrol cars had been thrashed by people and you'd see a patrol car on the corner jacked up on blocks, so they'd have to take parts off three different patrol units to keep one on the streets," Zimmer explained the pieced together look of cop cars in New Orleans.

"Didn't they have a limo?" Sheriff O'Connor asked. He had heard about a limousine confiscated in some kind of sting and it was one of several fancy vehicles the department turned into resourceful substitutes that covered basic need. "One of the oldest police officers there—I think the story was—had landed in the beach invasion during D-Day and was working for NOPD. He needed a place to sleep and they used one of the limos and allowed him to sleep in it," Lt. Dennis confirmed.

"Is the U. S. prepared for another large-scale terrorist attack?" I asked. Zimmer hoped we could "come together as a nation and support each other," but never really answered the question. Instead he offered what his gut instinct said, "I think we're ready to respond to it." Dennis was a little more aggressive with his opinion, "I don't think we're ready, truly, truly ready. I think we'll rise to the occasion, maybe not as quickly as people would like us to." Their words bounced off each other. Zimmer went first, "We rely on the government too much," then Dennis, "9-11 opened some eyes, but if you'll notice, it didn't last long."

Two of Victoria County's finest headed back to work. Sheriff O'Connor had Lt. Dennis make me a copy of the November 2005 issue of *POLICE, The Law Enforcement Magazine,* in which Dennis and others were featured in a search and rescue squad photo of one of their New Orleans missions. Another picture, from *The Miami Herald,* showed task force members trying to give water to a thirsty, frightened dog. Sgt. Ryan Mikulec also represented Victoria County, just as Zimmer and Dennis had done. And done well.

"The officers were very appreciative," Zimmer says, "one of the sergeants that we worked with—Dan Anderson—was always saying things like 'Get the Texas guys, they're ready to work.'"

Sheriff O'Connor pointed to Abel Arriazola, "I sent special weapons guys because we didn't know what the circumstances were. Abel was sent to take another crew the same Monday we were warned about Hurricane Rita." The seventh man, who entered the room last, had a striking dark complexion that was smooth and flawless. Since Victoria was one of the early forecast targets, Arriazola and company had to immediately pull back to cover home. But Rita quickly turned her attention away from Victoria eyeing Galveston, then Houston.

Other lawmen in the room were ready to talk about why Victoria County personnel went to help a Texas county many had never heard of. Our chat began, when each man, like a welcome-back-to-school assignment, told a little about themselves. Rita birthed a different kind of inclusive conversation with first responders who rarely get credit for jobs they are proud to do. Nor do they want credit.

Alan Roberts worked for the county as a Precinct Three equipment operator, he sat at the far end of the table to my left. His accent was unmistakably British. When asked his age, Roberts smiled, "30, ah, that'd be lying, 48, rather." We had our funnyman, the native Birmingham, England lad came armed with a bloody good sense of humor.

Next to him was Gary Burns, a 53-year old county commissioner, a native Texan, who spoke, looked, walked and talked like the Lone Star. He was lanky and blonde, with a full head of tousled hair, a good man who wouldn't be rushed to tell his story or opinion.

The microphone was pushed a few inches away from Burns to the face of Roland Villafranca, who worked for Precinct Two, as an equipment operator. The animated delight in his voice and a big smile on his face offered proof of his love for children. Stated with pride, the 43-year old native Victorian was eager to please.

The man of few words allowed even less be read about him, "Investigator, Victoria County Sheriff's Office." Abel Arriazola was 45-years old. While his name was clearly Hispanic, his face was international in that it represented many peoples. I saw Native Americans, Mexicans, Puerto Ricans, and other Latinos I personally knew.

Seated at the far end of the table, or appropriately, the position known as head of the table, was Victoria County's chief deputy. 55-year old John Kaspar spelled his name, gave his title and was silently dubbed understated strong man on deck.

"Their trees are our water, that's their livelihood, that's their everything," Roberts started our marathon discussion. The expert landscaper once had his own business before joining the county and had never seen "so many trees laying down." Burns dived right in. He knew from time spent in East Texas, that trees can't sit too long without water and care before timber is unusable.

"We were kind of wondering, it's so far from the Gulf where we went, [Tyler County] surely the hurricane didn't hit them, but the deeper we got in, these trees that were 60-70 feet high, they were as big or round as your car, we'd never seen anything like it," Burns recalled. Sheriff O'Connor quietly slipped out a side door of the conference classroom with its stage, white projection screen, and supplies. He returned with coffee. An assistant handed out bottled water to everyone but me. The sheriff poured the preferred caffeine.

Burns painted a bleak picture of Tyler County. He felt like the men had entered a vast swampland, a low income area that was surprisingly heavy on population. "These people didn't have jack," he cleaned up the slang, "I mean you couldn't get through the roads, nothing." No one has ever argued that Tyler County is a rich place, just the opposite, but the sobering reality of poverty touched men sent to be of service. They "rolled in," Burns says, with a limited amount of equipment and quickly found themselves calling Victoria County for more. Then Burns pointed to the man patiently waiting to his left, "He cut his leg real bad because we weren't set up with all the right equipment."

Included in the "we" that journeyed to Southeast Texas, were about 60 people from various agencies in Victoria County, all levels of government, including police, city work crews, state officials, and of course, the sheriff's department. The seven men that were chosen by O'Connor were representatives for colleagues. There was little doubt, these people *were* Victoria herself and that O'Connor couldn't be more proud.

"How'd you cut your leg?" I was in front of Villafranca. First he mused some about how Hurricane Claudette gave them experience in clearing trees and making roads passable, but that the more lady-like storm hadn't come close to preparing them for a swamp with debris everywhere and people driving "under huge pine trees that were across the road." Villafranca was the third consecutive man to use the word "swamp" and they all agreed the Victoria team, initial-ly, lacked the equipment to clear mammoth trees that had landed on homes and roads, leaving many trapped for days in said thickness.

The commissioner interrupted with his slow, raspy voice, "I lived there awhile." He had put in some young manhood post-college years and thought he knew it. "But the amount of trees," Burns paused, "I had no concept." Villafranca shook his head, "What really amazed me were the number of power lines that were down. That's how I cut my leg, a lot of trees were on power lines so we were trying to clear trees from the road."

With Roberts driving a backhoe, the men knew they had to be extremely careful not to cut at the base which might trigger a flip in the wrong direction. Villafranca's injury came early in the visit, "We went up and I cut one of the branches first and it fell. Then I went to cut the other branch to let it come down, see where it would fall. I was in the bucket when I cut it and moved the chainsaw over." When he did that, the second branch came crashing down right into his body. "It put 14 stitches in my left leg."

There was a triage center right near the men's living quarters. They were nowhere near the temporary home. "We were so far back off in the hills, it took us 45 minutes to get there," Burns began, then Villafranco interjected, "I think he [Gary Burns] was more about to kill me driving than my leg was hurt." Even Arriazola smiled.

"You know what he was worried about?" Burns decided to tell, "He [Villafranca] said, 'Don't send me home.'" The Englishman had a theory, "He was more worried about being sent back to Victoria, Texas than he was about his leg." Roberts confirmed Villafranca was-n't the only one concerned about something other than an injured body part. "And we were worried too, because he was our cook."

Sirens just outside North Glass Street competed with our laugh-ter, work continued for deputies around us. Villafranca remembered being "up in the bucket" when his leg was cut wide open, how Roberts lowered him, and the frantic drive to the triage, and later

219

being taken to a hospital where a team from New Mexico took excellent care of him. "Yeah," Burns had a vivid memory of what that entailed, "They had a bunch of women, they had about eight women to take care of him."

Villafranca admitted 14 stitches and extra bravery in front of the female nurses paid off. "They were screaming 'chainsaw cut, chainsaw cut,' and asking to take pictures of it," he smiled. 11 minutes into the hurricane discussion my own post-divorce senses warmed up. I was divorced, not blind. I sat in that room with some fine men, brave responders who heard the call for help and willingly answered.

Abel Arriazola scooted up closer to the table and a slim microphone attached to a reliable Sony mini disk. "Have you ever been that far back off in the Piney Woods?" I asked. "No, never," he started, "They got some deep woods in East Texas and that was an experience for me." Arriazola was among the initial crew that arrived with Team Convoy from Victoria County. "I'll repeat what they (pointing to his colleagues) said, power lines, the devastation of trees, and one thing that stands out in my mind is just huge sections and lines where you could tell a twister or tornado had gone through." Or in this case, he thought aloud, Rita.

"Our primary areas and responsibilities were different, ours being law enforcement and they were doing construction and crew work," Arriazola explained. Men on the law enforcement side of the Rita-restructured Tyler County house had been sent specifically to assist officers. Arriazola gave thoughtful, detailed answers, as did the men before him, impressive as a no-nonsense investigator who would not easily suffer fools.

"The anxiety and the desperation of not having any facilities, any lights or electricity, and it was extremely hot," Arriazola added, "all of that factored into *behavior*." For a moment I was back in Newton County with my football coach and the stern reminder of what happened to bad boys who required discipline. His compassion melted like butter when Arriazola described the horrible living conditions of fellow Texans who had to cut themselves out of damaged homes and trailers, the long time it took for some of them to get help, supplies and food. It was clear that he saw hunger, thirst and suffering up close and that these images would remain with him for a long time.

"The big thing for us was to support law enforcement, there were a lot of businesses like banks that were unsecured and a lot of merchandise," the cop talk was resumed in a heartbeat. Arriazola knew that Sheriff Jessie Wolf's small department, working around the clock, would get fatigued in a short time without backup. The plan: learn the land as quickly as possible and start riding with Tyler County deputies.

"In many instances, some of our officers got in our own patrol cars and just took off to help." Arriazola says more than crime sprees or looting, there were "homebound people" who were thrilled to see law enforcement. "We found ourselves doing a lot of humanitarian relief efforts."

Arriazola recalled "a lot of elderly people" on his routes and how it was just part of new job duties to check on forgotten folk deep in the thicket. "You've got to remember," the SWAT team investigator says, "there was no telephone." He offered a half-smile but erased it a second later when his own cell phone played on cue. The pause meant Victoria's chief deputy was ready to rewind things back to pre-arrival.

John Kaspar never forgot what Hurricane Carla did when he was about 12. More recently, another hurricane that started with "C" had hit Victoria and the cleanup was quick after Claudette. Not easy, but quick, because of hard work and team spirit. Kaspar instantly knew components in the aftermath of Rita were different.

"Going there, the first thing we noticed that had an impact was when we convoyed—we had 50-something vehicles. When we went through Houston, we had a plan to fuel up at a certain place just north of Houston." They arrived only to discover the lot wasn't large enough for massive equipment to fit and be strategically positioned to turn around. While Houston still had power and some gas, there were long lines.

Armed with a fuel truck, leaders of the convoy were determined not to use it for refills on the road. They would need gas in Tyler County. It took two hours to refuel all the vehicles. Once they did, relief workers were able to convoy "all the way into Woodville."

Chief Kaspar was the point man in Tyler County, the sheriff depended on him for updates about the mission and what they needed. The men generously passed around praise and gratitude.

Roberts talked, at length, about some of the guys that worked with him, day after day, cutting trees and piling debris. Many didn't have his depth of experience as "tree men," but they were "quick learners and hard workers." Roberts wanted to be a part of the team so badly, he put his health at risk.

"When I got there, I was only supposed to be on the backhoe, because I had just had major, *major* back surgery," he stressed. The Brit had only been back to work three weeks, after being off for months, when the opportunity to assist Tyler County was originally presented to staff. "When Commissioner Burns asked for volunteers, I was one of the first," Roberts says, "hands up." I thought he meant "hands down," but suspected it was the English equivalent.

"Why did you do that?" Roberts thought about his answer, then it clicked in his brain, "Because I have so much experience and I felt like you've got to help your neighbors. We wouldn't be nothing if we couldn't help each other." What Roberts said next was a stunning admission. "I learned that I was never prepared. My wife's not prepared and a lot of people I know are not prepared."

Roberts spent a minute reflecting on the way Rita had mocked and tormented innocents who believed a storm would come in, the wind would blow hard, the lights might go off and then everything would get fixed. His advice for future hurricanes was simple—flashlights, batteries, radio, water and a stash of food that doesn't require cooking. He had a speck of inconvenience when his family was without power for five days in Victoria city limits following the last storm that blew through. They thought things were bad then. "Not compared to what I saw over there with Hurricane Rita and people living out in the rural country areas, they were tough people and they still had a jolliness about them. We took them food and ice and even gave them our rations because they had no means of getting *anything*." Roberts, more a Texan than an Englishman, vowed to never forget what he saw in Tyler County. "They were so thankful for us being there, going there to help them."

Gary Burns had another aspect that spoke to how quickly the mission was adopted and approved by County Judge Donald Pozzi, Sheriff O'Connor and Mayor Will Armstrong. All the men who signed on were aware that Victoria County hadn't promised a single nickel above their regular pay. "We knew it would be long hours, nobody asked a word about money, about the hours," Burns explained, then Roberts chimed in, "Or where we were going to sleep or how we were going to cook." Without amenities to rival home, Victoria County volunteers managed to be pretty self-contained.

"I didn't know Roland and some of the other crews, and the city did a great job too, don't get me wrong," Burns pointed out, "but I had 10 guys with me and any one of them could've run the crew." Burns was fortunate. As supervisor, he never once had to stand over any man and tell him what to do. "I wasn't going to take Alan because he'd had back surgery, but he said he'd stay on the backhoe." That only lasted two days before Roberts broke his promise with a feisty announcement, "Screw this." That's when the scrappy tree man grabbed a chainsaw and dove right into the heavy labor of tackling thicker woods. "I kept after him, but I finally just gave up he's so damn hardheaded." Everyone agreed with Burns, who then turned to the man with a 14-stitch souvenir.

Burns praised the way Villafranca never missed a beat even after his leg was cut. I was presented a picture, that all the fellows conceded was a post-photo, after the wound had been cleaned up. To drive the point home, Burns painted a mental picture for the Kodak moment I stared at. "You could've put your hand in the hole in his leg." *Okay, thanks.* Roberts took a shot at the recovered patient, "But he's still ugly and it didn't help him any, but he can cook." We howled again, a roomful of Texans at a law enforcement bar inside the Victoria County Sheriff's Office.

Every morning in Tyler County, the men got up about 5 a.m. to cook and eat. They worked all day, came in after dark, dog tired, to eat again and sleep. Rita brought them closer, Roberts says, "We almost have a little brotherhood." He joked that some of the guys that went, still, months later, had beards, while others who didn't regret missing out on the bond. "It was a very great experience," the expert limb man summed up the feelings of everyone in the room, great, Roberts laughed, even when "somebody came in that first day and said, 'Y'all need to get out of here, they'll shoot you down here.'"

"Yeah," Villafranca reminisced, "I think I met ZZ Topp." Actually, one of the men noted, there were quite a few ZZ Topp sightings "back off in the woods." At this point in the interview, the comedy club mike was being shuffled back and forth so quick, a score card was needed to keep up with who said what, our laughs mixed in together comparing notes on new friends and fellow Texans in Tyler County.

"This one guy chased us down," Burns says, "and got a big ole jug of spring water, no shirt, long hair, beard down to here," he pointed mid-chest, "looked like he could whip all of us put together." Why? "He just wanted to give us this water," Burns remained disbelieving that the woodsman had no other purpose for flagging them down except to offer some neighborly hospitality. Someone laughed at the stranger, "You sure it was spring water?" More bar whooping and hollering, between the rowdiest patrons—Roberts, Burns, Villafranca and myself. The sheriff laughed quietly, as did his chief deputy. Arriazola smiled, but outright rowdiness didn't belong with such intensity.

"They even had one man who had an outside shower who told us 'Y'all get too hot, y'all go take a bath in there.'" Villafranca says they just looked at each other with one unspoken thought, "Ah, no, that's alright." They decided instantly it would never get that hot, not muggy enough to utilize a rigged outdoor shower, which was as homemade as that jug and its so-called spring water no one ever bothered to test.

"This was so far back off in the sticks that the morale was what I couldn't get over," Burns argued. He noticed that some volunteers, not from Victoria, desperately wanted to go home. It wasn't what they hoped. They flat out didn't like the country. "We rolled in, our sheriff's office," Burns added a disclaimer, "I'm blowing smoke now, is so well organized, it scared the hell out of these guys." Burns called his side of the mission "physical," while "John and Abel was a little different." Holed up in a church made livable by a backup generator, Tyler and Victoria made an impressive team.

"There were three old ladies right across the street in 100-degree weather sitting on a porch," Villafranca says, "and there we were with AC, good food, the sheriff did a good job of getting us good food to cook and to eat." He almost rubbed his stomach at the thought. "What was your best dish in Tyler County?" I asked, not a good question since I hadn't eaten since breakfast back in Jefferson County that morning. It was past 3 p.m. All the men were eager to have a say on "Roland's Restaurant."

The chef looked around the room and attempted to silence his patrons, "We may not want to do that." Villafranca thanked Prasek's, a Hillje, Texas restaurateur who donated 50 pounds of bacon and 100 pounds of sausage. "We had eggs, they got us some chicken, we had big ole pancakes, which helped everybody because we ate good." They had seen people living outside, in tents, in tarps, in trailers, crammed together everywhere, best they could and it had a profound impact on ability to relax and talk about teamwork at the end of some long, grueling days. Villafranca met folk who didn't even realize Rita was coming, "That was amazing." He rationalized it must've had to do with simple life minus cable or minus televisions period. Disconnected from life as most city slickers knew it.

"People would tell us they just saw the wind coming, one man said he could look out the window and see dogs blowing down the street." Villafranca was asked to repeat every statement he made after "we ate good." *Dogs blowing down the street* gave an unforgettable hurricane visual. Not to mention another good laugh. But most things associated with Rita affected these men—husbands and fathers—in a plethora of ways.

"A lady and her husband came driving up," Villafranca's words speeded to match the approaching mental vehicle, "and there were four kids in the backseat. They were all in their underwear, no shirts, no shoes." The woman caught Villafranca off guard, she had come to apologize, said she was sorry to leave help from Victoria County behind when they traveled so far to be of service. They were parents, like him, and needed to get their babies somewhere away from the deadly heat. The lady said, "Y'all come to help us and we're leaving." Villafranca was deeply touched by such sentiment in a county where the people had so little. He told the woman that he understood how much family came first, then he looked right at me, "Those kids were beet red and they were just hot." The room went quiet like Arriazola. Nobody moved.

The seven men who worked for Victoria County had too many stories to find space for here, but that day, it seemed therapeutic to tell them, to talk about what's good and right about Texas, our strengths and our flaws. "We saw a real sense of welcoming, not only from the sheriff, but from his deputies," Arriazola had genuine praise for Jessie Wolf and his entire department. "He's a giant man, but he's a gentle giant," one that out-of-town company soon chalked up as responsive to the needs of county residents and the requests of volunteers. "The primary reason we went up there was to support him."

"They didn't ask for much," Burns says of county residents who were mainly in good spirits. An average property worked by Victoria County crews included 15-20 huge trees that men, working in concert and with a certain rhythm, could move in 90 minutes. When astonished people would tell Burns and company that they couldn't pay, he always smiled, "We're not here for the money." That wasn't true for con artists who found a way to bilk a select few with coins in the mattress.

Burns lost count on the number of times he flat out heard people order them off property because proud Southeast Texans couldn't pay and wouldn't take charity. "This guy was driving down the road and he said he had two trees on his house, the man told us a guy with a crane came down to his house and removed those two trees," Villafranca excitedly found himself wrapped up in anger, "and charged him $3,000 for about 15 minutes of work." Disasters bring out the best in people. Sadly, they also have the ability to showcase the worst. Villafranca remembered the man's sad face when he realized they were in Tyler County doing work as volunteers and removing trees at no cost. Burns added, "And we did that, everyday, all day long, for free."

An elderly couple stood out. They examined a car in their yard that had been damaged and blocked by a tree. "I got some Gatorade and offered it to the lady. She refused, 'No sir, no sir, those are for you.'" Villafranca told her there was plenty to go around, but it was an uphill battle just convincing the woman and her husband to take a sip. Once they did, the couple Burns jokingly called "old as baseball," Villafranca says, "You would've thought she was drinking gold." They were just one family unable to escape their situation, trapped in their home. It had been 14 days since the man and woman had had ice or anything cool. The cold Gatorade *was* gold. The last day Victoria County volunteers were in town, they carried their ice chest to the couple.

"There's such a sparkle in your eye when you even talk about it," I gushed, knowing 'sparkle' was the wrong word for such masculine company. Not one man responded. Burns did believe destiny played a role in their assignments, none of them ever expected to be in Tyler County. A brief stop in Jefferson County first deposited the men in a nice neighborhood where they felt like everyone "had insurance" and would be okay. Before leaving the Beaumont area, men from Victoria County played angels for practice.

"They had a playground in the back of this church and it was completely covered with trees." Burns says they hit it quick and hard. No one was there. "We got a kick out of that and thought about how the preacher had left thinking the whole playground, the whole back of the church was tore up and demolished. When we finished, there was just one piece of playground equipment damaged." Ever the prankster, Roberts laughed, "The only thing he's [minister] going to miss is the one toy for the kiddies and the big trees. It's a miracle."

They left debris cleaned up and stacked in orderly piles, no note, no need to have names for men who left the good deed behind. "The Angels of Tree Mercy," I dubbed them, to big smiles. Again, no verbal response. While they were still in Beaumont, it refreshed them to connect with other men and women who knew the pride in being first responders. "We talked to some of the firemen there, the people who rode out the storm and there were about 10 families in the fire station," Villafranca says. Even with the doors boarded and fire trucks strategically positioned to act as a secondary line of defense, firefighters confided that many could feel the concrete floor underneath their mats shaking as they waited for Rita to weaken.

One evening in Tyler County gripped all the men for its potential to heap on more devastation. "We were going from one site to the next," Burns says of the nonstop work detail, "and they had a well blow out. Everybody was a little nervous." They needed to get around the troublemaker in case it erupted. As they traveled by caravan, the men from Victoria caught a sight that diffused some of the tension and provided comic relief.

"I see this guy up in the middle of the road, looked like some derelict cop up there," Burns laughed, "directing traffic, big bushy mustache. When we went by, I hollered at him, I said, 'Hey, I hear they're hiring in Victoria!'" When I didn't get the joke, Burns added, "It was our sheriff."

Only did I feel safe to laugh at that one after looking over at T.

Michael O'Connor and seeing the big smile on his face. Burns expressed it over and over, "Everybody pulled their weight."

Roberts wanted it on the record, "The actual hands-on experience is the best training you'll ever get in your life. You can read textbooks, you can look at videos, you get there, get down in the dirt and do it." Burns had one amen, "I guarantee you, if another disaster happens, these guys will be clamoring to go again."

The bond, the circle of camaraderie, won't be broken. "It's a lifetime deal," Roberts concluded. The pact included people who didn't go. Worried family members remained behind. Roberts' wife, Patricia and their two children, Alan, Jr. and Samantha, ages 15 and 13.

Burns has a 20-year old, Nick, who answered an ad to volunteer in New Orleans for a week and didn't want to come back. Like father, like son. Nick has a twin, Danielle. Burns is also blessed with a 23-year old named Lindy and a nine-year old daughter, Sydney. When asked his wife's name, Burns quickly stated "J. R."

What does that stand for, the nosy reporter wanted to know, not Ewing for a maiden name, huh? "Jessie Ray," he wisecracked pending doom, "She'd kill me for that." I asked how to spell it, the poor man didn't know for sure since he couldn't remember ever seeing it written anywhere.

Villafranca's wife is Tammie and he did know how to spell it, cracking up over a private joke on Burns. Clearly, the women in Villafranca's life owned his heart, particularly eight-year old Alexandra and six-year old Jocelyn.

Becky Arriazola and the dark-eyed investigator are the proud parents of Abel, Jr., 23, and Allison, 15. They sounded like a loving family, that news made me happier to gain access to a different side of things. Personal ads from men who made a difference.

"After seeing me go through this experience," Kaspar beamed, "I think they kind of look up to me now." Raised right by Linda Kaspar and her husband, are two grown children, John Jr., 31, and 25-year old Shelly. "It made me feel real good," Kaspar says, "how proud they were."

"I think my wife," Arriazola began, "after seeing what Katrina did to New Orleans, they were supportive when they knew we were going to help out with Rita." He was a man savoring a delicious feast, "They were *very* supportive of me."

Villafranca suddenly turned serious, "It kind of hit me real hard, my oldest is close to me and the youngest is closest to my wife." When he called home that first night to let them know they'd made it there okay, Villafranca asked his wife how the girls were. "Alex had told her mother that part of her was missing," he paused, "and I told Tammie, I said, 'I don't need to hear this right now.'" Everyone in the room was a parent. Everyone in the room nodded understanding. Roberts offered, "A part of you was missing too."

Ten seconds later, it was back to business, the bonded for life men teasing each other again. "You should've seen him when he had to call his wife the day he cut his leg." Villafranca accepted being a softy with the women under his roof. He dreaded the nightly question of when daddy was coming home, "Just stay with mama, take care of mama."

Burns mentioned being a single dad for 15 years. He and "J. R." were practically newlyweds. "I'd been married about a year," he started, when Villafranca dissolved into chuckles. The big private joke surfaced a second time. "Why are you laughing?" I demanded my share in the secret. "'Cause he forgot her birthday." We all started clapping hands and laughing. "Wait a minute, wait, wait, what happened?" I asked.

"We'd been taking care of a lot of people from Katrina," Burns couldn't believe he was coughing up such personal details. Muffled snickering floated through the classroom. "Everything was going along, I didn't even know what day it was, and I forgot it," he says of the wife's birthday. "You're newly married a year, is that right?" I asked again, "And you forgot? Oh man, you didn't sleep outside, did you?" The teasing got stronger. Burns slowly answered, "Pretty close."

Not one man had a safe secret that day. Roberts reminisced about the joy of being able to sleep in his own bed. What made it sweeter was being able to do so without earplugs. "Well, we had some world championship snorers," Roberts jokingly glared in the direction of Villafranca, "and I ended up having to sleep with earplugs." He waved his hands in a dismissive fashion, "Hope I never have to do that again."

While no one wished to see another Rita, or any girl stronger, the men are realists. Helping Tyler County inspired Roberts to build a new workshop with plenty of shelves, where he now keeps a box of MRE's, just in case, wrapped securely in duct tape. "My wife, she's not the world's greatest cook," it sounded like he was about to tiptoe into hot marital territory. Two weeks earlier his Mrs. had suggested they devour the ready to eat meals for dinner one evening she hadn't done her stellar cooking duties. Roberts nixed that idea real quick, "No, no, no. You go to McDonald's, them MRE's are staying up there because you don't know what I saw and you don't know when we're going to need those."

Even Arriazola had to laugh. Roberts was on a serious roll, vowing to keep the ready to eat meals forever, no matter how many times his wife missed cooking. "And let me tell you," he roared, "MRE's are a hell of a lot better than what she puts out, but I ain't gonna tell her that!" Like a scorned mistress, used and discarded for her talents, Villafranca asked, "What about *my* cooking?" Roberts stroked the ego, assuring us that the talented pancake-sausage chef had nothing to worry about, "Ooh, I wanted to marry him."

None of the volunteers from Victoria County waited for supervision or confirmation on what needed doing. They just did it by pulling together. Her highness, Katrina, was shown royal respect because it was New Orleans that inspired an already great game plan to another level. "We learned a lot from Katrina," Burns stated. "When Rita hit, Johnny on the spot right then, Rick Perry knew exactly what to do and we were mobilized in no time." He felt strongly that if not for Katrina, Rita might've turned out completely different. *More people would've died.*

After the tape was off, the men asked all kinds of questions. I told them my 'back off in the woods for Thanksgiving' story with Billy and the Deer Hunters. It was Gary Burns, Mr. Texas, who got the last word on bucks and does.

"We were on a dirt road the first or second day there, and we're eating MRE's for lunch," he paused, "and we looked from here to that wall," Burns pointed to the other side of the room. "Somebody had dressed out a couple of deer."

Hey, don't look at me.

EIGHTEEN

One by one, my Victoria County men left the room, amid a flurry of smiles, good lucks and verbal thank you notes.

52-year old *Thomas* Michael O'Connor handed out shoulder pats and kind words, answered a few questions, then closed the door. We had already done a brief phone interview, which was trumped by the precious time he carved out for our in-person chat. The big bushy moustache that Commissioner Burns had joked about was just a part of what defined the look of a true gentleman-sheriff. Physical notions aside, O'Connor certainly epitomized the description in professionalism, compassion and heart.

"Each generation's a Thomas, I'm a Thomas, my dad's a Thomas, my son's a Thomas," he paused, "so it got kind of confusing when someone would call out 'Thomas.'" The 5th generation rancher smiled at his obvious Irish Catholic name, "a dead giveaway." Not widely known outside ranching circles and South Texas, is what stands behind an established family name respected by real cowboys, cattlemen, entrepreneurs and others who admire the legacy of all those generations of men named Thomas.

When the sheriff, along with most county officials in Texas, was monitoring Rita online, via the State Operations Center in Austin, he wasn't surprised that Victoria was an early hurricane target. "I began to ask for air support and other things so that, when in fact, not as much in advance of, as it was for *after* the fact." He sounded like a lawman. "Myself, the county judge, and the mayor," O'Connor says, "we declared a mandatory evacuation."

One reason the sheriff negated the wait-and-see approach was what he termed "the education of New Orleans." It was a motivating factor in how Rita was processed and handled. "Once it [Katrina] hit them and then my troops were down there calling daily telling me what was going on, then all of a sudden, here comes another one." O'Connor couldn't take any chances and leave needed personnel in New Orleans "with Rita breathing down Victoria County's neck."

Once attention turned more to Rita and the direction began to shift to the Galveston area, then further east, O'Connor knew the hurricane would miss Victoria. A ton of people would be exiting Houston and Galveston. "Even though we're 125 miles west of Houston, we got a direct affect because we have a main highway for out of Houston that comes straight to Victoria." The amenities and population—Victoria County has 85,000 people—equaled hotels, service stations, restaurants and stores, with helpful attendants.

"As it made landfall, we were still in contact with the various Gulf Coast counties in the state of Texas. We were witnessing and hearing their plight, indirectly," O'Connor says. "I have ranching friends in parts of East Texas and around the Beaumont area." He kept in constant touch with them to offer a strategy in advance of Rita. "After the fact, communication was all down and we kept hearing 'Tyler County.'"

EOC officials in Austin were trying to figure out a way to help some of the most devastated areas, inland counties that weren't supposed to be battered and smashed by Rita. Those residents sincerely believed they were "the forgotten ones," three words that made O'Connor grab a map to see exactly where Tyler County was. He knew other places in East Texas, "but I didn't know about this small community of Woodville."

The fresh geography lesson resonated with O'Connor. "The SOC, the state, called us and said, 'I hear you have the resources,' and I said, 'Yes.'" When asked what Victoria County could put together, "a pretty good contingency" of personnel took shape with Commissioner Gary Burns and Commissioner Wayne Dierlam brainstorming.

"They said, 'We ought to send a crew,' and from there it grew." The city got onboard and other agencies wanted in. Before O'Connor and company had packed one bucket or chainsaw, one bullet or vest, they had 60 people with a wide range of talents and backgrounds—from utility and construction to road crews and law enforcement. 10-4, good buddy, they had themselves a convoy.

"We wanted to go to an area that needed it the most, we told the EOC out of Austin." O'Connor says the director in charge had one suggestion—"Go to Tyler County."

The Corpus Christi native initially believed they were headed to either Chambers or Jefferson. He'd already spoken with Joe Larive, the sheriff in Chambers, who could sure use the help. O'Connor set in motion a thorough and detailed plan for Chambers that his men bunk down at the home of a friend, a fellow rancher in the area. That was before he heard from the EOC again. "They said we really need you to go, with your resources, to Woodville." Thomas Michael O'Connor responded with two words, "Very good."

"Once they [Victoria County volunteers] got there and got established, there wasn't any planning for their arrival and my main goal—even though I so badly wanted to be there fulltime—was basically the ensign commander here." It was smart that O'Connor stayed behind in stretches. He received daily reports and requests for supplies and other things the men needed. "I'd send transports up there and I also went up there on multiple occasions, rather as a day trip or longer, to go check on them."

His approach was rolled sleeves and hands-on. "My main goal was to let them sleep well and eat well because they were going to work so hard that the fatigue would set in so quickly that they would be played out in a short period of time." Sleeping and eating were tied to duration and morale. He didn't want his men to not be able to back up Jessie Wolf's department, men and women who were already sleep deprived. "I told the sheriff, 'We're gonna be here until you run us out.'"

Victoria and Tyler. They sound like the names of a sister and brother, two kids that got to play together, work together. Both sheriffs say the bond is deep and everlasting. "He [Wolf] told me, 'Something happens to y'all and we're coming.'" O'Connor recalled the very first trip he made to get a personal assessment of the situation in Tyler County. "We pulled into the law enforcement center, the sheriff's office, there was this football player, big black gentleman, on a bench, just outside." O'Connor was like anyone else with eyes who first stumbled upon Wolf in person.

"I said, 'My God, who in the world is that guy?'" His chief deputy, stoic John Kaspar, deadpanned O'Connor, "That's the sheriff," to which O'Connor, unable to hide his shock, replied, "Really?" There was no electricity. Wolf was sitting in the dark Texas breeze. Once the temperature gets between "warm and hell" during the day, things usually cool down after 10 p.m., somewhere in the neighborhood of 89 degrees or so.

"Quite honestly, knowing what had happened in East Texas," he says, "how did this happen?" The admission was a double racial reference from O'Connor, being that the "what had happened" he assigned to the dragging and the "this happen" question was something Wolf himself was aware of. How did a black man in a tiny Southern town, that was predominantly white, get himself elected sheriff in a county that bordered Jasper?

The two men were introduced. "We started talking and I began to admire him and appreciate him more and more," O'Connor says. The sheriff liked what he heard about Wolf from other law enforcement. What he liked most was the way they complemented the other. There was room "for two sheriffs" at the same time in one small county.

"There were no power plays, no egos to manage, none by either. He was the boss, I'd work traffic and go wherever he wanted me to go." It was an upfront stipulation that both lawmen saw the humor in. Out of nowhere, the rancher took over. A surprise topic.

"Growing up as a cowboy, I grew up with black cowboys," O'Connor started my formal education. "Hispanic cowboys, vaqueros and what not, and there were generations of them that worked on the ranches." The Aggie graduate was a huge fan of history and a rich, combined culture of many peoples that gave Texas her zesty flavor. O'Connor respected who the cowboys were and learned lessons on humility early.

"I was raised in a family where stewardship is a very important aspect of life." The tenet has stayed with O'Connor. He has passed the legacy on to his two children, "You're never too important to serve others, especially those who can not do for themselves." A sister and cousin adhere to the same philosophy and a shared love of history. After Nancy O'Connor graduated from the University of Texas at Austin, her brother urged her to come home and document stories from the vast well of living sources—cowboys of all colors in their 80's and 90's. Before they were gone. Along with cousin, Louise

O'Connor, the sister he was so proud of, Nancy, logged thousands of hours to express a part of Texas history few have ever paid homage to.

"She's documented it all, had them in pieces, and we also have *Crying for Daylight,* the companion book by my cousin." O'Connor suggested I visit his sister in Houston to learn more about the exhibit and see it for myself. He cherished the passionate storytelling in photos, words and art that both women have compiled. "She [Nancy] has had showings and exhibits in Houston, Dallas, Los Angeles, New York, and all over."

O'Connor was mesmerizing. I was enraptured the way he fetched stories from another era. Memories decorated the walls of an ordinary police classroom while black and Hispanic cowboys dusted off their boots in gratitude.

"I had an elderly cook, 80's, black gentleman, he was a reverend on weekends," the sheriff started, "I asked him, 'Milam, how did you learn to cook?'" The man plainly stated, as if it were the most natural culinary thing in the world, that he cooked "by revelation." Meaning prayer, divine intervention, by the will of God.

"He was excellent, he was a camp-cowboy cook, self-taught." A plethora of mental impressions conjured up sights and sounds from old westerns as recording device and other equipment became poor substitutes for ranch style beans and thick juicy steaks. There was the undeniable aroma of strong black coffee. Dancing cards flashed in my head—the deck of men who needed baths and shaves but wanted nothing more than to eat, relax, sing, or be still with horses.

"Growing up," O'Connor says, "these guys were my mentors, the black cowboys." I saw a different side to the man compliments of decades gone by, years of shaping and training that he credited as the foundation for who he eventually became—a sheriff who sent deputies miles away to a county nowhere near home. To help. To learn.

As T. Michael O'Connor spoke, we seemed to drift in and out of the room, sometimes the room itself changed color and lighting. From dusky shadows and a pale moonlight to fierce bright sun baking the skin on our backs. No matter where the sheriff journeyed on the long trail, dust was a permanent part of the western visual. I never took one note. Who could not help but imagine Larry McMurty's *Lonesome Dove?*

Danny Glover, a man I've interviewed twice in my career, had a supporting role. He has always been a good model for what a cowboy ought to look like. Glover, Tommy Lee Jones and Robert Duvall exemplified my limited notions of the Hollywood version. Now a rancher gave me a sweet gift—the real McCoy.

"Black cowboys could speak better Spanish than the Hispanic cowboys," O'Connor smiled. When I told him that information was "a new one on me," he simply and very emphatically stated, "Yes ma'am." O'Connor was patient with the education of a woman he slowly felt more comfortable with as we shut out the modern-day troubles of lawbreakers and disasters. Who were these black cowboys? The subject was both delightful and fascinating. One, it was largely untouched by the entertainment industry and in historical accounts fed to young students in public schools. Sure, the information was always there, but a person had to know where to dig.

Besides Glover, (I was an adult for the two movies that even remotely portrayed his characters as anything close to a "black cowboy."), pre-*Silverado* and *Lonesome Dove,* there was entertainer Lou Rawls. The Grammy winner once portrayed a singing cowboy on a television show called *The Big Valley.* I usually watched this western to see Nick or Heath. Before Rawls, the only black person I had ever seen on the popular show was Silas, the longsuffering butler, whose primary job was to let white people through the door and pack picnic lunches. I loved the show anyway.

One night, and nothing prepared me for it, a black cowboy named Joshua Watson just showed up. He could work circles around the white ranch hands, and the Barkley family had hired him to help win the annual rodeo. Rawls not only lulled the cowboys into dreamland around the campfire with his magnificent voice, his character was pretty damn handy with a gun. Some chump made the mistake of calling him "boy" and the black cowboy had his iron out of the holster and cocked before the sodbuster could even lift his. Rawls, portraying a black cowboy, a sight unimaginable to a little Negro child, uttered something so spectacularly bold, at that time anyway, I've never forgotten the humorous line.

"You almost made it," he flashed the pearly whites, "to the other world." I squealed with laughter. My mother thought I was high on sugary Now-Laters candy, so tickled that the bad guy would get what he deserved with a Hollywood stunt gun. It was Lou Rawls, working and singing and roping and riding and breaking horses. And only using his gun if he had to. Years later, the Rawls parallel to Danny Glover came full circle when *Silverado,* a movie that featured a stellar ensemble cast, abandoned some of the stereotypical cowboy notions that allowed Glover's character defend himself against anyone who was a threat.

When Glover, utilizing a McHenry rifle instead of six-shooter, had to teach the lesson of his name not being "boy" and what a man could do with such a weapon, his character delivered another famous line never erased from movie memory: "Mister, I don't want to kill you, and you don't want to be dead." But these glamorized versions, be they ever so few and far between for cinema lovers, could not live up to what O'Connor vividly and masterfully described as the real black cowboy.

"One was a father figure to me because he basically taught me how to ride, rope, and do things and I was with him all the time." Spence Cook came to life in that room. He watched over us, listening in on the conversation. The mental campfire roared on. Cook wasn't just any black man who lived and worked at the O'Connor Ranch. The way the sheriff talked about Cook, *he was the spirit of true ranch life.*

"I was just kind of his sidekick, wherever he …," O'Connor's voice faded into the sunset and he never finished the sentence. Nor did he return to it. In 30 seconds it became apparent why the detour. When O'Connor was a young man in college, still at home, and before he transferred to Texas A&M, Cook was killed in an auto accident. "I was supposed to meet him because he was going to go into town to get something and come back." O'Connor paused before the next set of words escaped. "He never did."

An 18-wheeler spun out of control and struck Cook, instantly killing the longtime mentor. With matching eyes of stone gray, the salt-and-pepper haired lawman acknowledged the soul among us. "It was a significant loss for me but the spirit and the will continues." O'Connor used the same word, "spirit," I had thought seconds before. His eternal love for Spence Cook was real, the unshakable homage paid to black cowboys like Cook resonated far beyond anything Hollywood had offered me in childhood and even now.

As O'Connor waited to see which course an interview could

possibly take after such flashes of reality ranching, I offered the only gift available, the one black cowboy I had been connected to. "My Uncle Dayton," I told the sheriff, one of my mom's brothers, "saddles up for all the trail rides, looks like a cowboy, dresses like a cowboy and works on ranches and farms." In fact, I added, that same uncle loved his horses more than any wife he ever had. That finally got a laugh of approval, as I couldn't think of anything else to cheer O'Connor back to present. What a man Spence Cook must've been.

It won't make my uncle too happy that I compared all his ex-wives to horses. The truth is, I lost track of the marriages, never the faithful sidekicks he nurtured and brushed and treated like best friends. After the uncle-story, O'Connor repeated his earlier position, "You need to visit my sister."

Her exhibit contained a fair amount of visual pieces and some fantastic audio. O'Connor fondly recalled one that included photos of a cowboy-cook who always wore a brown paper bag rolled up like a chef hat. The sheriff's mother, Madeline O'Connor, was also a well-known artist who had pieces exhibited around the country. On a trip to New York with her, the young O'Connor was excited about surprising the cook. "I thought how neat it would be to buy him one of the best chef hats, the fanciest I could find." The cook could finally stop wearing that old brown paper bag on his head.

O'Connor was eager to see the man light up at white material elegant enough for chefs in London or New York to don. "He was most appreciative," O'Connor shook his head slightly, "but I never once saw him wear it." We both laughed when O'Connor says he always saw the white hat, just not high on the man's head. It rested "on top of the ice box." That memory, part of the exhibit, a man who "always put on the preferred paper bag" to cook in, taught the sheriff it was "just his way." Nothing fancy, the brown paper sack didn't affect the food.

O'Connor summed up the exhibit again with enthusiasm for a beloved sibling, "fantastic, fantastic photos." Then he kindly bestowed another synopsis to link cowboys and hurricanes. "With that kind of heritage and upbringing, I knew it was important, no matter where it is or who it is, whether it's New Orleans, or somewhere else, [Tyler County] you surely want to help."

Time and time again, in home after home, or what substituted for damaged homes, in trailers and motel rooms, I heard people testify that their respect for New Orleans was none diminished by the hurricane that wiped them out or forever altered their lives. They knew history meant Katrina had an earned deadly respect that was no match for Rita. Nor did they ever seek *comparisons.* Katrina broke hearts. Poor people without cars and access to credit cards or cold cash got left behind. There was no other way to account for the disconnect that afforded a new definition of "refugees." A disconnect that produced some of the most unforgettable images in television news history.

Human beings, not in some third world country, but in a modern American city, floating in stench-imagined, dirty water. Toxic nightmare. Dogs trembling, too shaken to even accept food or water. People trapped on a bridge being turned back by an overzealous, probably racist sheriff. Thousands more trapped in a psychological warfare of waiting for buses that might never come. A woman covered with a sheet in her wheelchair. Dead. Her last ride.

"That Monday that we were being warned it [Rita] was coming here," O'Connor redirected our conversation. "Mayor Nagin got on the news and was saying 'We're going to open up New Orleans and have everybody come back.'" Clearly, the premature welcome mat disturbed O'Connor. His men stationed there painted a much different picture. It wasn't safe.

"We had no say," O'Connor referred to the decision, "that was their issue." It was not at all humorous to me that every single time the embattled New Orleans mayor said something that couldn't be fully forgiven, explained, or understood, white friends and some black ones too, would clog my mailbox with letters like, "See what your friend Ray has done?" *My friend? I've never met him* I'd write back. Nagin, if no one else has guessed, seems in the hunt for redemption. He simply wants a chance.

Each man gets his own bag of rocks one cowboy had said to another around a midnight campfire in an old western flick. I never learned the name of that movie but would never forget the truth about rocks. O'Connor loaned me some new black cowboys to help me carry mine. Then 37 minutes into our chat, "Can I ask you a personal question?" His expression never changed. "Sure." I needed the money story confirmed.

"There is a salary with this but I've offered to utilize it for my officers." O'Connor was quite capable of supporting his family as a rancher and businessman, a fact that allowed him to turn his paycheck back into available funds for the department. For 30 years, O'Connor has enjoyed "parallel careers" of ranching and some capacity of law enforcement *without pay*. Two assignments that stand out were appointments by Texas governors. Bill Clements drafted O'Connor for a criminal justice commission and Ann Richards tapped him for the Texas A&M Board of Regents.

During our conversation, the sheriff mentioned the word "service" multiple times. Whether the men working with him were fighting "organized crime" or the aftermath of Rita, O'Connor placed heavy emphasis on what they should do—"step up and be responsible." From the start, his deputies took the post-hurricane vita seriously. "I said, 'When we go up there, we're not going for a vacation and piddling around. We're going to go make a difference and work.'"

As long as Thomas Michael O'Connor has passion for his job and is making a difference, he will continue to seek the position of sheriff. It is a good fit for the cowboy that still lives inside the man.

"Curiosity," I prefaced the last question, "how many acres are we talking?" The same way he thanked me for coming, O'Connor gave a final lesson in his answer.

"There's one thing in Texas with ranchers, and I'm not trying to be disrespectful, two things you don't ask cowboys in Texas—how many horses you have and how many acres you have." *That many, huh?* I do not say the words, but the man read my thought.

"It's probably one of the oldest ranches in Texas," he has no brag about the fact, then added, "and probably one of the largest."

NOTE: When I returned home the weekend after meeting O'Connor, there was a photo in The Dallas Morning News of Laurene and Albert Cunningham from "Echoes: Memories of a Black Culture" and "Soul Cages," excellent history and art exhibits from two women whose names I had just learned—Nancy and Louise O'Connor. Their brother and cousin is a man called 'T Michael' who will never forget the mentor named Spence.

NINETEEN

Teacake crumbs were all over the blue Dodge Durango I had rented.

Flying down the highway to a scheduled Sunday interview, a voice played in my head, "The Lord can't be happy with you not being in church. Try to go some of these times you're on the road." It was my mother. I had just left her in Shreveport, Louisiana, where I stopped for a book event at the Shreve Memorial Library.

"Joyce, where are you?" Angel San Juan rang as I refueled. Weeks before, we had compared notes, after reading the same *Associated Press* story, about another city trying its best to recover from Rita. We were both impressed that Lake Charles, Louisiana, by all accounts, a very poor city, agreed to foot the bill for 10,000 evacuees in hotels when FEMA threatened to stop paying the tab. It would be my first question to a man named Paul Rainwater, the city administrator.

As I drove another tree-misshapen highway that caused the foliage to look anemic, Angel's voice was full of electricity. "Do you remember that nice man you met, Judge Ron Walker?" He had a presence impossible to forget. Walker had visited more than an hour with us as we chatted with his son, Judge Layne Walker, in the younger barrister's chambers. Angel replayed election results from Jefferson County where voters had ousted Carl Griffith. There was a mountain of new hope and restored faith in the gavel they decisively handed to Ron Walker, the man who will help guide a big chunk of Southeast Texas into the future.

Around lunchtime, I walked the length of an adjoining parking lot to the Lake Front Hotel in Lake Charles. Steps on the pier had dropped into port water, a few above were spared from the watery grave. Near those wooden planks were a line of ducks. They swam, or not, effortlessly, wind-aided. Many just rode the waves. There had to be an advisory, the gusts testified as much, 45 or 50 mph. A chain link fence ran from one end of the pier all the way behind the pink and purple and blue stucco of Harrah's next door. It was a crime scene, like others my career allowed me to report on. In the distance, a big bank building was closed. There wasn't enough money in the vaults to begin to cover massive damage and repair costs for what Rita had done to Calcasieu Parish.

Choppy waters kept pushing the ducks across the waves. A black woman's hair stood on thinning ends. An American flag whipped its whistling melody in the center of port-owned water. Not far away was downtown Lake Charles, sketched by the fair skyline. The camera came in handy for digital recording. Two women monitored my business behind the hotel.

"Hey, would one of you mind taking my picture?" they looked at each other and decided there were two of them and only one of me. The younger woman took the camera and shot from twin angles. "Are you a guest at this hotel?" she wanted some form of payment for her work. They were a mother and daughter, who had their lives destroyed by Rita. Two of the 10,000 evacuees.

"I lived in Holly Beach," the photographer stated, "now I won't get to ever take my children back. It's gone." I wondered how an entire beach could be "gone." They walked with me a few seconds fighting the wind and clinging to papers. One promised to call me later. I failed to get her room number. We parted when they recommended the hotel chicken quesadillos.

Paul Rainwater had been waiting for my call and was somewhere mingled in with that downtown skyline I had earlier observed, working he said. We agreed to meet an hour later in the coziness of a first floor suite with impressive gold-plated neighbors like "The Bill Harrah's Suite," which was 116. There was also "The Lakeshore Junior Suites" before that, nailed to the door of 100. One that really stood out, "The Showboat," was Suite 107. And just to the right of my entry was a double suite, 133-134, "The Las Vegas Suites." The two-bedroom paradise was reserved by big spenders *before* Rita.

Lake Charles residents were friendly, the few I encountered. Hotel employees were accommodating, opening doors and answering questions. One brought me a newspaper. I read *The Houston Chronicle* as I waited for a man with a Native American sounding last name. Looking out my window, Francis Scott Key would've felt right at home penning his famous words.

Our flag's reflection shimmered off the bouncing waters and sent a patriotic ripple through me. What a comfort it had been over the months to see American flags of all sizes, some brand new, some tattered and torn, flying high on trailers, buildings with missing windows and doors, houses minus roofs, even on pummeled cars. The flag was a strong message that Americans were still standing after Katrina and Rita, living amidst the debris, death and destruction that attempted to defeat so many thousands.

At 1:29, the very prompt city manager knocked on my nameless suite. We were both casually dressed, he in khaki dungarees and a shirt. I had instantly liked him on the phone days earlier when the face time was prearranged. And then I liked the look of him in person. It seemed one of the few occasions a person's voice actually matched his/her face. It was a nice face. Handsome. Professional. Bluish gray eyes that had seen partly cloudy to partly clear days. Large and inquisitive. Mr. Rainwater came armed. He thoughtfully explained the large brown file was mine for the taking. It contained emergency management material, detailed information on how well prepared the city of Lake Charles, less there were doubters, really was.

Rainwater, not a Native American name, smiled at the oft-made assumption, was headed to Washington, D. C. the next day with a contingency of others from the area. There were concerns that Rita wasn't being taken seriously enough. He acknowledged Louisiana wasn't attempting to compete with Texas as far as reimbursement for money the state spent in good faith and was owed by the federal government. We both, almost at the same time, recalled how Gov. Rick Perry, in the days before, had been in Washington with Louisiana Gov. Kathleen Blanco, and governors from Mississippi and Alabama, Haley Barbour and Bob Riley, respectively, to testify on hurricane matters.

About the proudest I've ever been of Gov. Perry had to do with the direct language he utilized in demanding the federal branch cough up the $2 billion dollars owed to the Lone Star State. He called Rita, "the forgotten hurricane," the same three words that crossed party, racial, gender and socioeconomic lines to form a common bond of humanity.

"Why did you decide to house 10,000 evacuees from Katrina and Rita?" I stared into the southern sky eyes. Rainwater supplied seven uncomplicated words: "It was the right thing to do." An hour later, he left the Lake Front Hotel. I had no idea of ever seeing the man of faith again. But Paul Rainwater and I would meet less than four weeks later to resume our conversation and dissect his Washington mission.

That evening for dinner, I rang room service and followed the culinary suggestion of the woman from Holly Beach. I wanted to finish our conversation but she never called. I settled in, channel surfed, landing on a Lifetime Original Movie about a girl trying to bring black and white students together for an interracial high school prom, instead of two as had always been in the past.

For One Night starred Raven Symone and was set in fictional Mercier, Louisiana, near New Orleans one of the characters said. Later, a local weather report called for clouds Monday morning, and possibly, rain. By 7 a.m., I was packed and ready to take the wheel again for an appointment in Cameron, Louisiana with Clifton Hebert. The man in charge of Emergency Operations for the parish.

Rita was pressing business down Highway 27. Men in hardhats worked, others required no headgear. They hammered and toted and measured. A few waved, speaking to another invested stranger who slowed down to gawk and make mental notes. There were men on the roof and in the front portion of St. Peter the Apostle Catholic Church. Damage was heavy, the men in good spirits.

As I drove all over Cameron Parish, scenes defined my childhood Louisiana with refineries in the distance. Oil platforms no longer looked steady in the Gulf. An arrow pointed toward Grand Lake. A sign to Holly Beach. A never-ending plank ran on both sides of the highway as I traveled the length of the water. Gray drizzle was a nuisance. Then it was real rain in need of wipers. I pulled off the road when I realized where I was.

A weatherman's chilling words were automatically recalled, "Rita made landfall at 2:38 a.m. in Johnson's Bayou." She came ashore where I sat in the rental car. None of it seemed believable, except remnants of Rita were still visible in pants pockets ripped inside out. A crushed house. An empty store. Structures that leaned, not sound by any engineering estimate. I drove away. Soon I made a right turn onto Louisiana 82. "Go 17 miles," I read the Mapquest paper out loud.

Down 82 were a handful of scattered oil-related businesses and trailer homes and manufacturing sites. I could see white trucks creeping along. The rain stopped. The rain trickled. What was left of Holly Beach slapped the unsuspecting writer who gasped at the woman's description in Lake Charles: "gone." The postcard had been replaced with debris, downed foliage, things dead and unwanted, left in the once whitish pebble-colored sand. I saw cars, nose first, the rear pointed in an unnaturally perverse angle, *home was that way.* No more. A blue and white boat was simply abandoned on the side of the road, its owner gave up trying to secure it.

I was lost. I had gone past PR 545, the right turn for Bayou Road. Houses on legs had paint stripped away. Others were absent, only the stilts remained. Slanted trees cried for attention, human hands to stand them again or clear them forever. There was no one coming to Cameron Parish. Two people shooed me away, they fished near the edge of the highway. Dinner that night would be fresh. Rotten wood marked numerous locations that were once beautiful spots. Orange construction strangled me, Texas prison stripes for Rita-consumed land where luck had run out.

It was long past the appointed time to meet the man named Hebert and find the Parish Road numbered 548 from PR 545 that would lead to Smith Road and Cameron's courthouse. Suddenly, the rain drove harder, beating its sigh against my windshield. The sure marker that I had gone too far—"Welcome to Port Arthur, Texas." I stayed less than a quarter mile into Arthur before turning around and going back. I had to see Cameron Parish all over again. "Wiped off the map," were the words a woman named Julie had uttered by phone. I pulled over once I forked back to Johnson's Bayou and called the lifeline. I was not ashamed of being lost. All the highways merged together.

Julie Burleigh worked for Clifton Hebert. I could tell by the sound of her voice that she was a good woman who cared about our Pelican State. The line was busy. I retraced all my steps, factoring in a sooner turn instead of keeping straight as I had done before on Louisiana 82. A few minutes later, I was face-to-face with an old-fashioned ferry closing and instant proof that the town of Cameron, the parish seat, was just on the other side. Two flashing words kept me from a hidden destination: "FERRY CLOSED."

Burleigh finally answered, "I've been trying to call you." The ferry had shut down some 48 hours earlier and wouldn't open again for three days. Disappointment dripped in her voice. Burleigh felt sure that after all the circles I'd driven in, the drizzly mess, the grayness of a day ready to be forgotten, that I'd never see Cameron. I'd never meet the voice that was Cameron, the Cajun enunciation of the smallest things. I'd never meet her husband, Kirk, who had done such a fantastic job on repairing their damaged home, government officials asked to post a picture at its website to give encouragement to others. How terrific.

The journey of a million miles continued on. I had missed Cameron proper. An appointment in Port Arthur meant time for the small parish had vanished. It took a few minutes to wind my way from the closed ferry to Hackberry, and eventually, back to Interstate 10. I was about 20 minutes away from my next conversation when the woman I was flying to meet canceled. I was sick for Cameron.

Checked into my Beaumont hotel room, I sat on the side of a king-sized bed for no smokers and wept. The marshy landscape seeped up in me, the way it had sprang from a trashed shoreline. Holly Beach was no more. Cameron Parish seemed the ultimate in forgotten. I believed even the "forgotten ones" in Texas would acquiesce their title if only they drove around lost with no way out as I had. Cameron had captured my whole heart. At that moment, I truly felt despair that I wouldn't see the town or parish again. I prayed. It took a long time to get off my knees from the dreary hotel carpet. A blue divorce sometimes merged itself with the brilliant drama of other people's lives. It was the native Texas Christmas bow left intact on shreds of ripped Louisiana-grown wrapping. I was both, blessed to be so. Blessed to have conversations with my neighbors.

Next on the hurricane agenda was a man, who had agreed by phone, to retrace a 50-hour bus evacuation route not sanctioned by the state of Texas. Shelton Boyce knew the journey would be rough.

He didn't know there would be more than two people in the car. I called to confirm our ride and hung up trying to wrangle in my emotions. For some reason, I thought of author Joan Didion.

Though she was no bigger than a small bird, fragile and brave, I was terrified of going onstage with Ms. Didion for an interview program I co-hosted in Dallas. Before taping began for *The Writers Studio,* I almost suffered a panic attack. The fear had little to do with nerves. I was terrified of listening to Ms. Didion describe a 40-year union with husband John Gregory Dunne. He had suffered a heart attack at their dinner table and died. Then she lost their only child. My heart ached for her. One word or tears welled in Didion's eyes and I felt sure I would weep in front of the live audience in 2005. Her book, *The Year of Magical Thinking,* a short time later, won the National Book Award.

I fell asleep in my clothes.

TWENTY

2005 was the year of hurricane thinking with special guests Dennis, Katrina, Rita and Wilma. Months later, we were still crazy. Something whispered *don't stop.*

Shelton Boyce shook hands. We got in the Durango on a bright Tuesday morning. He had worked for the Beaumont Independent School District as a bus driver for almost 10 years. Single, 30-years old, Boyce had a friendly face. He settled into the passenger side, holding the small gadget I gave him like a pro. We were on a roll until Boyce mentioned his birthday would never be celebrated the same.

"How ironic, we were at work and doing a day of harmony, a presentation at the Montagne Center on the campus of Lamar University. We had all seven middle schools of the Beaumont Independent School District going over." Another ordinary Tuesday, not unlike the one we had just undertaken, slightly after 9 a.m., Boyce remembered things quickly changed from a celebratory field trip for students to one of horror and panic.

After the first plane hit the World Trade Center, Boyce believed it was some kind of tragic accident, crazy, unexplainable, but an accident, nevertheless. "An hour or so later," he excitedly started, back in the 'oh my God' moment, "I heard 'We're being attacked, we're being attacked. What's going on?'"

From the Walden Road hotel, we zipped onto Interstate 10 Eastbound. "Up until that day, believe it or not, I'd never looked at my birthday as 9-1-1." Upset by the pain and anguish recorded at the one year anniversary mark and with memorials all across the country, Boyce didn't feel much like a party. Only the passage of time has made the September date of birth feel like the blessing it is. He is a survivor, along with millions of Americans who won't ever forget the day innocence was murdered by hatred, trembling produced by terrorists who flew planes into hell.

Robert and Mercie Boyce knew their only son was special, sensitive, and someone they had instilled a sense of compassion. "The most important thing my parents have taught me is to be respectful to my elders, and to respect others and you will be respected in return, and to always put God first in my life and know that I can accomplish anything that I set my mind to."

We soon neared the exit that deposited us onto Highway 69 North. Juvenescent features made it easy to see why so many young passengers confide in "Mr. Shelton." The kids who climb aboard bus #325 know him from the testimony of former passengers—siblings, cousins, and friends—that Boyce has driven over the years, tenure providing him unwritten expertise on how to handle riders who rarely trust anyone over 18. It is the kind of experience a fatherless bachelor hopes will come in handy whenever he walks down the aisle and starts his own family.

As we sped down the exit ramp, a serious mission temporarily erased our smiles, his students, relatives, and the gorgeous day. When the freeway pavement changed from 10 to 69, so did our moods. "It was on a volunteer basis," Boyce explained the driver duty that afforded his position in the unforgettable 50-bus, 2,000-plus passenger convoy.

Five years before, Boyce had driven people out of Beaumont for the evacuation of Andrew. He felt sure Rita would be the same. "We had such a good time because all the drivers, we went up there, to Lufkin and then on to Diboll, and sat down and just had a good time." The storm turned and headed toward Louisiana. They went right back home. When drivers were needed again for Hurricane Rita, there was "no fear and no hesitation." It was also an opportunity to make extra money, enjoy coworkers and ride out the storm with people he liked.

"Our transitional point was Smith Middle School because it had ample enough parking for buses to come in, people to park their vehicles and easily accessible to the interstate." They rolled out on Thursday, around noon. September 22, 2005. "Beaumont to Lumberton, usually, is roughly about 15 to 20 minutes," he pointed down the road as we hit Hardin County, "not very far apart." When it took Boyce two hours to get from Lucas Drive in Beaumont to Lumberton, the jovial man had one disconcerting thought: "We are in for a long haul."

At that point, authorities had not diverted traffic in the same direction to help ease the congestion. Around 6:30 on Thursday evening was the first time that Boyce noticed all lanes were finally moving in one direction. Northbound. As we drove, he measured things, mentally, and remarked many times on how different the route looked from the faraway September weekday.

"Sabine Pass, Port Arthur, Orange, all those areas were trying to get up this way," he shook his head. One reason Boyce submitted to the ride was my agreement to not ask that he drive it again. I hit the gas.

"Altogether, we had 50 buses and I was bus #25 in the first group." Boyce paid attention to numbers, particularly after his 9/11 birthday in 2001. "Thankfully, my bus was equipped with AM-FM radio and air conditioning, so I was pretty much able to keep my passengers calm." Boyce assured the 36 people riding with him, particularly after they hadn't moved much in the first two hours, that they needed to be patient and relax. The numbers game was a long way from being over.

"We were just inching along, people started to get frustrated, constantly asking me questions. Finally I said to myself, 'Calm down Shelton.'" Boyce used the slow motion time to tell riders he knew as much as they knew. "If you would be cooperative with me, whenever I find out information, I will gladly pass it along to you." Again, he thanked his Maker for air conditioning and a working radio. It provided relief and a form of entertainment for people tired of looking out the window at the same trees and stores. Boyce tuned into music, news, and weather reports coming in every few minutes. Bus #25 also had a working intercom system that allowed him to communicate with convoy leaders, drivers at the front who guided people they would come to know much better than anticipated.

Via cell phone, passengers were exchanging disturbing information and rumors. It created an air of greater panic. No one dared spit out or confirm an ETA—estimated time of arrival. They had one hurricane goal after rolling the dice like everyone else with nowhere to move or maneuver. It looked like outrunning Rita might be fruitless.

"While we're approaching the Crestwood Baptist Church,"

Boyce pointed out the window to our right, "here was one of our first stops for a restroom break." Yellow school buses lined the side of the narrow highway, one after the other, a parking nightmare. Most spaces on the church lot were already taken by other vehicles. "Everybody just ran off to use the restroom." Church officials couldn't believe what they were seeing. Crestwood was overwhelmed. In two hours, a 25-bus convoy had only reached Lumberton, and the second half, another 25 buses, were right behind them.

Along the route, residents stood on sidewalks, sometimes in front of their own personal residences, holding up invitations. "I saw signs that said 'Stop here' and a lot of people on the side of the road with signs that asked 'Need water, need juice?'" They were "ordinary people" who opened their hearts to help the only ways they could think of. Folks lined up and down Highway 69 North had never seen anything like the throngs of travelers stuck on school buses, in cars and recreational vehicles, in trucks and vans. Seeing the signs and the kind strangers who held them up made Boyce know "God does have his children working in the fields."

After creeping out of Lumberton city limits, there weren't many options for breaks until the next town. "We moved like a snail trying to cross the street." His voice stretched in jest when Boyce mocked the ride, "It was just crawl-l-l-ling." Then he echoed the words of neighbors he'd never meet, "Rita brought families closer, she broke down racial barriers for some people." The storm forced a lot of Texans to look at each other "by the content of their character."

With everyone, as Boyce put it, "in the same boat," Rita ruled the waves of fate. As we drove, in relative comfort and nearly non-stop, Boyce recalled how the knowledge that loved ones were okay eased his mind that day on the bus. An older sister, Nita, 33, had evacuated with her family. His 17-year old sister, Megan, and parents, both 51, had gone to a friend's home in North Texas. But not without some heated discussion.

Initially, Boyce's father refused to leave Beaumont. The professional driver made one ultimatum to a stubborn man he had never before spoken to in such a tone. "Either you're going or Community Funeral Home will be coming to pick up you up because I'm gone kill you myself." That same sense of humor kept Boyce from losing it on the long evacuation trail.

"We all had cell phones, my cousins and other relatives, we were keeping in touch with everyone." Still on 69 North, soon we were out of Hardin County and into Tyler County. Warren was a few miles down the highway, which, at that stretch, was two Northbound lanes and two Southbound lanes. "In the median," Boyce instructed me to use my imagination, "to your left there, were cars pulled over with tents set up. Folks were on the hood sleep, on the ground sleep and I guess these people were just plain tired. They had been on the road so long." Boyce had never, not in all the years he drove for a living, seen motorists asleep on the median.

Some were out of gas. Others stopped in their attempts to preserve gas. "We were moving like a snail before, then we graduated to a turtle's pace." Between the towns of Lumberton and Warren, the moaning and complaining grew louder and more frequent. The most popular things Boyce heard in the first few hours were predictable, especially given he had "a lot of family units" on his bus. *When do we stop again? We need to use the restroom. I'm hungry.* It was prerecorded and even played on the rare occasion when no one spoke.

Fortunately, there were several people onboard who had brought food from home. For the few who ran out, people shared chips, soda, water, and other goodies. "My bus, we were one big family." Boyce might've put the school bus in park and walked away if not for the people who hung in there and "kept the faith." Like the parents who maintained discipline by flashing combs straight from Sunday service.

We passed a sign, "Woodville 23 miles." When Boyce saw that same green marker a few months earlier, he assumed it meant there might be a couple of places they could let weary passengers have a break. He hoped the Tyler County seat would only take a short time to reach. Instead, "it took an eternity" to creep those 23 miles. That's when a few people went ballistic.

"We were able to stop, but unfortunately, there was another group of buses that weren't from Beaumont that had been there before us." Boyce wouldn't name where the other buses originated from, even though he knew, out of his wish to not slander an entire town. He acknowledged ugly things had happened. "When we stopped, the Beaumont people were blamed, of course, it wasn't us." Right then, Boyce realized a tide was turning. It was upsetting to

Boyce that what "happened" in Woodville diminished the balm of goodness. "People were already Katrina fatigued."

Texans had to evacuate with their evacuee-charges. "More than anything I faced on this journey, what got to me the most was, I mean, my heart went out to people from the New Orleans area, and I asked, 'Lord, how could this be?'" Boyce had been taught to never question God. Yet in the many conversations he had with the Creator before Rita, he always returned to one particular question. "Lord, these people just evacuated. Do they have to go through this again?"

Heartbreak over a beloved hometown, full of the walking wounded, Boyce wondered, as we drove faster, what psychological havoc enveloped their minds. At the same time, he voiced sadness at how so many could downgrade Rita. "We are the forgotten few," he ached. "If I had the opportunity to say that to George W. Bush, I would let him know we are the forgotten few." Boyce had plenty of company who, in the months after Rita, have loudly, and at times, angrily, agreed.

"It's really indescribable, a lot of my co-workers don't like talking about it. I, myself, believe one of the greatest forms of healing is for you to talk about the situation you're going through." Expression has been therapeutic in helping him to cope, to come to terms, to move on, beyond the storm. "I related Hurricane Rita to the death of a loved one. It comes, it devastates you, and it leaves you."

We arrived in Warren. A driver on the southbound side high beamed us that Smokey was out in full force. It was an old highway signal that still meant slow down. We counted churches, passing First Baptist, a church of Christ, then Bethel Baptist. Along that part of 69 North, we were briefly down to single lanes.

Stuck behind a logging truck, suddenly our smooth ride came to an abrupt halt. This was not something that usually happened on an ordinary weekday in the country. As we sat a few minutes, looking at faces in other vehicles reminded Boyce of spending hours behind the wheel of a school bus staring, waiting, praying. There was no way to pass. Traffic on both sides was backed up. Boyce became anxious.

As we tiptoed into Hillister, we were down to less than a quarter tank of gas. Passing Ivanhoe, we marveled at how green everything was. On top of the soft Texas carpet, there was another color.

Black. Piles and miles, we saw the charred remains of fallen timber. It had been burned and left for pickup.

"When we were driving through here," Boyce was reminded of something, "it was dark, at night, so all you could see was lights on cars and cars for miles and miles and miles and miles." A percussionist in the band at West Brook High, the sight of so many lights had carried him back down memory lane to a favorite tune they played. "The song was *I Can See For Miles*." As 36 passengers tried to sleep, block out worries and fears, Boyce hummed the catchy tune in his head, fully aware that marching, quickstep, was a much faster mode of transportation than the big wheels they relied on. Boyce hummed out loud. Then the song stuck, literally, for miles and miles, for hours, for days. He couldn't get it out of his head.

"It's just awesome how God works and how God moves. It's just like the Bible says in Lamentations," Boyce smiled. "His mercies are new every morning." That was a first, someone quoting to me from Lamentations. "He let us help the Katrina evacuees and put us through that so we could be prepared for Rita." Just outside Woodville, Boyce uttered the very thing that resonated with thousands who had compassion for New Orleans, but so little time between the two hurricanes to pull themselves together and pack, flee Rita.

"After everything had happened with Katrina, we had a family from New Orleans come and worship with us at St. John Missionary Baptist Church," Boyce says. "Rev. stood [Dr. O. J. Beasley] in the pulpit and he told us that it could've been us, it could've been us." No one had a way to foretell, three weeks later, it would be them. A prophecy come true, Boyce called his minister after Rita hit, "See what you done."

He also phoned Dr. Beasley while driving the route. "I said to him, 'Rev., see where you got me at? I'm behind this wheel driving all because of you!'" Joking aside, Boyce confided to Beasley that he was ready to quit. The convoy was 10 miles out of Longview on Highway 259. Boyce had traveled ahead of his story. He rewound to present and the hours being pursued, in a slow-speed chase, by Rita.

"How ironic, that we are sitting still, six months later, in one lane of traffic," he says. We saw the sign for County Road 1044. Highway crews continued to detain us. It didn't look like they were doing anything except talking in the middle of the lanes. All around us, to the left and right, were crates demolishing timber, surplus wood being sprayed by watery mists. It was mountain after mountain of wooden victims and water shooting from all sides to prevent the former trees from turning into a humongous bonfire. Ironic that wood was watered, as it waited for gasoline, a red dirt hole and matches, to be put down and set ablaze anyway. We started to slowly move again.

The Fellowship Church had a sign, "People reaching people for help." Boyce pointed to the building, "That was one of the churches we stopped at." I asked, "How did it go?" He shuddered, "A travesty." Boyce again reiterated that every single person did their best, but small churches with a handful of facilities weren't meant to manage hundreds of people at once. "Trying to get all the buses in and people to use the restroom, it was quite small and they were giving out as much as they had. People started taking stuff."

This saddened Boyce. A few evacuees were "misbehaving in a church house." Tired travelers saw no end in sight. Boyce could also see residents in each small community frustrated at the traffic and huge crowds that needed more bathrooms than were available.

Slowly, we pulled into Woodville, moving, Boyce says, just as they had moved in September. "We were so tired." A construction crew helped recreate the route. Boyce required no visual aids or bumper-to-bumper traffic. He would never forget.

"Like this empty Wal-Mart parking lot," he gestured to our right, "we wanted to pull over there and get some rest. They told us no, keep moving." That day, there were 18-wheelers parked, with drivers, who appeared to be doing the same thing. There were also RVs and smaller vehicles. Boyce repeated what could not be understood during the evacuation, "They would not let us stop." I asked who "they" were and he responded, "Mostly DPS troopers."

The gas needle edged closer to empty. We pulled over for water and fuel. Thousands on this same route had purchased whatever they could find in 2005 until there were no more supplies or stores shut down. When Boyce told Department of Public Safety officials that bus drivers "were tired," and quoted the "10-hour limit," state policy that required a person get eight hours rest, they were in for a rude awakening.

"We were instructed by DPS, *by state troopers,*" he loudly emphasized, "to forget that rule, it was thrown out." Boyce recognized the state of emergency Rita had tossed everyone in, but his fear was that a "bunch of sleepy folk," tired and deranged, were behind the wheels of school buses, not only responsible for their own lives, but for the lives of 2,000 others. "Who was negligent?" he asked.

With each order given by DPS, Boyce became more agitated. "Crazy, loudmouth me," he started, "I said 'So you telling me I can go out and rob a bank and I won't get sent to jail since we're in state of emergency?'" An officer was not amused. "Were you putting people's lives in danger?" I asked. Boyce looked at me with such a serious look, it gave his answer powerful validity, "Yes, in grave danger."

We got back in the car after the Dodge sucked up $66 dollars worth of gas. The first sign we saw was "Zavalla 23 miles." A short distance later, "Lufkin 47 miles." Relieved when he came upon the markers a few months earlier, there was renewed hope. "This was the halfway point to Lufkin. When I saw that, I breathed, somewhat, a sigh of relief." He truly felt the two convoys of 25 buses were closing in on their evacuation destination. Things were supposed to work. "That's where we were instructed to get shelter, the Red Cross was supposed to meet us there. There'd be food and water, the necessities." Boyce says there was a big surprise waiting in Lufkin, Texas.

We soon hit Colmesneil, population 638, a beautiful piece of property with a never-ending white picket fence. Horses and cows mulled about in their cliques. Picturesque homes of white, green shutters, blue trim, clean trailers stood next to leaning trees, done damage. Our law enforcement conversation continued.

"There were times that DPS troopers were covering up their badges with their left hands and their right hands were on their guns in holsters." Boyce was adamant that cops didn't want passengers and drivers to know their names or badge numbers. Again, he had ventured ahead of the route. "That occurred on 259 Northbound." We drove on, behind schedule because of highway work.

"Born, bred, fed and reared here in Texas," Boyce's voice went up, "they work for me and are supposed to be my protection, helping us out." At one point, he says, ugly words were directed at convoy leaders who dared complain. One DPS trooper was tired of hearing the pleas for rest, "Well, if your drivers just can't drive, we'll round up some troopers that can drive these buses." The threat was not taken lightly. Drivers forced themselves to stay woke without the help of caffeine, since there was no way to tell when bathroom breaks might come again.

"We pushed ourselves to the limit," Boyce sadly says. In the delirium, he began to see Christmas trees running alongside the road. Boyce got on the intercom and lowly told other bus drivers he was "fading." They were too. Many chuckled at his holiday remark about the trees and offered their hallucinations. "One woman said every time the windshield wipers went back and forth, she would see deer jump across the road." It was worse than counting sheep and she definitely didn't need any help falling asleep. Still, the woman shook off the nerve shattering deer. Trading stories helped. Several drivers took turns on the two-way to lament the fact they were bone-tired. Eyes *and* ears played tricks. "Another guy thought his wipers produced gunfire, we were all just delirious."

Soon we were in Jasper County. "The closer you get that night, the better you feel?" I asked. We were 35 miles outside Lufkin. "Most of them [passengers] were sleep and that was kind of good." We breezed through Zavalla. Less than 30 miles away was our des- ignated hurricane stop. Boyce was reliving every mile in his head.

Thursday night had turned into Friday morning, September 23, 2005. Daybreak broke. Light poured into the buses. A few sleepy heads moved from side to side. Hundreds of Beaumont residents finally reached Lufkin. They wanted to exit buses. That wasn't going to happen.

"About 7:30 that morning, they just told us there wasn't any room." The convoy was swiftly directed to Nacogdoches. Every hope that had been clung to was dashed. Gone. Never existed. "Lufkin is the shelter point for us," Boyce began, then listed all the cities that ordered evacuations thinking Rita would hit them. "By the time they [Jefferson County officials] ordered a mandatory evacuation, all the shelters were full."

First the convoy went to a small area and "tried to squeeze 25 buses in." They parked, according to Boyce, across from a Diary Queen on State Highway 103. "We had a tragic accident to happen there. A lady was walking across the street, back from using the rest-room. She was struck and killed by a passing motorist." Several passengers remembered 81-year old Charlotte Ranger. They were traumatized. "Some of the other drivers saw it and I was blessed to not see it because it has stayed with them."

Exhaustion made the short drive next door seem like 150 miles instead of 15. "On the way to Nacogdoches, they heard we were coming, and told us not to come, to keep rolling." Boyce was somber as we drove around Lufkin, then found our way out. An Earth, Wind, and Fire song, *September,* featured a line in the chorus that could be slightly altered for those trapped on buses. "Do you remember the 23rd of September?"

Indeed, it was a Friday in 2005 when hundreds of Texans felt unwanted, unprotected and uninspired by some of the things they heard and witnessed. Out of despair, some thought they were turned away, denied help, refused entry because they were black. Even a handful of whites on board, agreed it was because they were black too. But Boyce believed it was more a combination of factors.

Just as Lufkin was overwhelmed with people, so too was Nacogdoches. Boyce had no concrete proof that law enforcement agencies were contacting each other from one county to the next or one town to the next. He assumed it was either them or city officials. "How else could they know before we arrived that 25 buses were headed their way?" Sounding depressed, a little forlorn, as he faithfully retraced the route, Boyce remembered the new day with the same old phrase to greet them. *No room.* "We were in a state of emergency and no one could help us?"

The buses barely slowed down. "We kept going, we bypassed Nacogdoches. There was no need for us to even venture in." I sensed the journey to recreate the route was getting increasingly difficult for Boyce. Yet he bid me continue on, the way he had. "No" was the password on everyone's lips. "Where were you going?" I asked. "We had *no* idea." Convoy leaders were placed in the unthinkable positions of having to strategize on the move about where to take hundreds left in their care.

"One of our convoy leaders was born and raised in East Texas," Boyce says she knew the area fairly well and called some folks in San Augustine to explain their plight. They were no longer on 69 North or 259. Boyce was turned around. "By this time, I had lost all direction and didn't know what highway we were on." An old pro who drove chartered buses on weekends and school buses on weekdays didn't know where he was, though he knew Texas like the back of his hand. Boyce was reduced to following. He drove. He had one color in his head—green—for a line of Christmas trees dancing in the pines.

At one checkpoint, Boyce was uncharacteristically defiant and territorial. "I'm not letting no state trooper get on this bus and drive it." A childhood friend named Derrick Levergne had experience driving 18-wheelers. He was a passenger on the Boyce Bus and offered to take over. "I showed him where all the controls were, and he drove." Levergne knew the kid he'd gone to elementary school with was beyond tired. Boyce gave quick lessons and told the trucker, "If you can give me two good hours, that's all I need."

"What did that, getting rest, do for you?" I asked. In 2005, his body was shutting down. In 2006, his whole frame relaxed, "It did me a world of good." There weren't a lot of people on the other buses who could step behind the wheel. Boyce knew his deal was heaven sent. "God always has a ram in the bush to help you, Derrick was my ram." Everybody was drained, "physically, mentally, emotionally, psychologically." It was clear in the way many stared straight ahead. Life was blurry.

Boyce got on the two-way with an announcement no one objected to: "Okay, let's pray, we need strength, let's pray." Plenty of company was qualified to lead those appeals. Some of the drivers, local ministers, got on the intercom and prayed. "That lifted us." One driver had a beautiful voice and knew another way to inspire broken spirits. "He sang *His Eye is on the Sparrow* and near the end everyone was like 'Come on, keep singing, keep singing.'" This encouraged the rolling crowd, separated only by the various buses that doubled as pews. "We had church over the airwaves, it inspired everybody."

They were desperate to find a city willing to play host. "We get into San Augustine, instead of 25 buses, all of a sudden 50 buses showed up." The other part of the Beaumont fleet "caught up and one of their main convoy leaders had bailed out." The man simply walked off, couldn't take anymore. 50 buses settled into San Augustine, more than double what they were expecting. If they had a number at all.

"We got up there and they said, 'Okay, but we only have food for 200 people.'" Texas neighbors were doing whatever they could. It wasn't their fault, Boyce shook his head. They were at San Augustine High School. It looked, to Boyce, like soup was being served. Something quick and hot. He remained on the bus to eat a snack because food for 200 should automatically go to passengers without resources or food from home. As the food ran out and we drove on, Boyce says, "They had an injunction and we were court-ordered out of San Augustine!"

Boyce says it wasn't something made up to threaten the crowd. "I guess fear and they didn't have any room, they told us, 'The storm is headed this way so you've got to get out of here.'" Like most officials I spoke with in towns along the evacuation route, they wanted it clear that race had nothing to do with how Beaumont evacuees on school buses, or any others, were treated. San Augustine County Judge Wayne Holt says his county fed everyone and there was no injunction. Period.

"We are a pass-through town," Holt says. "We already had over 5,000 people [evacuees] in the county." To Holt's way of thinking, a town with only 2,000 residents where the largest facility available was the First Baptist Church, officials were plenty busy. They didn't need or have time to get an injunction. Holt has heard the rumors that people think his county is racist. "We tried to do everything we could for them."

At that point, drivers were "begging and pleading" for rest. They had been behind the big wheels since noon Thursday when they left Beaumont. Soon it would be noon Friday. 24 hours later and Rita was inching closer. They quickly departed San Augustine.

"I stopped looking at highways," Boyce was geographically challenged. The little nap and snack invigorated him for a new itinerary. "They were taking us into Tyler." It only took a matter of minutes before Smith County [Tyler, Texas] officials got wind of the shaky plan. Convoy leaders, he says, were flatly told to stay away since the storm might produce zigzag damage throughout East Texas, areas that certainly wouldn't take the brunt of Rita's wrath, but surely would feel the outer fringes of high winds, heavy rain and power outages. "By this time, the buses were being escorted by state troopers," a fact that Boyce says caused mass confusion.

"Those people led us in a circle three times," they kept passing the same exits and roads, the same highways, convenience stores and little towns. "They weren't giving us much help, just telling us to get out of Dodge." Convoy leaders tired of the circuitous route and directed 25 buses to park on a lonely stretch of road. One convoy driver gave a brash, arms-folded announcement, "That's it, we're not going anymore." Buses came back around to Highway 259 and didn't budge.

"People had given up, they were calling relatives, asking them to come and get them." Passengers were tired, frustrated, and two words kept being repeated in the pre-storm minutes that ticked away: "Help us." The phone call that Shelton Boyce had made to his minister was revisited.

Rev. Beasley was only 22 miles from Longview. Boyce asked him to "meet the bus" he intended to park and never look back. He was fed up and told the pastor, "I'm not driving no more. These people got us going all over the place." Beasley listened carefully. He and his wife had evacuated to Henderson, right near Marshall, where she was originally from. Beasley calmed Boyce, counseled him, advised him to not abandon the passengers. What would become of 36 lost lambs if the shepherd left no one at the wheel? The man he admired who always demonstrated such great faith bulked him up. Boyce pulled himself together and drove on. We drove on.

"I tip my hat to the three convoy leaders that stayed with us and hung tough—Sandra Robinson, Esther Bethea and Benny Huckaby." None of them could guess, just as Boyce did not, a ride that started in Beaumont would ultimately end up a life-altering detour. "Believe it or not, we had some drivers," he began to pound on the dashboard, "drive the whole 50 hours without one ounce of sleep." His faith was severely tested in such a way until Boyce told God what God probably knew all along. "I just can't do this no more, I'll move out of the way and let you take full control." No doubt, God was at the wheel long before Boyce made the declaration. It was like that country song, *Jesus, Take the Wheel*.

"One of the passengers," Boyce wasn't sure who, "finally said 'Call the governor.'" This was a verbal illusion in a political desert. Boyce thought he'd imagined the words. Next thing the bus driver knew, Rick Perry had been contacted. His office was on the line,

Austin wanted an update. Help wasn't coming from anywhere else. Few were confident that putting any leftover hope in a Republican governor, who didn't resemble the majority of registered Democrats on those buses, would net a solution.

After Gov. Perry interceded, some drivers did allow DPS personnel to drive their buses. Wherever they were headed. No one was sure. DPS officials never came onto bus #25, Boyce felt his temper was too short. He also didn't want to risk saying anything else comical. There was still at least one officer who thought he was planning to rob a bank or loot a small town.

Much of the last portion of the route was muddled in Boyce's mind. He could only remember leaving the Tyler area, not to be confused with Tyler County, but the city of Tyler, Texas. Boyce soon heard Canton was the new destination. As some DPS troopers/employees drove B. I . S. D. school buses, a few officers remained in police vehicles, escorts alongside, like a never ending funeral procession without sirens. Out of Angelina County. Out of Smith County. Into Van Zandt County. And so we drove.

"When we got into Canton, those people just poured out their hearts." Boyce was sure the entire state had heard about the 2,000 evacuees from Beaumont. He later learned that Canton officials got a call about 10:30 Friday night. "We got into Canton at 6:30 the next morning [Saturday]." They went to the Canton Civic Center first, to a staging area where basic needs were assessed. With short notice from Austin, Canton officials hustled and had the welcome mat out. Evacuees from Beaumont finally had their first extended break from school buses, *after* Rita made landfall some four hours earlier.

"I guess, they were equally nice to everybody, but, being a Christian believer and being rooted in the word of God, when you're among other Christians, it's so sweet."

They were not in Canton long before Gov. Perry sent buses that carried most of the evacuees to different places, including Reunion Arena in Dallas, a former detention facility there, and a Salvation Army camp in Midlothian, Texas.

When Boyce made it back Beaumont, it was late on a Friday evening. "That Saturday, October 1st," he started, "I was down at Ford Park talking to a guy from New Orleans. He was part of the military based at the staging area of Ford Park." The man told Boyce a lot had been swept under the rug after Katrina. He spoke in hushed tones, asked if Boyce knew about 1200 people who had been housed at a New Orleans gymnasium and the reason it didn't make the news. "Because the people all drowned," the soldier whispered. Boyce felt like he was back on the bus.

Another Katrina evacuee told Boyce it had been well documented among black New Orleanians—an oxymoron—that one thing of bad weather was true. "If a storm ever came through *they'd* let go of the levees and try to wash half the population out."

We traded conspiracy theories gathered over the months from Louisianans as we wound back to Beaumont.

Two churches, one large and one small, were located directly across the street from one another. The larger building, Fellowship Missionary Baptist Church, was very nearly destroyed by Rita. Chunks of the bricked frame torn away, it looked like the skeleton of a giant dinosaur. Its sanctuary unusable.

Across the street was a white wooden structure that reminded me of a simple country house of worship. Tiny frame, one story. Not a shingle was missing from the House of Prayer Missionary Baptist Church. I photographed amazing grace. Boyce and I drove away making plans for a soul food Sunday and his specialty—fried okra.

"I don't think anyone in their right mind will ever forget Sister Rita."

TWENTY-ONE

I haven't known the sheriff of Jefferson County as long as Chief Ron Hobbs, who heads up his Narcotics unit, or Major Jimmy Singletary, who works in that division. But their history together may be enough for both men to forgive me for getting Mitch Woods to tell this story, not once, but twice. To make absolutely sure I heard right.

"Jimmy and Ron and I were bunked down in my office for Rita. We were sharing that space the night the storm came in. After Rita passed, knocked the electricity and water off, that Saturday everybody had been going about their duties and getting things done," Woods set the Texas table. Later that evening, people returned to the courthouse for a staff meeting in the conference room. It was almost too hot to think, let alone stir.

After a series of meetings, people began to drift back to their various makeshift rest areas. Hobbs, Singletary, and Woods were in his office with the blinds closed and soon joined by Chief Zena Stephens. "Somebody made the comment, 'Man I could sure use a cold beer, a cold beer would be really good right now.'" It was hot. They were sticky. Humidity added 20 degrees to a miserable weather environment. One announcement perked the men right up— Stephens had some cold ones up in her office that she had brought from home. Woods had two in an ice chest. The party was on. A simple wish came true and the shared pleasure cooled everyone off. But the beer must've conjured up other simplicities taken for granted.

The foursome began to carp and complain, Woods says, about how hot and sweaty the long day had left them. "We couldn't open windows, we couldn't get cool, I began to whine and said, 'You know, my normal routine is I take a shower before I go to bed every night and I'm probably not gone be able to sleep tonight.'" They had been rained on that morning and perspiration streamed from their clothes all afternoon. Woods looked around the room and told some of the closest members of his staff, "I'm not gone be able to sleep tonight, I'm gone be miserable. I can tell that right now." As Woods savored the icy thirst-quenching taste of suds, he shook his head, "Man, if I could just get a shower or bath, I'd probably be able to sleep so much better."

Hobbs had an insane vacation idea, Woods says, that wasn't so crazy. "All of a sudden, Ron goes, 'Hey, we could go to my house and bathe in my swimming pool.'" For a second, nobody said anything. *Was Hobbs serious?* Woods knew his narcotics commander had a pool. It never occurred to him, particularly in the aftermath of a devastating hurricane, that it could double as a giant bathtub. Then someone spoke. It was Mitch Woods who broke the silence, "Heck man, I'm in, let's go." Chief Stephens quickly excused herself with four words: "Not me, I'm out."

When Woods reiterated his enthusiastic willingness again, "Well, I'm in," Hobbs did what good friends do, he followed the lead: "Me too, let's go." The skeptic in the trio had remained silent. Singletary had time to think and he slowed the bubble bath train down, "I don't know so much about that, I don't know." But all Woods could see was cool, clear water by then.

"Don't be a wuss," Woods jokingly told Singletary to get with the adventurous program. The vote was 2-to-1. "We all got up, changed, put on gym shorts, t-shirts and flip flops and we got towels, soap and loaded up in Ron's vehicle and headed out across town." The trip produced vivid reminders that inconvenience had come to stay.

"Pitch black darkness" greeted the trio. "Everything just looked so different at night with the lights out." They weaved by objects, dodged debris, and picked their way around, "so accustomed to visual landmarks." Rarely do residents think about what their cities and towns would be like without anything flashing, beaming, welcoming, guiding and lighting their way. No traffic signs. No stores open. No gas stations. No malls. No restaurants or well-lit buildings. No neon signs anywhere, "just total darkness outside."

Woods and his swim team were on Eastex Freeway where DPS units were manning all the exits. This was customary during the curfew. Exits had to be blocked because things were not safe with busybodies and a few looters on the prowl. "We pulled up and turned our emergency lights on and he [the trooper] walked over and we said, 'It's okay, we're with the sheriff's office. We're going over to this guy's house to bathe in his swimming pool.'" The trooper started laughing and shined his light into the vehicle to take a headcount of how many grown men were headed to the post-hurricane party.

"Yes, we were in an unmarked vehicle, of course, and he shined the light on all of us and started laughing again, 'Y'all go ahead.'" Besides the few, like Zena Stephens, who knew the water themed plan, its three participants, and a stranger within the statewide law enforcement brotherhood, not that many people in Jefferson County have ever heard the famous "pool story," not straight from the sheriff's mouth anyway.

"We get to Ron's house and use flashlights to make our way into the backyard. There were limbs and trash everywhere, all through the neighborhood and the streets," Woods says. "We literally had to pick our way in and drive over trees to get there." Rita, fresh in everyone's mind, they all agreed, "The neighborhood looked horrible." Woods stopped smiling for a couple of seconds to mentally revisit all the lines and trees down, to this day, still something unimaginable. But there it was right in front of him.

"We get in the backyard, strip down, and Jimmy's a little homophobic. He says, 'Turn the light off, I don't want you shining the light on me.'" Woods was back in fine form, smiling and laughing, eyes filled with clear humor, despite the admitted knowledge that Singletary won't be thrilled to see this story in print. The "light" that Singletary referred to was actually headlights from the unmarked vehicle Woods and company drove up in. There was no electricity anywhere. Before they could jump in, it took several minutes to find the buried water underneath a pile of tree limbs and shingles and debris Rita had tossed in for a game of hurricane volleyball.

They got in. The water was colder than the beer, refrigerated icemaker cold. Chilly cold. "After a few seconds," Woods sighed, "man it felt good." Once they adjusted to the temperature, it was soap and shampoo heaven. They went to work scrubbing, of course, mindful of Singletary's orders to stay in their sections of the pool.

"Of course, the humor that goes along with this," he says, "was three grown men naked in a pool together, bathing." *Yes, sheriff, I got the naked part.* They were clean. They dried off. For a moment, everything with the world was alright and looked better. "Man, it just felt good to be clean." But the pool story didn't end there.

After another day of the mercury baking citizens, they went back to the pool for a second night and had Refreshing Bath Number Two. There still wasn't any running water at hurricane headquarters inside the courthouse. "For three nights in a row, we bathed in that swimming pool." Then the consensus was in. "We pretty much felt like the pool was not fit to be in after that third night." Woods laughed really hard, and I was nearly on the floor, when he added, "That was probably it."

We talked a little longer that day. Woods always remembered to ask how I was holding up, what I had seen out in the sticks. "Holly Beach, Highway 82, the route out of Port Arthur, you go out of Port Arthur over on Pleasure Island and go across the causeway into Louisiana," he paused, "you went that way." Woods tried to draw me an invisible map of where I had gotten lost two days before on my way to Cameron.

"That was always a spur of the moment short motorcycle ride over there," he fondly recalled. After Rita hit, Woods flew over and did an aerial assessment. "To go over there and see it, to see Holly Beach, just gone, just gone, nothing there."

Later that night, something the sheriff said made it hard to sleep. *Cameron wiped off the map.* Sure I'd seen parts of the parish—Johnson's Bayou and Hackberry—but not Cameron. My brain wouldn't rest and it was almost time to push out of the region. Head back to Dallas, New York, and then London.

Thursday morning, at what I considered my grandparents middle-of-the night bacon and eggs breakfast, I was up and dressed by 4 a.m. When I hit Interstate 10, it was still too dark to see what I had 48 hours earlier at a more decent hour—those refineries in the distance and oil platforms waving in the Gulf. I couldn't spot the abandoned boat, but nothing could shield the fact that Holly Beach had been picked up and carried off, hidden from all those who loved it. Gone, "just gone," I could hear Mitch in the car with me. Then, that other George, as if I'd planned it.

Radio stations in a rental aren't fun. When I hit 101 FM and they were playing my Mr. Strait's *Stars on the Water*, it felt tailor-made. He was singing about hurricanes, even mentioned Beaumont, New Orleans, deep into Mississippi. Not long after, I spied another one of those infamous blue state signs *Bienvennue en Louisianne,* "Welcome to Louisiana." Blue like the tarp. Calcasieu Parish.

After crossing the Interstate 10 bridge, I took the Cameron/Creole exit, which finally wound to Highways 14 and 27 South. The Southwest Louisiana Rifle and Pistol Club was still standing, little around it had been left untouched by Rita. A thick forest looked like Big Foot had walked through. Mashed up landscapes were painted to my left and right. I passed a huge house… resting on top of a barn as if it was the most natural architectural thing in the world.

I slammed brakes as my mother's voice on the cell phone screeched to coincide with the shoes, "Be careful." There was a relic bridge to maneuver and I'd be in Cameron. "I can't go across that thing," I told the same woman who always shut her eyes when we traveled together in the Pelican State and had to cross high bridges over water. Which was most of the time. Marshy foliage came tip-toeing up to the edge of the concrete. I slowly crossed the Gibbstown Bridge and held my breath. A man was pulled off to the side of the road when I got off the rollercoaster ride. We nodded heads. He was taking pictures of another house on the side of the road. Relocated by Rita.

Posted signs confirmed what Julie Burleigh had said, "Cameron to your right, Oak Grove, go straight." There were unlivable houses without windows, *Wizard of Oz* legs and trunks buried underneath structures. The wicked Witch of the Gulf was not dead. Entire insides of buildings were blown clear through making it easy to see from front door to rear in a blink. Boom. Shotgun houses. I got to 82 and 27 and a four-way stop. Abbeyville was on up the road, 86 more miles. I turned right and saw a blinking highway message, "FERRY IS OPEN."

I wouldn't need the ferry from that side. I was finally in Cameron proper. Nothing anyone had forewarned, in stark detail, prepared me for the ride down the main drag or the spirit of the parish. A woman who had been a voice on the phone for weeks.

Clifton Hebert, head of EOC, had just driven away. I didn't know what he looked like. Burleigh had me on the line again, "He's coming straight at you." She described his truck. I stopped in the middle of Marshall Street and flagged down Hebert. He didn't have time to talk. 90 seconds later, I was seated in a trailer marked "Number 7" in the lot, face to face with Julie Burleigh.

"The school is smashed," I told her, "like the bank and the gas station, and, well, everything." She smiled, "We had two elementary schools—one in Cameron and one in Creole. The kids are going to Grand Lake in Northern Cameron Parish now." A shared school building means one set of young residents get to attend two-and-a-half days, then Cameron children get equal time. "They've been awesome about sharing their school, the teachers sharing their class work and the information they have because the teachers here lost everything."

Cameron Elementary had about 300 students. Some of the instructors had been there more than 20 years. They cried when files, photos, and mementos were washed away by Rita. Homemade cards from students, Christmas gifts, pictures, special reports favorite students had penned. Gone. Burleigh pulled out a picture of Wakefield United Methodist Church. The hurricane blew out pews, communion trays, musical instruments, everything was "just gone." Except the soul of that sanctuary. There was a frightening uniformity in Cameron, a new building code that Rita willfully created and complied with—almost every structure—home, store, church, school or business—was totaled, annihilated, or smashed. In many cases, a caved in shell was left to house what must be cleaned and gutted. *Gone,* I heard Mitch again.

A group from Adams State College in Colorado was in town to clean up the church. "They also cleaned an older gentleman's house yesterday in Grand Chenier and an older lady's house today, stripping out stuff for her." Thanks to small groups and through the efforts of AmeriCorp, help trickled in. Cameron hasn't turned anyone away, "We had a little church group from Kansas that just showed up on our doorsteps and they said, 'Send us wherever, we just want to help.'"

Home after home, in rows, on the drive in, looked violently aired out by wind and water. Stilts—houses with legs—beautiful

Louisiana island habitats, were down, drowned, or damaged. "What are they called?" I asked. "Homes on pilings," Burleigh explained. "Mine is 14'4 off the ground, at my base floor, some are made of cinderblock, some are made of cement, and mine are big wood pilings that came from the Gulf."

Seals sit on top of the pilings, then the base floor sits on that. Much of what they used came from an old bridge that was being torn down to throw out. "You're going to have to drive with Kirk to my house to see it," she laughed when I questioned sturdiness.

"This is all Main Street," Burleigh pulled out another photo of what Cameron looked like right after they were allowed back in. Unrecognizable Main/Marshall Street. We sifted through pictures of what was Hibernia Bank, only a morsel of a sign remained. Darla K's had been revamped, back in a limited capacity, "It's that little brown building off to the side, used to be a store."

Gone was Wendall's Electric, a drug store, the Script Shop. "Our post office was sitting right there," Burleigh pointed to the vampire space in the picture where people once stopped to post and pick up mail. "It's all gone."

I asked about Gov. Blanco. "She's been here, I've never seen her. I heard the president showed up, but Blanco didn't stay long." It was the first time in all our phone conversations that Burleigh's voice sounded distant when she talked about how little time there seemed to be to look at what Rita did to Cameron. "The president flew in and he flew right out in a Blackhawk, he walked around a little bit right there at the courthouse visiting with them and he hasn't been back." Then she noted Mr. Bush had just visited New Orleans again and also Mississippi, so she emailed someone the following dissertation: "What's wrong with Cameron? Are we *that* small that we're not noticed?" Burleigh wanted it written somewhere in the record, for all time, that people have suffered in Cameron and other small places the same way they suffer in larger cities.

When Katrina evacuees made it to Cameron, an entire wing of the hospital was turned into a makeshift compound to house families and keep them together. Burleigh was one of the first volunteers, "I went back for two weeks almost everyday staying until 10 or 11 o'clock at night." After her day job, Burleigh would go straight to the hospital, carrying food, clothes, encouragement, all she could, to people she had so much compassion for.

"I met some really neat people there, I really did." Those who didn't have family, especially the older residents, lit up whenever "Miss Julie" came around. "I had one lady in there that had walked for miles and she was not in good health. Finally when she was picked up, she was brought to the interstate where a bunch of others were waiting." They were supposed to be transported from that designated point, but "she sat for hours in the sun" and it took its toll. Everyday, Burleigh massaged the woman's aching, sunburned legs. Another woman didn't walk to safety, but had issues related to that very activity.

"She was quite a character," Burleigh says of the senior citizen housed with a daughter. "She would not walk, she would not take any kind of exercise, she just refused." The woman had pretty much made up her mind Cameron was a good place to die. She was content to wait for her final nap. No medical staff could reach the displaced Louisianan. Then Burleigh showed up and issued a challenge, "No ma'am, I don't take 'no' for an answer. When I come back tomorrow, you *will* go walking with me."

Burleigh returned the very next day. The little lady was perched in a chair out in the hall waiting. Not on the deathbed she had earlier glued herself to. She waited for the feisty Cajun to come back and care again, to boss her around a little more. "She said, 'Look Julie, look where I walked to.'" Burleigh was well aware that her new charge was in pain, but something else outweighed the significance of physical hurt. "She wasn't going to lay there and die with me around. I wasn't going to allow that."

There were more than 100 people from Katrina in Cameron Parish, many of them at the recreation center in Johnson's Bayou and maybe 35 at the hospital in Cameron. People opened their hearts and wallets, "They cooked for them, they took care of them." There was still a sentiment that if it happened again tomorrow, Cameron would respond exactly the same way, with no regrets and no resentment. They too, like many others, loved New Orleans. Yet they also possessed a desire for America to accept and understand Rita was a separate hurricane. Ignoring her won't change what happened and how they were abandoned caregivers first tending the needy, then their own wounds.

"That's tough to swallow, it really is," Burleigh shook her head. "It feels like we're just left here by ourselves with no help." She mentioned a P. O. D. site, a Point of Distribution, where everything from food and water to ice and tools is kept for residents without other shopping alternatives. Supplies were stacked in FEMA-borrowed 18-wheeler trailers. "Are you telling me seven months after Rita that people still have to come to the P.O.D. site for help?" Burleigh almost shrugged, "We have no grocery stores within a 50-mile radius, at least 50 miles one way."

Lake Charles is where most people traveled to shop. "And with fuel prices, they're fighting their insurance companies, and fighting FEMA. People just can't afford to be running up and down the road." Several have asked why Burleigh keeps the distribution site operational. Her answer is basic, like the needs of those who shopped there. "We are still in recovery mode. We're not in the rebuilding mode, but the recovery."

Part of the lateness might be attributed to how long it took to let residents back in. Long after other parishes and counties allowed citizens to return, Cameron was waiting. "We got in the second week of January 2006." Julie and Kirk Burleigh had evacuated, first to Mount Pleasant, Texas, to check on a son who attended college there. 20-year old Lucas is a real cowboy. "We noticed a lot of kids up there from Southern Louisiana, that rodeo and stay up there, so we decided to go meet them." It felt good to offer comfort that their families back home were alright.

During her two-day stay in Mount Pleasant, some of the students actually located a satellite picture of Burleigh's house on the Internet. She could count her 13 oak trees, and managed to check some of the damage. "The water was still high, but you could see the staircases below my house. When we got back those staircases were no longer there." They had been washed out into the Gulf.

Her neighborhood, once comprised of 60 homes, won't ever look the same. "There are still four homes there, one on the other end of the subdivision, and three on my end." When weekends rolled around, tourists packed the parish, driving through, taking pictures, walking around, in shock. "You're talking three to five years to get Cameron back on its feet, to get the people back. A lot of them aren't coming back, they don't want to go through this again."

An irritatingly loud phone shattered our one-on-one. "Cameron E-O-C," Burleigh answered, "This is Julie, how can I help you?" Her voice was not only liquid therapy, it was genuine and warm. You believed it instantly. She hung up. "I guess you could say I'm a Jack-of-all-trades," Burleigh laughed. "When they first threw me in here, there were five soldiers—Chief John Harris, (Retired) First Sgt. Brian Fletcher, Christopher Erbelding, Staff Sgt. Mays, Staff Sgt. Stephan—and they were from Army, Navy, Air Force and the National Guard." Her job description was unwritten, defined on the spot by whatever was happening. She recalled how several of the men worked though their own families needing them at home to deal with damage from the storm. Many had just returned from Afghanistan, then dealt with Katrina, had no break and was told to head out for Rita. Her phone rang again.

Written information from *Louisiana Spirit* was in a stack of papers I nosily picked up from Burleigh's desk while she spoke to another resident. Counseling was available. Volunteers of America specialized in mental health and well being. Included in a brochure were warning signs on what to look for in someone anxious, stressed or depressed. Or all of the above.

"I guess I'd been here two weeks and started looking through that," Burleigh pointed to the list of signs, "and I was going 'Oh gee, that's me.'" Burleigh had to get a grip, "Back off now." She called it "scary" how many persons, self included, had some of the indicators, signs of a person in potential trouble. "We had four heart attacks, massive heart attacks, two older ladies and two gentlemen. Two of them were close friends of ours. They've all died *since* the storm."

Burleigh's voice is unmistakably Cajun, thick with the missing letters of a southern Louisiana pronunciation flavored with pride. "It was all stress-related to Rita," she says of illness and deaths. "One lady saw her house on TV and she had lived there all her life. She had lived through Hurricane Audrey." We both re-read the checklist for 12 warning signs of suicide and put the pamphlet away.

Her raspy voice cracked slightly. "It's like you're forgotten about. Nobody calls. Nobody comes." Work crews, from Montana to Manhattan, from Texas to Tucson, have all asked her the same thing:

"Where is your media? Why is this not being covered?" For those fortunate enough to have met Burleigh, they leave "ambassadors for Cameron Parish," as Burleigh accustomed herself to a quick counter response. "Why don't you be our media? Go back home and tell people what you saw."

Burleigh has six neighbors who have vowed to return, she hoped more will do the same. "Every time I see them, they're like, 'I miss home so much.'" For now, the fear and wreckage and hurt are too fresh. "They need time to heal, time will pass and they'll see things are improving and that their parish is growing." Burleigh is convinced that Cameron will bounce back. She is the effervescent cheerleader more believable than a large banner draping the front of the courthouse: CAMERON WILL RISE AGAIN.

"Someone told me that they weren't going to rebuild until after the new hurricane season passes, they're scared," Burleigh says. She felt "blessed" that her family had good insurance and a fair adjuster who handled their claim quickly. Her phone rang again. Things picked up as the morning zeroed in on 9 a.m. She put the receiver back in its cradle, "These people are still shocked, walking around in a daze. My next door neighbor has no home left and he stayed for two days hauling important stuff to his attic. [before evacuating] There is no sign of their home left."

For the first two months after parish residents were allowed back in, the man would pull up in his driveway, stare out at where his house used to be, a square patch of grassless earth and never get out of his car. "After five or six minutes, he'd drive away."

"Last year, we said if a storm comes and takes everything, we're out of here." She and Kirk Burleigh, who, just one day before, celebrated his 50th birthday, considered resettling on a small ranch in North Texas. Married for 30 years, with three children and three grandchildren, they sat down after Rita to talk legacy and life in Louisiana. They talked family. 25-year old Erik lives with his wife, Sarah, and babies, Dylan and Brianna, in Moss Bluff, Louisiana. 23-year old Jenny lives in Grand Lake with husband, Steven, and baby Trenton. Texas would put the Burleighs near their youngest, Lucas.

"After the storm hit, I asked him [Kirk] 'What do you want to do?'" Her husband owned Cameron Fire Equipment, a 50-year old business started by his father. He was born in Cameron Parish, she in Opelousas. "He can listen to something over the telephone and tell you what's wrong with it," Burleigh laughed at her husband's talent. He was always working, she says. The soul of Cameron was one to talk. She regularly put in seven-day workweeks and spent a lot of volunteer hours at Camp Cameron, a FEMA base where people who needed it could live.

"It's got tents, cots, blankets, and sheets and stuff for people to stay. Hot showers. Hot meals are catered in and an overnight laundry service." Part of her job was to make sure contractors and volunteers at the camp "had badges and can go use the…" her voice trailed off as the door opened. Kirk Burleigh came in.

A marital smile that spoke to their mutual respect and love for one another was blinding. "Your ears must be burning," I quipped as introductions were made with Mrs. Burleigh blushing like a 16-year old child bride. The man's tanned face and hands were the definition of masculinity. There was a soft leathery quality about his skin. When Kirk Burleigh spoke his voice was more Cajun than hers. He laughed a mischievous little grin and sat beside us, content to listen to his wife and play catch up in the conversation.

"There was a time I was in the courthouse talking to someone and some guy was in there saying 'Man, I can't believe I drove through this driveway the other night and got flat tires from boards with nails.'" Julie Burleigh knew immediately that the FEMA employee had driven through their yard. *What was he doing there at night?* They had put up the rigged boards, piled across their entryway to prevent non-neighbors from getting in. People were stealing things right out in the open, in daylight hours. Night was worse.

For a few minutes, the dialogue jumped from New Orleans to Beaumont, from Katrina to Rita, from men to women, from culture to cuisine. We talked about qualifications, or lack of, for 23 candidates running for Crescent City Mayor. "I find that the only thing many outside Louisiana understand is New Orleans," Burleigh says. We all agreed that much of the "understanding" leaned toward tourist-educated symbolism. Except for those who truly knew the city. People knew the French Quarter, Bourbon Street. They turned away from the Lower 9th Ward or the city's public housing units.

Burleigh recalled one woman in the parish hospital who had evacuated before Katrina with her three kids. "I asked her why she had never left New Orleans and what the attraction was for staying when life was so impoverished in that kind of soup bowl." The woman explained it best she could to Burleigh. You had to be raised there, she said, part of the culture she was born into meant, "If you leave, someone in your family will die or you'll curse your family for generations." Burleigh again outlined how much people were willing to do to help their fellow Louisianans, pre- and post-Katrina. "We were just helping them and now we're running for our lives trying to survive too."

The tie that binds Katrina to Rita should've allowed for more attention to situations like Cameron and other places. "I feel for those people in Mississippi—they've lost like we lost." Silence. Then the blamed culprit: politics. This prompted a whole new discussion for three people who grew up in Louisiana—we talked about a man I once met who actually read my first book while serving, and is still serving, a 10-year federal prison term in Texas. Edwin Edwards was the name that always came up when Louisianans gathered to talk politics.

"He was the most dapper white man I'd ever seen," I told both, and we cracked up about all the "crooked things" and hands-in-the-cookie jarred moments. Our conclusion came from Kirk Burleigh— "If the man could get out tomorrow, the people would vote for him." *I guarantee.* Then Burleigh gave a history of life as a native son.

He was born in a little clinic in Creole and was a toddler when Audrey roared through. A place dubbed the old Henry House was where Burleigh lived, "Almost 50 years later, it went through Rita and is still there." How can you not have a spicy personality after being born in Creole? Sounded like a stereotype, but this man loved his life, his parish, the work his father trained him to do and what ancestors meant.

"My father's father, my grandfather, passed away and they buried him on the day Hurricane Audrey hit, June 27th, so we were all evacuated for the funeral. Otherwise, we might've been statistics, instead of survivors." His family felt the death was life's way of beginning again. Someone "up there" was definitely watching over.

They returned to Cameron Parish, still grieving, doubly so, the personal losses were tenfold. 390 lives were lost. 391. As a boy, young Kirk learned the example of service to community from his father. "Your hometown people just pitched in [after Audrey] and did what had to be done. We didn't have FEMA then, we didn't have help. You just did what had to be done."

Julie Burleigh nodded to what her man was saying, then added, that the poor people who assumed they qualified and sat around waiting for help wish they had just done it themselves. With a tractor, they tackled the hard jobs, cleaning and clearing, tossing and throwing. It was worth it to both. "For the tsunami, they [government] were there," Burleigh says, "but all of sudden, the people in the United States need help and it wasn't there." Then she talked about what Texas and Louisiana being neighbors should've meant in Washington.

"I thought he'd [Bush] be there with everything he could find to help his home state. And Louisiana, being on the edge of Texas, we could suck a little bit off." We laughed at her geography. "Born and raised down here," Mr. Burleigh picked up the mantle, "your heart's down here, you really have to feel it down deep in your heart. If I had my heart in my hand, where would I put it? Right back on my lot in Cameron." These were the kind of plain people with extraordinary lives who drew me to outdoor chats, talks in tents and trailers, discussions and disagreements about divorce, love, marriage and race. Thank God I was sucked into the eye of their *personal* hurricanes.

The Burleighs had always contemplated the 'what if' and decided to cross that bridge Rita built with stipulations. They both said if his dad's house was gone, the business was wiped out, and their house destroyed, they were "out of here." Worried about what they would find, two of the three did happen. The longtime Burleigh home was gone, the business the elder man built up with his own two hands had been demolished, but the house where Julie and Kirk grew to love one another as a young couple to present day, was still standing.

"You can't run from life," he says. Amazing statement, considering just moments before entering the trailer, his wife had said, "I'm not going to run." This was the completeness people crave, a marriage of hearts and minds. So alike, so together, ready to protect one another for the right to live and die where they choose.

"People say 'How could God do this to us?'" Julie Burleigh remembered overhearing comments at a Wal-Mart. Her answer,

"God didn't do this to us, God maybe woke us up and said, 'Hey, we take things for granted.' It took this to wake us up." The door flung open again. We paused like old people in rockers on the front porch to see who'd come to sit with us. A silver-haired woman announced to Burleigh, "All these men need badges." At first, Burleigh told the group she couldn't do it right then because I was there. Her husband and I agreed to chat while she went to work.

"These are firemen from Lake Charles, they've been good enough to come down and help us out. They all live in Calcasieu Parish just north of us. We've had firemen from all over the country—West Virginia, the Carolinas, everywhere." As they took seats, Burleigh keyed some information into the computer and continued talking, "We have 275 caskets right now on the side of us in the multipurpose building that we're having to rebury." *What? Caskets?*

Real caskets were washed up, by Rita, out of their original burial sites, out of the ground, out of cemeteries. It took time to identify the ones they'd located at that point. The process called for notifying families, putting the bodies/remains in new caskets, remarking the sites and burying again. "We're still missing up to 70 bodies that have not been found yet, are somewhere in the marsh or water. We still have 100 that aren't identified coming from way back."

Zeb Johnson, the man who headed up the daunting project believed a few of the caskets were actually washed back in by another girl named Audrey. "Testing for DNA is expensive," another route that would speed up the identification process. But where would Cameron get that kind of money? Burleigh was a professional juggler who could multitask at a carnival. She looked at us from across the room.

"Joyce, why don't you talk to these guys?" she pointed to the firefighters.

TWENTY-TWO

"Who wants to be first?" I asked the volunteers to *volunteer.* By the looks on their faces, you'd swear the woman doing the courting was a two-headed, bug-eyed monster who ate men for dessert after interviewing them. I was back in Newton County and none of them knew what was so funny. They were worse than my high school football players.

"Come sit right here for one second," I pointed at my selection, which was followed by wild laughter from the chorus of colleagues. Someone said, "Man you like to talk, go ahead." I wanted 26-year old Jason Hinton because he already had a badge from a previous tour of duty. Hinton looked like a kid about to get immunized. He bravely took furniture men dubbed "the chair," another George Strait hit.

"People needed help. We'd expect them to come help us if anything ever happened. We're all in it together." Hinton reminded me that Lake Charles had suffered too. Another reason the single firefighter wanted to volunteer was he felt sure Rita was "the forgotten hurricane." Hinton was nervous, fidgeted a bit in the chair, then added, "We're so close to Cameron, a lot of us fish in this area and it was pretty tragic." He'd heard all the handed down stories of Audrey. "With this one, with Rita, there's nothing left. Audrey killed people, Rita killed property." Enough said.

"Hi, who are you?" I didn't wait for the next volunteer firefighter to step up on his own volition. In my finest Texas twang, I coaxed the next man to take Hinton's place in front of me. More cat calls and laughs. The man I singled out just stared at me like the microphone was some kind of weapon. Following his heart, he refused my invitation. I urged like one of the drag characters from the long-running *Tuna Christmas,* "Come on in, come on, please, have a seat right here."

Others egged him on as my patience petered out. "I'm just gone snatch me some men, somebody come on." From across the room, Julie Burleigh yelled, "Go ahead." She needed more time to enter each man into the Cameron Camp system that tracked the identities of volunteers, residents and contractors.

"Give him a piece of candy," someone suggested. "He'll talk, he'll talk," another firefighter joked. Finally, Brandon Conner approached the chair opposite mine, "Better ask me one question at a time, because ADD is tough." *Oh, a wise guy.* "Don't give me that," I was used to mothering men his age. Both he and Hinton were handsome pages from the annual calendar of hot firefighters.

24-years old and pretending to be shy, I started to slap him, as I often threatened my kids, "into the middle of next week." Conner was almost the same age as my oldest and had the same name as my youngest. I was definitely back in Newton County. Conner had been with the department three years, gave short answers, and like the others, had "good home training." Conner ended every sentence with "ma'am." When I couldn't get anything out of him, I changed the drill. Plus he was being ribbed the entire time I pounded him with questions.

"Give me an artist," I pushed when he offered something generic about listening to all kinds of music. A whisper from behind us, "He listens to Merle Haggard." Conner also kept trying to turn the questions back on me, which prompted more motherly directives, "Stop trying to interview the interviewer."

It was an off day for these men. The fact that they were spending free time in a parish that had so little and needed so much told me all I needed to know. Mainly, I had my answers without anyone saying a word. I was just having fun. "The way I look at it," Conner started, "I feel this is people's homes and it's great that so many want to return." That was his longest response. His most meaningful was three words, "To help out." Then Connor gave a dissertation on hurricane destruction being "the nature of the beast" and warned it will happen again.

"Who wants to be next? I know I'm picking on everybody…"Again, silence. No takers. "Charles is next," the lone female volunteer in the group ordered. "Where you from?" Conner didn't want to vacate the hot seat. I answered him, but had my sights on the older firefighter. "What's your last name Charles?" He hesitated, then responded in a muffled voice, "King." I had my hook and showed no shame in using it, "Come on, we might be related."

He spoke louder to such an idiotic notion, "No, no, we're not related." More laughter and prodding, then an answer to a pretend question. "He likes to ride motorcycles." *Good, now be quiet.* Someone else pointed to a more willing subject, "This one is from New Jersey." I gave Charles King a pass, for the moment.

"Okay, come on Mr. East Coast." As the next man walked up, Conner exited the chair. Both men received jovial applause from the gallery. I had cast my net for a man who flatly said no, twice, leaving me with one thought.

As I sat there, King eyed me, sure the victory was his. I remembered an old movie, *Adventures in Babysitting,* where a blues singer detained the bad guys who chased the youthful babysitter and her charges. Albert Collins stopped the mafia-looking dudes with his guitar and one sentence, "Nobody leaves this place without singing the blues." I kept my eye on King and pretty much decided nobody would "leave this trailer without talking to me."

27-year old Daniel Paladin was born in Monmouth County, New Jersey and had lived in Louisiana five years. Three of those were spent working for the Lake Charles Fire Department, of which he was very proud. "What kind of route leads from New Jersey to Louisiana?" I asked. The cutup crew beat Paladin to the punch, "A woman." Serious laughs. "Yeah, that's what got me, a woman. My wife is a native." When I asked how they met, the same pranksters spoke again, "In a bar."

Paladin has made brave adjustments being the only male in a family of women. His eyes lit up when he talked about Chris, his wife, and their two daughters, ages three and one, Imogene and Analise, respectively. The rest of our conversation went like this:

"You feel like a Louisianan now?"

"Trying to convert," a co-worker helped out.

"Yeah, I'm getting there, yes ma'am." (Paladin was more southern than he knew.)

"Why are you here today?"

"My whole family has been, basically, in the public service sector, between police and fire. My dad is a police officer, my mom is a police officer. Six uncles were all police officers and my dad was also a fire chief."

"Are you proud of what you do?"

"Yes ma'am."

"So am I. Thank you."

To that, Paladin actually blushed and relinquished his seat for another interviewee. "Who's next?" I decided to let the remaining firefighters toss for the privilege. "Charles King," they yelled out. King again expressed his disdain for talking into a palm-sized Sony minidisk. I didn't dare insult him or purr at him anymore, for I knew why King didn't want to talk. Had seen it before. These men were humble, modest, hard-working fathers, husbands, ordinary citizens who didn't ask to walk into a trailer on their off day and find some stranger waiting to stick a microphone in their faces. It was intimidating, to say the least. No one moved to sit in "the chair." Burleigh kept creating new badges for the men.

Out of the blue, Jason Hinton surprised us, "I got a special birthday too." He was off mike. "Come back over here," I gestured. He sat down with one condition, "I get a free copy of this book." Hinton sat a second time to reveal his "special birthday" was June 27th, the anniversary of Hurricane Audrey. "Thank you Jason."

In unison, two firefighters chanted, "Charles King, Charles King." As badly as King wanted to dash out, like Josh Alfred who kept eluding me in Newton, my Lake Charles offensive line wasn't about to let that happen. King was outnumbered and there was no escape from the long lost Dallas cousin.

"K-I-N-G," one of the men playfully spelled it for the record. "Thanks, but I know that one," I smiled. Slowly, King made his way to the chair, mumbling something about the interview not being necessary. "Come on now," I urged, "don't be mean." I soon had my theory confirmed on why King didn't want to talk.

Older than the other men, he was 42 and divorced. The father of 17-year old Alex was visibly concerned that whatever he told me, in front of the men, might be misconstrued or used as ammunition later. King's tenure and title should've trumped that—he was nearly 11 years with the department and a captain.

"Mr. King, why are you in Cameron today?"

"Well, it's kind of a long story, we don't have that much time."

"Give me the Cliff Notes version."

"We started out helping the people from New Orleans," he says, "in shelters and stuff like that. A few weeks later, the tables turned on us and we were in the same predicament." King was sincere. There was a duality to his voice and tone that emitted both hope and hurt. The captain didn't want his emotions to betray him. They very nearly did when he defined a feeling of "being hit twice."

He spoke methodically, the selection of words precise and predatory. While the other men more joked than anything else, King's demeanor was the real McCoy, on target with, I suspected, *their* deepest innermost feelings. It hurt like hell to see Cameron down. How could Lake Charles be up and running when a close neighbor, a sister-parish, months after Rita, couldn't even manage to stand?

Having so few Americans believe Rita was a serious storm just hit King like the burning building good men never give up on saving. They bring more water. Fight harder to knock the blaze down. "Really, you'd have to see it to believe it," he shook his head, "and the media's not covering it." All he could remember was a week or two, "That was it." Cameron was old news. So was Lake Charles.

"Yeah, I feel that we've been looked over some, but that's the way it is," he says. "You don't hear anything about Rita." I thanked King for talking with me. Never told him that because of his courage and willingness to sit in that chair, another Louisiana memory pricked at my heart. Damn. Rita unearthed memories from last year and decades before. I saw Percy Johnson through and through occupying the Cameron space across from me.

King, while it shouldn't matter for any discussion on Cameron, is a black man. Johnson was a name from my childhood in Louisiana, one of the original plaintiffs in a lawsuit that resulted in the integration of the Shreveport Fire Department. Johnson was also the first black fireman promoted to the double-rank of Instructor and Captain. He was one of the handsomest men I'd ever seen. In Louisiana or anywhere. Of course, I was just a kid, a girl with a crush. He was tall, dark and intelligent, you knew it instantly from hello. He treated people with such kindness and care that a hobo or drunk might as well have been royalty. What did I know? I was just a kid. The man was a hero to little squirts like me. Most of the people at the church we were both members of, also looked up to him. Johnson had a motorcycle, he had taken my older sister riding. I was too little. He was different. His heart was beautiful, it matched a spirit tailor made for saving lives. And he was always nice to me and my family. We were proud to know the man.

Some years later, married and raising my own family, I was in a Houston newsroom, working for a Westinghouse station, checking *The Associated Press* newswire when a familiar name rolled across the page. It was my husband's birthday. September 1984. A bulletin had just come in from Shreveport. Percy Johnson had entered a burning building. He never came out. There was an explosion. Thick black smoke took forever to go white.

I broke down and sobbed in the newsroom. Three days later, Captain Johnson became the first Shreveport firefighter to die in the line of duty in more than 40 years.

I saw his face, happy and handsome, a man I thanked God for making. We don't get enough heroes as kids or adults. So when a real one comes along, we, none of us forget their bravery and willingness to walk into the fire.

The cheering section nudged the next man toward me, "Get on the seat." Laughter was indeed a good way to keep the heartbreak at bay. More than that, it was just good clean fun, therapeutic for what ailed all Louisianans in that room.

"How are you today?" I asked 39-year old Reginald Larkins who had an adorable baby face. He and wife, Michelle, were raising three children, Courtney, 15, Tamara, 10, and Reginald, Jr., who was seven. "Katrina was more like, the people needed help and we needed to help them." Larkins was straightforward, like the decision to put in hours on days off. "With Rita, it was more like shock, 'Oh my goodness, it happened to us too.'"

Larkins had a working man's good life, the family he loved and protected, and eight years with the department. "I've just made captain," he talked some about job duties and community service, then asked a question of his own. "Where's our help?" Larkins didn't like complaining. Nothing in him defined a man who did much of that, yet the frustration kept creeping in. "We're used to helping and now we need help, it's totally different."

The Fitchburg, Massachusetts native has lived in Louisiana since he was six-years old. He smiled, "They still call me Yankee." Before leaving the witness stand, Larkins testified that pre-Rita, there were more cliques of people who stayed with their own. "After Rita, there was an obvious need to learn more about your neighbor, help your neighbor, walk in his or her shoes." Larkins believed that strife gave survivors no choice except to come together.

Background chatter in the trailer was more intense as everyone discussed strategy and what needed to be done first. I interviewed five firefighters from Lake Charles, but seven people, a numerical fact that had not escaped my notice, came in the door together. *Seven people entered Trailer Number Seven.* A man who had said nothing the entire time, just mostly smiled, wondered if I would ask him to participate. I beckoned for the lone man wearing a suit to join me.

A quiet dignity, his age, and something about Gurjet Kohli, told me he wasn't with the Lake Charles Fire Department. "No, no, no, I'm a physician." The 50-year old native Indian lived in Alexandria, Louisiana. "The camp needed a doctor and we rotate." Kohli was being paid by the state agency that picked up the tab. Doctors volunteered for the program. Kohli did some of everything for firefighters, workers, contractors, and "anyone in the parish" who needed help. Minor injuries. Immunizations. Advice on illnesses.

"We're part of the public health department so it's more about that." Kohli had put in five "very humbling" days that reminded him of the movie *M*A*S*H.* Then Kohli laughed, "But we've got more equipment. I've worked all my life in these kinds of environments. For me, you figure, electricity is a blessing."

Before Rita, Kohli had only seen the aftermath of a Category One storm and was stunned by what he saw in Cameron Parish. "It was big, it is big." Kohli has shared much of his experience with wife, Aditi, and colleagues from all over. They have a 20-year old son, Aditya, translated, it means "son of Aditi."

"I was born in India, did all my education there and worked in Africa for awhile." Kohli was employed by Huey P. Long Charity Hospital before traveling back to India where he developed medical software. As a physician, Kohli had experienced, firsthand, numerous conditions, but never anything like Rita's aftermath in Cameron. He repeated, "This is big, it is big." Then Kohli pointed to the woman behind him, my seventh man, "I was just talking to Dorothy here and she lost everything, her house and everything. She has been all over the world too."

Burleigh was knee deep in work. People streamed in and out of the trailer in need of help or coffee or a few kind words. Her husband, a real Cajun comedian, had slipped me a piece of paper while I was interviewing firefighters. I almost fell off my own chair when I read what he had written. "KATRINA MADE ME A DEMOCRAT!" Kirk Burleigh came and sat next to me again.

As we talked, volunteers with new ID badges left. I thanked each for allowing me the privilege of "interviewing" them. Just meeting them was a great honor. The men had made jokes, downplayed their involvement and didn't want any credit for the work of responding. Then Burleigh gave an explanation for the changed political affiliation.

"I was in Lake Charles yesterday and I was behind a vehicle with that," Burleigh says he read 'KATRINA MADE ME A DEMOCRAT' on a bumper sticker. We laughed and fell deeper into a joint comedy club routine. I asked if he'd heard of the famous East Texas t-shirts some residents had donned with "FEMA" written across the front and what some people thought it stood for. "No, what?" Nobody knew what we were laughing at so hard, "Fix Everything My Ass."

I loved to listen to Julie and Kirk Burleigh talk. Their Cajun voices had character, tough and tender. It was nice to hear the pronunciation of certain words, minus the hard R, like the way they both said "Lake Challes" and "New Ah-leans." It carried me home. Burleigh looked over at his wife. If he didn't come to the trailer-office, they rarely got to see each other after Rita. He watched her with a pleasing glow, "I've seen her sick as a dog and still go out and help people." She still amazed this man after 30 years.

Burleigh glanced up and caught both of us staring at her. The husband was paying compliment after compliment about her love for kids, their coaching baseball 20 years, and how she showed up for work every morning at seven and didn't quit until late in the evening. The couple exchanged a secret look between them, an 'I miss you' kind of brief exchange. Then she gave an order, "Joyce, you need to talk to her too."

Dorothy Carter was the 7th person in the group of volunteers who came in together. The 49-year old woman did not work for the Lake Charles Fire Department or the state. However, like the others, she initially offered gentle protests, "No, no." I looked at the long hair coming from underneath a baseball cap and a feminine toughness that equaled little time for sitting still. Carter was used to being on the move.

"Come and just talk to me for one quick second," I fudged. She knew better and told me so. "There is no such thing, and there's no quick second when you start talking to me." Carter was a story, anyone could look at her and tell. She had outwitted some hard knocks, believed in working, paying taxes, doing for herself, helping those who needed it. A second later, she confirmed part of the external truth.

"I was born in Georgia, I've been here 16 years," she started. The volunteer firefighter was a resident of Cameron Parish, the town of Oak Grove. Her department: Grand Chenier. Carter talked fast, her words excited more by the lady she sought to defend against—Rita.

"Total destruction of the area," she explained how unbelievable the sight was to anyone who came back. "How much everyone lost." Homes. Cattle. Property. "Their whole lives were uprooted and they are completely devastated." I noticed a defense mechanism in how Carter kept saying "they" and "their" instead of "we" or "us."

"People who've gone through Hurricane Audrey and Hurricane Rita," she sounded incredulous, "and they're willing to come back. They still want to come back, but everything is so slow." Carter pointed out weather trivia, "They have a major hurricane here every 48 years." She listed 1919, 1957 and 2005. Why should people come back and try again when they've lost everything? Carter shot back, "They have their land, and this is their home." When I directly asked about her situation, Carter's facial expression lost a smidgen of its toughness.

"Well, I'm here and I'm going to rebuild. If it happens again, I'm going to rebuild again." There were tears. Carter willed them away. Not today her eyes seemed to bulk up and harden. The married mother of two daughters, 24-year old Nina, and 19-year old Kumiko, was in the Merchant Marines for 20 years. That explained the world travel and gutsy veneer. She was in good shape. I couldn't see Carter inactive for long periods. She craved work, an honest day's labor.

"I do this on my own time, I do not get paid," Carter was one of 20 volunteer firefighters before Rita came through. In 2006, Carter was one of two who worked on a regular basis. "It's myself and Mark LeBeouf, my fire chief." Carter and LeBeouf have maintained all the trucks, made sure they're serviced and ready to roll.

"No one's willing to help, they're volunteers and they're crying, 'We're not getting paid so we're not going to do it.'" Carter was angry and disappointed, a combustible mix for a proud woman unaccustomed to begging people to do what they've promised. "Does that break your heart?" I asked. Her voice was more agitated, higher and strained, "Yeah, it does." She added, "This is their community, like mine, and I'm willing to give all the time I've got to be able to do it."

Despite water that filled her eyes, Carter never dropped one visible tear. Yet I knew this woman was crying on the inside, aching, wanting, waiting for more people to reinvest in Cameron Parish. She was disciplined as any solider I'd ever seen, yet there was also a very feminine side. She was a wife and mother and seemed slightly embarrassed to admit, "I never see my husband, he rarely sees me." Carter explained "Neil is also a Merchant Marine," one who was busy preparing to return to an assignment aboard a ship. She wasn't sure where.

Merchant Marines often work for private contractors on tankers, freighters, wherever they're needed. The job sometimes took Neil Carter away for up to six months at a time. The couple communicated by phone. Email mostly. It was more difficult when she performed the same kind of grueling labor. They, literally, were two ships that passed in the night. "It takes a special person to be able to deal with someone being gone a lot." Her husband wasn't there to lean on. "He was in Ohio when Rita hit, so I had to pack up everything on my own."

"Have you even taken a breath?"

"No, no, I've been going the whole time, nonstop, but it is also what keeps me going."

"Why not stop?"

"I don't have time to get depressed. It might overwhelm me and that might be the reason I'm not willing to stop."

Burleigh finally finished entering volunteers into the Camp

Cameron system and stood over Carter. "This is my awesome worker, *she's* what keeps me going." When Burleigh hit a brick wall, she called the fireball.

In the months since Rita, Dorothy Carter has lost a lot of weight but her energy level has skyrocketed. "She won't admit it," Burleigh smiled, "but I kind of made her mad. When she went to Abbeyville to pick up a bunch of supplies from a group over there that was donating, she [Carter] jumped across the back of my truck and fractured two ribs." Carter was "hardheaded" because she wouldn't have the ribs taped up or looked at. "Finally, one night when the Kentucky firemen were here, they talked her into going in for treatment." Even then, Carter was determined to drive the truck in case there was an emergency she needed to respond to.

"Just in case," Burleigh facetiously began, "there's a fire in the middle of the night, she was going to jump up with two cracked ribs and go help fight this fire." Sure enough, Carter ended up driving the truck, in so much pain, she could barely shift and steer. "I could hardly move, I was in bad shape," Carter interjected. So there she was on the streets of Cameron Parish working, responding, blowing and going, just generally being "hardheaded" and stubborn. That's when Burleigh pulled rank.

"I called her boss, the fire chief, and said, 'Dorothy's hurt and has fractured two ribs trying to mandate the fire truck and keep it going. She needs to go home and take medicine and go to bed.'" Armed with two large firemen, Burleigh went to "Dorothy's place" and "retrieved the fire truck," essentially swiping the keys, taking them so her friend would stop long enough to rest for one minute. "She wasn't happy with me, but wouldn't admit it," Burleigh could finally laugh about hiding those keys.

"Well, I did stay home three days, the pain is still there but I can get around a lot better," Carter says. "She was exhausted," Burleigh seemed to be reminding her "awesome worker" once more. "She has worked so hard for this parish and for these people and they don't see all of that." Like Carter, Burleigh had "a big problem" with the volunteer firefighters who insisted the nightmare Rita left wasn't their responsibility because they weren't being paid. This touched off another nerve in Carter, "They weren't paid before either!"

Listening to Carter and Burleigh inspired people to volunteer, they were human magnets. "We're not here for the glory, we're here to help people," Burleigh says. She won't ever leave Cameron behind. "Your life is here, your family is here, your heritage is here. If the hurricanes come again tomorrow, it can't wash away the mental and spiritual connection to home." In the Amen corner, husband, Kirk, was savoring the time they were actually in the same room together, reiterating every redeeming word.

"The greatest feeling we've had since we came back—my wife and I—when we woke up the next morning, after that first dark, rough night, was a fresh cup of coffee in your hand and you walk out and are looking at *your* yard, *your* trees, *your* property." Kirk Burleigh didn't see the tear I wrestled with at the firm manly way he said, "my wife and I." That nearly made me lose it. They were, they are, a team. Life in Cameron was "a warm security blanket" that just wrapped itself around them. I was in the middle of a movie I hoped would never end. The door to the trailer opened again.

"I noticed she was recording, [pointing to me] that's okay, I'll come back." As if on cue, being around Burleigh meant I had to be more aggressive to keep up. I gave the familiar invitation, "Just sit right here, in this chair, for one second." They all laughed. Except Kristoffer Barikmo, which is pronounced Christopher.

"I teach high school at an all-girls Catholic high school," Barikmo was in charge of a group from Kansas City, Missouri. The 27-year old taught social studies, history, and government. He saw Cameron as a unique teaching tool. The students were on Spring Break and Barikmo had also given up personal time he might've spent with wife Kelly. His greatest wish was that the students be forever impacted by what they saw and by what they did.

"The person that organized our trip did some work in Louisiana when she was in the AmeriCorp program. After the hurricane hit, she knew this was an area that needed help because it was so hard hit. You see a lot about New Orleans and Katrina, but you don't see much about Rita and what happened in Creole and Cameron." The group from Notre Dame de Sion High School knew Cameron Parish was the right choice.

"Every year we do a Spring Break service trip," Barikmo says, "and once the hurricane came through, everybody kind of knew, this was where our trip would be."

There were nine students and two chaperones. "They're all sitting out in the van now," Barikmo looked over his shoulder. The juniors and seniors were anxious to learn where they would work that day. Hard, backbreaking labor. Manual labor. No computers. No cell phones. No handheld games. No iPods.

"They all do nightly reflection on the day's activities," their teacher beamed with pride. "Last night, there was a lot of angst in the group. They were just saying that it [cleanup] looked, almost, unconquerable, standing in another person's life, looking around, not knowing where to start."

This was, Barikmo felt, a perfect opportunity to teach a lesson not written down in any book. He told his students that the work would be accomplished by taking it "piece by piece." They thought that an oversimplification but moved forward when he issued the real challenge: "I asked them, 'How are we going to tell the story of Cameron Parish?'" Barikmo cautioned students not to answer out loud. He didn't need verbal responses, but preferred they ponder the conundrum as they returned to Kansas City.

"That's the most important part," Barikmo told them, "remembering the people we've met, remembering the places we've worked and remembering the things that we've done." He felt strongly that living testimonials from others who had seen Cameron up close would make believers of Americans unaware of the suffering. "In all my classes, I talk about how much we need to teach everybody how to be citizens, and not just citizens of our community, but citizens of the world."

The bulletin board in Barikmo's classroom, where students file in and out everyday, has an important question posted. "WHAT IS YOUR MARK GOING TO BE ON THE WORLD?" We thought about the binding hurricane that had brought us together in a trailer. More volunteers needed Burleigh to come meet them. They wanted badges and directions and work orders. Amazingly, one was a group of carpenters, sent by a more famous, *itinerant* carpenter.

I met the nine students. They got out of the van and talked some about what Spring Break would forever mean in 2006. Kirk Burleigh was the designated photographer in charge of several cameras. Before we said our goodbyes, his wife put a thick photo album in my hands. It was their personal recorded account of Rita's fury and aftermath. Burleigh hugged me, "You'll need it when you're writing."

She opened the book to one of the pictures, "These are our new duck-hunting bed and breakfast stops." A joke about an open-air structure, once a full-fledged home, pushed out into the middle of a giant marshy field, stuck in a swamp.

"Follow me," Kirk Burleigh knew how much his wife wanted me to see the repairs they'd made to their longtime love nest. We drove a short distance down the road and turned off the highway into their subdivision. They were still living in a trailer a few hundred yards from the house on legs I'd gotten an earlier lesson on.

Final repairs were being made. Burleigh was in the homestretch. We took more photos after I was offered water, Coke, "or something stronger." Burleigh joked that some of the best ideas for inventions were discussed over the grill and a cold beer. A neighbor they both wanted me to meet was standing outside.

Cedric Hebert had one thing to say when I spelled his name, pronounced Ay-bear, correctly, "I'll be damned." To that, I responded, "I'm from Louisiana." *Just don't tell Texas.* "You are?" he looked surprised, then the one-word approval, "Cool." Hebert was right about one thing. Most reporters who haven't logged time in Louisiana can't spell or pronounce names like *Thibodaux, Natchitoches, Opelousas, Plaquemines,* or *Hebert.*

"How old are you?"

"50-ah...37."

January 20, 1954 was the neighbor's true date of birth. We walked some as we talked, canvassing between his property and the new friends who let me in, minus the boards with rigged nails. I saw a salty, haggard look, but there was also something about Hebert like aged scotch, the good stuff. He had muddy eyes that made it hard to tell what color they were. He had the look of a good man who had lived, truly lived.

"Actually, I was born in Lafayette, but I've been down here all my life." Hurricanes were nothing new to Hebert. "I went through Audrey, and eight people drowned in them trees right there," he pointed to the death limbs, "the Millers." The idea was to tie themselves to the trees as a safety precaution, "but they tied themselves too low."

"This storm [Rita] was 10 times worse than Audrey," Hebert took his time between sentences. "Me and my wife lost three properties—her house, which was her mother and father's house, and this is our main house, we got 1 ½ acres there," he motioned to neighboring land in the distance, "and her business." Rebecca Hebert owned an auto parts-mechanic business. "The insurance don't want to pay, they don't want to give us nothing." Then I saw Hebert's eyes. They were tired of all the lies and hoops he wouldn't stand or jump.

For a long time, he didn't say anything. We didn't move from where the earth planted us. "But that's alright, we'll make it." Of everyone I spoke with that day, talking with Cedric Hebert was the most difficult. His eyes were dark and unnerving on some level. Yet, when he trusted you, those same eyes opened wider, welcomed you into his world. He knew I could spell his name. He knew his neighbors were willing to vouch for me so Hebert cut me some slack.

"You're not going to leave this area, are you?"

"Never."

"What do you love about Cameron Parish?"

"The people, the friends," Hebert sighed heavily.

"What would you like the national media to know?"

"I'm an armed guard for the biggest landowner in the parish and I've been catching FEMA people hiding on the back ridge to get out of work. They're not doing what they're supposed to and getting paid $40 an hour and they're hiding, smoking marijuana and drinking beer." I asked if he were absolutely sure this was happening on the "taxpayer dime" and Hebert answered with one word, "Exactly."

Catching contractors wasn't enough to satisfy him. "I'd like 'em to go to jail." So much of his heart could be read in those deep dark smoker's eyes. "We took a lick, then they come down here and spend our tax dollars, that's ridiculous." Another pause. Hebert continued, "I've caught several thieves." The statement out loud was enough to make him mad. Then he bristled at the naïve suggestion I made on having backup to bring the alleged culprits to the attention of law enforcement.

Hebert frowned hard at me, "I don't need no help, I'm Cajun. I'm coon ass. I don't need no help." For a minute, Louisiana gal or not, I forgot where I was. The coon ass remark deposited me right back to the early 1970's and the first time I heard another Cajun use

293

the same hot sauce. It was Gov. Edwin Edwards. He had opened the commencement address at my sister's high school graduation by taking the podium, "I'm proud to be a coon ass!" Then I insulted Hebert again.

"What have you done? Did you let them know that they need to get the hell up out of here?" For several seconds, which felt like minutes, Hebert didn't answer. He studied me and puffed on a cigarette. Then he glared at me some more, unsure about my real motives for recording his every word. After an uncomfortable examination of every inch of my person, from head to toe, and a mental dialogue with self, Hebert finally answered. The verdict was in. "They not gone come back."

It wasn't what he said, but how Hebert phrased it. Like some bodies might be floating around behind us in the marsh. Then he looked at me, his expression unchanged. I should know better, if I was from Louisiana as I had claimed, to continue that line of questioning. "Alright, I won't ask for any details." That was smart, since he hadn't volunteered any. Hebert burned a hole right in the center of my forehead with his hot laser stare.

"Tell me about your legacy here," I redirected the interview-chat. "Well, I like to hunt, I like to fish and this is paradise," Hebert says. Ironically, his 24-year old daughter, Claire Thompson, worked for FEMA. "She was a contractor in Vermilion Parish and they took a lick too, mostly trees, shingles, stuff like that." Hebert says a lot of people are hurting like Cameron, "You don't hear much about Mississippi, all you hear about is New Orleans." We sat down on some steps of the trailer home I'd just been in with Kirk Burleigh.

"She [his daughter] brought five [contractors] of them down here," Hebert paused again, "three of them started crying when they drove up to my house." He was not bitter. But other emotions weren't under such well-managed regulation. Hebert didn't try to conceal or camouflage the anger, disappointment, hurt or sadness. Above all, he was proud to live in Cameron and determined to see her back at full strength someday.

"We can take care of ourselves," his gravelly voice was its most full-bodied, "friends and family."

"Anything else you want me to know?" I asked

"Yeah, can you get me a house?" he flashed a baby smile.

"I wish I could."

"We'll take care of ourselves. It just upsets me…"his voice suddenly stopped, then, "How in the hell are we gonna rebuild?" Hebert continued to smoke. We watched Burleigh go back and forth, working on something, occasionally he would join us. "Look at all these license plates," Hebert pointed to contractors mulling on land adjacent to the ground we were on.

"Montana, Michigan, Colorado, why don't they hire us?" The question dangled like an upside down animal caught in a trap, swinging from Washington to Baton Rouge to Cameron. "I volunteer for the EOC and operate some marsh buggies looking for coffins," Hebert highlighted one example of locals able to do work in the familiar environment of home. "As a matter of fact, we found my sister."

In the background, running up and down the road, were FEMA contractors, independent contractors. We saw them on heavy equipment and in a string of white pickups. We counted vehicles in the parish to do business and make money.

"They got 10 Bobcats from Maine and rented them," Hebert remembered another solid example to bolster his thesis on a depleted local economy. "They don't know the area, they don't know the marsh. All they gotta do is ask us, 'Can you get this thing out of here?'" For a moment, I was lost, not sure what point Hebert was trying to make. Then it was clear, "We'd know what to do, where to go." Instead of asking the locals for help, Hebert painted a distressing picture of waste and paternalism.

"What they did, they stuck two Bobcats in the marsh, ruined 'em, cost taxpayers $13,700 to get 'em out." Hebert likened it to behavior beyond fraud or waste, "Stupidity." My own personal Cajun had no qualms about unleashing his true feelings for those crooked workers who came into Louisiana with superior attitudes, who at the end of the day, "know nothing about Louisiana." Hebert held a frown an uncomfortably long time. It was hard to tell whether he liked a person or not, he took more than a few minutes to decide. But history and love for the state that reared me, told me, intuitively, to stick with the belief that Hebert would never have talked as long as he did, or at all, if he thought there was a phony bone in my brown body.

Long gaps of silence between us made it feel like we had commiserated in some other life or at some previous Ground Zero. "All they got to do is ask us," Hebert admonished the guilty ones, "we been running these marshes all our lives. All they got to do is ask." He looked straight at me, relaxed his thick brow again, "We'll do it for free, but they paying them." No, Cedric Hebert didn't like politics and liars.

"I can't figure it out," his voice crawled like a blues song stuck on pain, "I just don't understand it." Angst from Hebert's soul. He was tough. He was loyal, to Cameron Parish and the life it had afforded him. Burleigh was back at our side making jokes about using my books to prop underneath the leg of an old rickety chair.

"You're a writer?" Hebert's eyes widened some and I could see more color in them. His approval rested in the common bond we shared as artists. Hebert is a fine musician. He knew exactly what it meant to follow a dream and chase words that few believe in, until they're bestsellers.

A documentary had already been filmed about his life, the MOE-D BAND, and the fantastic music they performed. But Rita, destroyer of so many good things, put the film's open on hold. Hebert has every confidence the documentary will get its moment in the cinematic sun. His passion for music that spoke to the real flavor of Louisiana is the best gift Hebert could possibly give to others, keep for self. A happy man came out when lyrics and harmony were topics. He suddenly disappeared to go do something.

"This is my last one," Hebert handed me a music CD, titled *MOE-D TOO,* with an attention-getting cover, artwork, that if available in more music stores, would surely draw new fans to it. A little boy has no pants on, white socks, a royal blue t-shirt, yes, that same tarp color, his back is turned, while he pees on a tree. Nedia Trahan was the artist listed. Thanks, for what looked, to me, like a Louisiana sundown in the marshes, where boys will be boys.

"Are you sure?" Hebert had caught me off guard with the gift. He deliberately chose not to answer. Those eyes struck again. When I let out a wide ear-to-ear Mary Tyler Moore expression, Hebert zapped me with more warmth, "You sure got pretty teeth." I resealed the piano face and tried not to blush. People don't usually talk about my teeth while they're out in the open like that. Unless it's my dentist.

Studying my newest addition to a thousand CD catalogue, (I own everything from Prince to Barbra Streisand, from the Rolling Stones to Anita Baker, from classical to country, from blues to gospel.) I couldn't locate Hebert in the group of six men on the flip side of the disc. A dark-haired heavier man he acknowledged was him in the photo didn't much resemble the person standing in front of me. Rita had taken 40 pounds off Hebert, the hurricane diet plan called for stress and very little sleep. Throw in worry and the pounds just fall off. I liked Hebert and his dry wit. We predicted a knock-down rocking shocking comeback. After all, MOE-D had opened for another singer I liked—Merle Haggard, who was a big fan and supporter. They'd definitely be back with tunes I now know all the words too, songs like *Chickens On The Run, See Ya Later Alligator, Jai Te O Bal,* and *Old Fool In The Mirror.*

"Man, she locked the door when she got out," Burleigh thought it was funny that I hit the keyed lock when exiting the Durango. "Ain't nothing gone happen to you out here," both men agreed and I knew it too. "Habit," I explained the automatic procedure that always accompanied getting out of a car in Dallas, at malls, at home, at grocery stores, at the bank, at the post office. "I never leave my car unlocked." We popped the hatch on the navy blue boat where I had the last few copies of *GROWING UP SOUTHERN* in a box. I gave Hebert a copy. He examined the 1968 Civil Rights era-photo of a nine-year old girl who still wore the same bang. Now I had Hebert off guard.

"For some reason," I showed the middle-aged teeth again, "white men just love me." Hebert and Burleigh looked at each other and cracked up, to which, the coon ass, not to be outdone, fired right back, "I'll bet they do." They knew, just as I hadn't wanted to leave Julie Burleigh back at Trailer Number Seven, I didn't want to part from their company either. We sat a few more minutes trading stories. Our conversations soothed a state sitting amidst the ruins left by a hurricane named Rita others may have forgotten. We never will.

One story Hebert told was about Bubba Boudreaux. The name sounded familiar, like a Texas-Louisiana identity fusion. According to Hebert, his good friend was the first "white" musician to ever play at The Apollo Theatre in Harlem.

Boudreaux had been denied access when the people in charge

determined there were enough clubs and venues for white boys to play at. Why invade The Apollo too? Apparently, the singers Boudreaux backed, along with the band he played with, felt much differently. Percy Sledge, known around the world for his signature song, *When a Man Loves a Woman,* flatly stated that if Bubba wasn't coming, he wasn't singing. Ditto for a man named James Brown, who later was crowned the indisputable Godfather of Soul. Basically, Brown added that if Bubba didn't play, he didn't stay. Boudreaux was in. And the white boy could jam.

"You've never seen an MRE?" Burleigh asked in wonder as I prepared to leave. No, I really hadn't. He ducked into the P. O. D. trailer and came out with two brown packages. "Here," he smiled, "they made this especially for people down here." The ready-to-eat meal was No. 22, "Jambalaya." Burleigh hugged me goodbye. Hebert looked at me one last time and turned away. We did not hug. Our hearts connected.

An ancient ferry was the slow boat that allowed me to sit in the car and stare out at the port's murky waters. I cherished new friends who anointed a less lonely life with gifts of music, food, and redemption. I had not known how strong my love for Louisiana was until Katrina and Rita attempted her murder.

TWENTY-THREE

Instead of a handshake, this time I embraced Paul Rainwater as my friend. Instead of a hotel suite on a Sunday afternoon, this time I was welcomed to his turf, Lake Charles City Hall. It was Wednesday, April 12, 2006. Officials were busy with early voting for fellow Louisianans who wanted to cast their ballots for New Orleans mayor.

"Our clerk of court, Lynn Jones, is just really working hard with the folks in New Orleans to do everything we can here. I think it says a lot about them wanting to come back to Louisiana, to vote at home." There were chartered buses from Dallas, Shreveport, Houston, and other cities.

The first time I ever laid eyes on Rainwater, the Lake Charles city administrator had arrived with a brown cache of documents to bolster a thesis on hurricane priorities. The first item was a four-page letter addressed to "The Honorable Mary Landrieu." At the bottom of that page was the Lake Charles city motto, "Cherishing the Past, Embracing the Future." A delegation, including Rainwater, was headed to Washington, not 24 hours after our March meeting, to present their case in person.

"Dear Senator Landrieu: First and foremost, we from Southwest Louisiana want to thank you for your support in our efforts to recover from Hurricane Rita. You have been very vocal in your effort to help us and we sincerely appreciate it. This letter is intended to give you information to support your efforts and remind you that we stand ready to work with you in this effort. However, it has become very evident that others in our nation's capital have forgotten about the destruction that occurred as a result of that storm." *Forgotten.*

"We are not asking them to take our word for it. Just this week Governor Rick Perry testified in Washington, D. C. and according

299

to AP wire reports he requested Texas be given $2 billion dollars, because "states slammed by Katrina are getting more generous help than his state, *which bore the brunt of Hurricane Rita."* Governor Perry's significant funding request indicates his belief that Hurricane Rita was a destructive storm."

The third paragraph began, "We do not intend to compete with our Texas neighbors for recovery money." Washington has the following numbers from Louisiana:

- 19,000 homes or 25% of housing stock was destroyed [Calcasieu only]
- Another 35% of homes were damaged there
- Power was out for up to three weeks in some areas
- Half the trees in Calcasieu Parish were destroyed/damaged
- Lake Charles Regional Airport suffered more than $20 million in damages and the passenger terminal damaged beyond repair
- Chennault International Airport, home to Northup Grumman, suffered $40 million in damages and was closed four weeks
- Damage to other aviation industry businesses is approximately $90 million
- Port of Lake Charles (12th largest in the country) had to be closed, resulting in supply disruptions to production facilities. Damages of $50 million have been reported; the community has lost hundreds of jobs in its petrochemical complex
- During power outage, six casinos were shut down. Harrah's two riverboat casinos and hotel were damaged beyond repair; 2,000 jobs were lost
- Damage to the educational system, including McNeese State University and Sowela Technical College, along with the four-week closure of all public schools, cost Calcasieu Parish about $57 million dollars

- Parish-wide highway damage, an early estimate, stood at $20 million

"Cameron Parish, our sister parish to the south, was totally dev-astated. Although there was no loss of life, Cameron suffered the loss of a way of life. Approximately 90 percent of the homes in Cameron, the parish seat, were destroyed. Other communities suffered similar or worse fates. The major industries—oil, agriculture, seafood and tourism—were destroyed. It will take years for the residents to recover. And Southwest Louisiana will never be fully recovered until Cameron is rebuilt and back in business again."

The framers of this heartfelt letter to Sen. Landrieu went on to describe in vivid detail an example of lost revenue for Cameron Parish, dependent on four wildlife refuges. 300,000 people a year visit the Creole Nature Trail alone. Rita severely damaged all four wildlife habitats and people lost a way to put food on their tables.

Unemployment in Calcasieu Parish more than tripled from 5.3% in 2004 to 16.2% in November 2005, another reality that pushed elected officials in the region to sign their names to the letter and hope it wouldn't be misconstrued. "Hurricanes Rita and Katrina have impacted 30-40% of the economy of our state," jumped from the final page, as the letter wound to its end. Eight signatures represented the masses—Randy Roach, mayor of Lake Charles; Willie Mount and Gerald Theunissen, both of the Louisiana State Senate; Chuck Kleckley, Elcie Guillory, Ronnie Johns, Dan Morrish and Brett Geyeman, all of the Louisiana House of Representatives.

Other interesting papers in the thick file included a piece from *AMERICAN PRESS EDITORIAL*. It was titled, "Hey, Congress, how about us?" The date was March 10, 2006. Here's an excerpt: "Why do Louisiana Gov. Kathleen Blanco and Texas Gov. Rick Perry have to go to Washington to beg Congress to send more funds for Hurricane Rita relief? All of this is a stark reminder about how Congress is out-of-touch with what needs to be done to help Southwest Louisiana and Southeast Texas get back on track."

It continued, "Louisiana Seventh District U. S. Representative Charles Boustany, Jr. is aware of the problem with Rita amnesia in Washington. He sent a letter to [Dennis] Hastert and [Nancy] Pelosi when he learned about the congressional visit to New Orleans and Mississippi, urging them to include Southwest Louisiana in their fact-finding tour. Hastert responded in a March 1 letter that he considered including a tour of Southwest Louisiana in their recent visit, but it was not possible."

I was eager to hear if Rainwater and company had made more of a dent in person *after* their Washington visit. "A group of us, our chamber of commerce, parish government, city, some folks from Cameron Parish went with us, and various mayors went to Washington D. C. to visit with, not just our congressional delegation, but we met with Senators Susan Collins, Don Mulvaney, and Dennis Hastert's office."

The Rainwater Review was "mixed." He felt some had extended a warm welcome to them, while others may have gone through the motions. "Sen. Joe Biden, who had been down to Louisiana, two weeks before, met us in Sen. Landrieu's office and we had a really good discussion with him about some things." Other dialogue came across as disturbing and unwarranted.

"One staffer, and I won't say from which office, but it was not from Louisiana," Rainwater verified, "said the rest of Congress feels like 'Louisiana is being a little bit emotional about how it wants to rebuild.'" *Emotional?* The staffer, according to Rainwater, also told the delegation that Washington powerbrokers would need to be convinced Louisianans were using "cerebral analysis" in the rebuilding process.

"That was a little bit upsetting because there's a perception in some congressional offices, on the House and Senate side," Rainwater explained, "that somehow, we're not going to spend the money wisely or that we're going to rebuild in areas that shouldn't be rebuilt." Rainwater is an intelligent man and sincerely committed to doing what is best for the people of Lake Charles and the entire state.

Like Rainwater, I have heard similar concern, in an almost paternalistic tone, as if to suggest Lousy Anna ain't too swift. *Not the sharpest knife in the state drawer.* There must be more than a few people in Washington who have asked behind closed doors, and doors not shut at all, why Louisiana should be trusted to spend billions of dollars.

"They're going to rebuild in Key West if a hurricane hits Florida, they rebuilt San Francisco after the earthquakes. Why the difference with Louisiana?" he asked. Rainwater and Mayor Roach have had many debates over how upsetting it was to hear dialogue bantered back and forth over whether to rebuild at all. Rainwater found it difficult in our second meeting to say some of the things that were on his heart, carefully choosing his words. Not blamefully, just honestly.

"I know the folks from FEMA, most of them are good public servants, but I think Washington D. C.—and I've experienced this before—the further you are away from the problem, the least you understand about what effect you're having on people's lives, the culture, the way of life." Rainwater was like a lawyer pleading for some alternative other than death or the runner-up sentence of forever.

"There's so much discussion about how the levees should be rebuilt or whether or not New Orleans should be rebuilt." His pronunciation of the Crescent City had the right blend of authenticity that only a native is in possession of to season his/her state's business with all the right flavor. *Nawlins should be rebuilt.*

"One of the things that bothers us is we've got some of the largest liquefied natural gas storage facilities in the country, if not the world, here in Southern Louisiana, and they're talking about a levee system that would prevent the rebuilding of much of Cameron Parish." Rainwater repeated a truth from the letter that preceded him to Washington, "Calcasieu Parish and Lake Charles aren't going to fully recover until Cameron recovers because it's part of our economy and our tourism."

While thousands of blue roofs remained in Lake Charles and unemployment was still abnormally high, Rainwater talked about faith, endurance, and people in the struggle. "Congressman Boustany is doing the best he can to make Congress aware of 'Rita amnesia.'" People in Lake Charles, at least in large numbers, are back to some degree of a "normal life," but still shaky. Smaller communities, like Cameron, are filled with self-reliant, caring people who could use more assistance from Washington.

"We've met with some high-level federal recovery officials and they talk the big picture and they don't really have a plan on how to get from A to B." Rainwater's next statement hit hard, "You know what you want to say them Joyce? You want to say [to some officials]

'I'm not stupid.'" Apparently, those with overtly insulting opinions about Louisiana have forgotten that many of the people they're talking with have been in local or state government for much of their careers, understand issues like flood elevation, insurance, banking, housing, free market, "and how capitalism works."

The word "stereotype" was only a few seconds behind. Rainwater believes that what is quaint about the state has probably also worked to hurt the state in the eyes of beholders who don't understand it. "Even people from our own country come in and say things like 'What are parishes? What's this form of government? Why don't *you people* from Louisiana…?'" his voice abruptly stopped in despair. The list of legislative putdowns was endless. The list of everything that's best for Louisiana, many days, was being compiled by people who've never even bothered to step foot in the state. Many who do show up are armed with preconceived notions that are hard to overcome.

Rainwater's comments took me back to those same young men who had changes of heart about dating a woman from Louisiana because she might leave a headless chicken or rooster on their porch, wore garlic to ward off evil and regularly made voodoo dolls of those who wronged me. In all my days of living in Louisiana, I never practiced any of the commonly known stereotypical recipes to injure enemies.

I guessed that my second meeting with Rainwater was peppered by a double dose of frustration and concern. He was sure that no one had questioned his home state when the 256th Brigade Combat Team deployed or when he and other native Louisianans left for duty. The National Guardsman has been to Afghanistan, Iraq and Kuwait, "We're proud U. S. citizens."

One afternoon on the Washington trip, Rainwater recalled lunch at a nice Italian restaurant. "You couldn't help but hear the conversation next to us, they were talking about Louisiana and that it should probably be colonized." The city administrator shook his head. A pitiful thing to have heard while on a mission to rally support for a section of a financially-strapped state that had done so much to aid people in their time of need, only to find itself stabbed by two vicious storms. "That's the attitude of some people, that maybe Louisiana should be a colony instead of a state."

No wonder Rainwater returned with mixed emotions. Yet, he remained upbeat about the future of Calcasieu and Cameron Parishes. "There are some very caring people in the federal government and U. S. Senator Collins from Maine—we had an excellent meeting with her." She not only listened to their concerns, but took notes. Rainwater acknowledged that Sen. Landrieu and Sen. David Vitter have represented Louisiana well and that both care.

"What was inspiring to me [about the Washington meeting] was you had Sen. Collins, a Republican, and Sen. Biden, who's a Democrat, both of them talked very much about what they want to do for Louisianans." Rainwater left convinced that both had "a genuine compassion" for what's happening in the state.

"I think what we're all afraid of is that this is going to be forgotten very quickly." With June 1st right around the corner when we met the second time, Rainwater also had mixed reviews about the approach to public education. "What we've noticed is that FEMA has been doing hurricane awareness at festivals, and I guess that's a really nice thing to do, but I'd rather them be involved in providing housing or helping the person who didn't get their $2,000 expedited assistance, which, by the way, they've cut off." It did seem far-fetched to preach awareness to folk piecing together their lives in the aftermath of back-to-back storms. "You can't go under the mindset that FEMA is going to take care of it for you."

Rainwater says Don Powell, coordinator for federal recovery and rebuilding, was in town the day before my visit. Powell met with city officials, Sen. Vitter and Congressman Boustany and applauded the great job Lake Charles had done in post-Rita recovery. "The mayor has asked him to use it [their plan] as a model of cooperation with FEMA." The reality, Rainwater says, is not all parts of FEMA move slowly.

Rainwater favored keeping what worked and taking a close look at what bogged officials down. For example, the Stafford Act wasn't designed for storms. Mostly, it was created for emergencies of a short-term nature with little room for flexibility. Katrina, Rita and Wilma were big girls who didn't fit well under Stafford guidelines.

"There needs to be accountability at the highest levels, but you also need to create an environment where people can make decisions and be held accountable for them." Then the Rainwater that first attracted me, "Spend the money where you need to spend it to help people." This was the same man who knew it was "the right thing to do" when FEMA stopped paying the bill for 10,000 displaced residents living in area hotels/motels. And the city of Lake Charles picked up the tab, jointly, together, suburbs and all.

"It wasn't just me," Rainwater again humbly pointed out, "it's the mayor, it's a group. But for me personally, it's about service." Besides Mayor Roach, other area mayors who haven't flinched or hesitated when it came to supporting hurricane evacuees include Ron LeLeux of Sulphur, Dudley Dixon of Westlake, David Riggins of Vinton, Margo Racc of Iowa, and Jerry Bell of DeQuincy. Lake Charles has never stood alone.

Whenever we talked about Washington and red tape, Rainwater was on the edge of his seat and used his hands more as he spoke. But when the subject turned to helping people, he often leaned back in his chair, a satisfied man with a wonderful wife and beautiful kids, the blessings mentally counted.

"Our fire chief, David Manuel, said it best, this area has a very strong sense of Christianity, of Christ, and I don't mean just going to church." Rainwater practiced what he called living the walk, not just through words and talk, but very much through actions "paid forward," two words I heard as much as "random acts of kindness" on the long journey. "I think what you saw in this community during the storm, during Katrina, during Rita, after Rita, was the philosophy that we have to take care of the ones who can't take of themselves."

Lake Charles, the 4th largest city in what is sometimes considered "the poorest state in the country," has an undeniable pride in its rich culture and heritage. They have embraced the concept of who neighbor really is. "I'd rather live in this community than any community of a per capita of $135,000 dollars a year and everyone has graduate educations, so what," Rainwater smiled. Content to live in a place where "people care about each other," he recalled stories after Katrina that strengthened a potent truth.

"There was a 12-year old boy that had been separated from his parents. And the crowd was about 10,000," Rainwater started. A state trooper found the child wandering through the throng and brought him to the city administrator. Since a command center was already operational, Rainwater accepted the pint-sized stranger. "It was late at night, I took the little boy, an African American child, and I think this says so much about people. We talk about race and issues of race, this was a little black boy. I brought him in and there were a lot of our firefighters, they were tired and had been out doing medical evaluations and basic triage stuff. Just helping."

Rainwater told firefighters the child was afraid and had lost his parents in the exodus from New Orleans. "They took him and covered him up, asked if he needed anything and told him to get some rest because he'd be safe there." A state senator from Vermilion Parish, Nick Gautreaux, was able to locate a sheriff's deputy who drove the child to Baton Rouge, where he was eventually reunited with his relieved parents.

"Another little boy, three years old, he couldn't tell us anything, so I just took him to a FEMA National Guard." The female military police officer enjoyed her mothering duties but had to get back to more serious work—the line for security was being severely tested with so many people pouring in. "I took him down to our operations center and held him, everyone just showered him with attention. He was such a little sweetheart." Rainwater kept the toddler close as he continued to focus on work.

"Everyone held him. Everyone wanted to hold him, they all wanted to be a part of it." In that group of caregivers and first responders, there were no black firefighters, a fact that never bothered the child, who was African American. Hurricanes crushed the notion that color was prevalent when people needed help. "It's about humanity."

The boy didn't talk much, typical for a baby in a roomful of uniforms and strangers. They were all fussing over him with comfort food like cookies. He was offered two kinds of the sweet treat, but didn't select, so was given a raisin cookie. When the child started picking off the raisins, everyone quickly discovered he would very much prefer chocolate chip. Little things brought out the human connections more common than color.

Besides Sen. Gautreaux, there were too many names to list, many I didn't know, like Representative Ronnie Johns. Others I knew from state history classes, like Landrieu. In Louisiana, theirs was a family many considered a political dynasty. Lt. Gov. Mitch

Landrieu had worked hard after both storms to bring attention to the plight of his fellow Louisianans. His sister was a United States senator, and his father, Moon, was the last white mayor to preside over New Orleans.

There was story after story of people helping people. But there were also negative images that others were more comfortable utilizing to define the whole of Louisiana. Rainwater mentioned an overzealous sheriff, not named but known, who had allegedly fired shots in the air, to warn people fleeing New Orleans not to try and enter his parish.

There was also the story of Richard Cole, the parish tax assessor. "I mean what does a tax assessor have to do with emergency response?" Rainwater laughed. "Nothing. He set up a group of guys that cooked 87,000 meals, along with Sowela, our vocational institute." There was no pay, no promise of reimbursement, just a willingness to feed hungry people. "I know there are compassionate people in D. C., it's hard to see sometime. Down here, there's no room for PR, [public relations] you don't have time for it. You have to take care of people."

The DeQuincy, Louisiana native met his wife, Linda, in college. They have two children, 20-year old Matt, who's in school at Savannah, Georgia, and 16-year old Danielle. He has high hopes for the next generation that will lead Lake Charles and the state. A solid way to invest in their future would be to put back some of the money earned off the coast of Louisiana in the oil and gas industry. Not a popular topic.

"We're working on a housing initiative right now. We've received a million dollars from Conoco-Phillips and $100,000 from Wal-Mart, $150,000 just yesterday from Excel Paralubes, which is a local company here." Rainwater vowed to keep collecting private dollars and leverage the money with federal funds to build affordable housing.

"The people of this area are inspiring. They gave food, money, their time, all out of wanting to help." Meeting Rainwater helped me. I flipped through a recovery plan he'd given me weeks before. It included things like public comments from town hall sessions. There's a section on what locals treasured most. Answers included "food, culture, festivals, close knit community, Patton Hot Sausage, ferry rides, magnolia trees, Zydeco music, French heritage, can do attitude, spirit of Louisiana people, oak trees along Enterprise Boulevard, homes in the Charpentier and Margret Place Districts, I want to go crabbing in Cameron and Calcasieu Parishes, and peace." Leadership during both Katrina and Rita was roundly praised.

As I drove back into Beaumont, I saw a billboard on Interstate 10, "RE-ELECT OUR MAYOR RAY NAGIN..."

Later that evening in my hotel room, I turned on the news. PFC Chase Edwards had been killed in Iraq and would be escorted "home." His body was flown into Houston and being driven down Highway 90 into Beaumont. All along the route, in community after community, were Americans who saluted, waved flags, showed their respect to the family. I do not know Chase Edwards, but it is important to include his name here, particularly in a chapter about service.

Edwards was, according to the news story, set to be buried in Lake Charles, on Good Friday. I saluted the 20-year old as other Texans and Louisianans did.

TWENTY-FOUR

How ironic that I was working on a book about a parish in Louisiana I had named Canaan, submerged in a decades-old racially-motivated crime, when Katrina hit.

Even more unbelievable, I had never heard of Cameron until Rita tore it up. I spent seven months driving in and out of hurricane devastation and left the Canaan book on hold to find a real promised land many don't see for its vast potential.

After Lake Charles, I left a rambling message for Sheriff Mitch Woods—my last bit of business in Southeast Texas—and checked out of Beaumont. I rarely drove under 90 mph almost the same way I had come in seven months before, always, always with George Strait. I remembered Mitch calling me once on my cell phone during an earlier jaunt as I neared Jefferson County. The music was so loud, he laughed, "Turn that music down, flying down the road like a renegade."

Over the months, people asked what my favorite Strait tune was. It begins, "If there's a plane or a bus leaving Dallas, I hope you're on it." The song is simply called *Run*. Where was I running to? What was I running from? Who was capable of making me want to run? Without the answers I prayed for, I ran, for months. The last mile led *strait* to church, then straight to New Orleans.

60 miles east of Dallas, I was in Canton, Texas for something known as "First Monday." Except it was Thursday. Weather wizards had predicted a 50-50 shot at rain and the sun played peek-a-boo all the way down Interstate 20. I was on my way to New Orleans, but planned a brief stop in Canton.

As I veered up Highway 19 toward historic downtown, I passed droves of people milling about, looking, eating, walking, and crossing the street near flag-waving attendants who directed cars onto grassy elevated lots. They wanted the parking business at $4 a vehicle. It was a carnival atmosphere. Shorts, t-shirts, cell phones, sun hats, Indy 500 motor oil caps, funnel cakes for sale. Last sign I passed made my stomach quiver with the words, "Fried Twinkies."

A few minutes later I pulled into the Word of Victory Outreach Center. It was just after 10 a.m. and I thought of Martin Luther King, Jr. No matter what else has been integrated in America, churches don't seem in any hurry to follow. Dr. King once called 10 a.m. on Sunday "the most segregated hour in America." Mercifully, it didn't apply the Sunday after Rita when hundreds of black people stopped at a white church for two loaves, five fish, and a shower.

Reserved parking for "Pastor Mike Burns" and "Janet Burns" were posted on the lot. I took the visitor's section and receptionist Phyllis Clardy kindly pointed me to the minister's office. After exchanging a few pleasantries, Dr. J. Michael Burns invited me into his private office, where I wasted no time in applying for my Canton citizenship. "What's going on up the road there?"

Burns smiled, "That's First Monday, a huge flea market and it's been here 100 years." Indeed, the tradition started on a Monday and was then held the first Monday of each month. As it grew, merchants and vendors came from all over to sell food, wares, and services. The Van Zandt county seat hosts some 7,000 vendors for the affair that once billed itself as a way to "swap dogs, antiques, junk and donkeys."

Today, First Monday Weekend kicks off on the Thursday preceding the first Monday of each month. According to the Department of Public Safety, up to 300,000 have attended the four-day market each month. So it would seem Canton was used to laying out the welcome mat for out-of-towners. Just probably not in the middle of the night.

Pastor Burns had received a frantic call from Rickey Malone, Director of Community Services for the city. Malone was overseeing things at the Canton Civic Center, a 34,000 square-foot facility, where officials were processing and serving evacuees. Malone picked up the story from there.

"The governor's office had called us and they needed a favor. There were buses from Beaumont and nobody could take 'em." The state told Malone there were as many as 2,500 exhausted Texans stuck on school buses. Days before, Canton had a practice exercise when Malone had been the point man who assisted a National Guard unit from Oklahoma. Similar circumstance.

A call came out of nowhere that military leaders needed to "sleep 250-300 men" on their way to New Orleans. Dozens of vehicles were part of the convoy. Pastor Burns agreed to let the battalion commander use the church as a military base to rest tired personnel. Victory did such an outstanding job that the church was later presented a special medallion for service beyond the call of duty.

From the National Guard experience, Malone knew Burns was the right man for the new assignment. "I called him and uttered four words, 'I need your help.'" The Canton Civic Center overflowed with people and city officials wanted them as comfortable as possible. *Could Victory accept 200?* The answer meant an entire town, a region would get involved. Redeem itself without even needing to.

"People volunteered, cooked in shifts, did medical evaluations, we had some of everything," Malone says. "It just worked out." The city of 5,000 had half that number come to spend the night. Up to 2,500 people filed off buses. Canton needed more food, cots, water and supplies. "We went to a place that was closed, a medical facility, and the owners told us to get what we needed."

They carried away wheelchairs and mattresses for the elderly. Other items. The National Guard, probably remembering the kindness of Canton earlier, dispatched a doctor and some nurses who examined frightened, disheveled patients from Beaumont. They saw every manner of suffering. Dehydration. Diabetes. Heart problems. Exhaustion. Depression. Insulin Depravation. "It was just terrible," Malone remembered. "There were a lot of mentally handicapped people. They were real upset."

Support from outside Canton also strengthened their resolve to treat Beaumont evacuees with a measure of dignity many passengers had been denied. "Mineola is a city not even in our county," Malone says. "They sent a $200,000 fire engine with volunteer firefighters and they helped work with the sick."

Promised cots from FEMA never arrived. No one held it against an organization still working in double overtime on Katrina. People who heard the plight of the "bus people" and their 50-hour odyssey began converging on Victory with sheets, towels, pillows, sleeping bags. No one could imagine being cooped on a bus for two days. Other churches in the area, including First Baptist Church of Canton, where Dr. Mark Roberson is pastor, rolled up their sleeves for both Katrina and Rita.

"We housed over 250 people after New Orleans. We had some stay, they like it here and won't go back," Malone checked his figures. "Katrina saved us time, it also made people from Rita more comfortable. We were able to cater to the people." Malone was clearly a perfect match for the position he loves, "I'm from here, my whole job is to make Canton a jewel. It brings tears to my eyes to know that we're known for love of fellow man, black or white."

200 people were asked to go just a half-mile away to Word of Victory and leave the bustling scene at the Canton Civic Center. The thought of even getting back on a school bus for one minute must've seemed like being asked to voluntarily administer flashback shots of rolling torture. Pastor Burns called Malone two hours before he expected and greeted the city employee with two words, "We're ready."

Each person was "gingerly brought in" where a Victory member would meet with whole families and assess their needs. Within 20 minutes they were allowed to eat and take a free, unencumbered breath. "It was remarkable to watch," Burns reflected. Members had hustled to transform the same gymnasium that doubled as a sanctuary on Sunday into a dining hall and giant four star hotel room for guests who could now sign the same invisible register as National Guard soldiers who bunked there before them.

As we walked through the gymnasium, children from the Victory School were laughing and enjoying lunch, calling out the pastor's name with full mouths. To the right of their cafeteria tables was the same kitchen that cranked out hot meals for evacuees who looked upon the servers as "angels," the word I had heard over and over from Beaumont passengers.

Beyond the kitchen receiving line was a door just off the huge basketball courts, the door that led to paradise—complete co-ed showers. Most churches can not boast dormitory showers, but Word of Victory had the water that cleansed shot nerves, easing tired bones and the emotional strain of uncertainty. There is no feeling on earth compared to the aftermath of soap and water and clean clothes.

In September 2005, Victory had hosted a gospel meeting. The

nightly speaker was a British evangelist named Jon Colyer. Right before Hurricane Rita, the man made a startling prediction related to a vision. Looking out at the crowd in the multipurpose room, then designed for worship, Colyer told parishioners that rows and rows of people would be sleeping where they were sitting. After Colyer was back in Birmingham, England, his vision for Victory came true.

"How has this experience changed your church?" I asked. "For one thing," Burns answered, "it made us understand how much we were capable of doing. We always believed we could do more and this helped us to see we got to really practice what we believe." The "benefits and growth" for individual members have been tenfold as Victory continues to pursue outreach efforts for "white, black, it does not matter."

As I prepared to leave Canton, Burns handed me a copy of something. "We found this on our information table on the day they [Beaumont evacuees] left, so one of the ladies, Sissie, wrote this, I guess." The Sunday after Rita, some of the evacuees worshiped at Victory. "I preached a simple message on The Good Samaritan."

Driving away, more people had arrived for First Monday. There were booths, vendors, cars for miles. Quiltland boasted a big sign, "HOMEMADE." Several quilts were displayed on what looked like an old-fashioned clothesline. A dreaded childhood memory of pinning wet laundry made me smile. The quilt I wanted was the $49 dollar special of an American flag.

Red, white, and blue and the words from Sissie's poem, pushed my car toward New Orleans. Here's what the woman scribbled on a piece of paper:

I heard a man speak about compassion
The help of one stranger
And of neighbors looking on while passing
He spoke of Samaritans and others
Whose hearts are cold
Of strict adherence to religion
And the love of God from within the soul
He spoke of the change
The change to come

How we need to reach for the light
Before this life is done
We were taken in, shown untold grace
What would have become of us
If not for this place
My faith in people is restored to me
Thank you, People of Victory

* * *

The French Quarter Festival was in high gear. Streets closed. Orange and white construction horses. A gaiety that seemed wrong. Seemed appropriate. I wrote down the various license plates and lost count of how many states were there. The United States map seemed to be in New Orleans. It was some kind of blinding smoke screen. Everything looked fine, up and running, warm and cozy lie. The truth too. I bailed, tired of the noise, traffic, and jubilant crowd.

I checked into a Metairie hotel. Five minutes and a shaky elevator ride later, evidence of Katrina started to come from behind the Mardi Gras mask.

Front desk delirium had installed me in a room with two standard beds. One bed was on the floor, and the other, incredibly, stood at attention when I entered the room. In all my years of opening hotel room doors, never once have I encountered a naked mattress, water-damaged and smelly, half in the air, left to air out and dry in its frame. It reminded me of a car embedded in the Holly Beach sand.

The wait staff back downstairs said I was mistaken. They would never give a guest such a room. A closer look at the hotel, and a much closer smell, peeled paint was everywhere and Lysol could not cover the stench. Not one person offered to knock a penny off the overpriced-to-begin-with rate. Someone was dispatched to see the upright bed. Okay with me, go see not only the bed, but the whole crummy room. I did not lose my composure, not then.

I went to eat. I was so thirsty I gulped down a glass of iced water without thinking. *Don't drink the water stupid.* All my bottled water was in the trunk. Across the causeway a familiar sign, unplanned indeed, smiled a pre-Katrina memory. It was the same Borders

Books I had done my only New Orleans-area signing for *HATE CRIME.*

I crossed the Pontchartrain out and made a hasty retreat after losing the initial battle to the Chamber of Commerce. I left New Orleans like an unsatisfied sailor on a weekend pass. My Monday was messed up. I had the blues from a weekend covered and colored by too many tourists in town. Plus, a mayoral election added a few thousand voters who had come to have their say on 23 hats in the ring. Three were considered serious contenders. That night on the local news, (in a different room without flying beds) Mayor Ray Nagin and Lt. Gov. Mitch Landrieu were headed to runoff city.

A few hours later, I was back in Dallas to wait out Jazzfest and the other 30 days of festivals that were nearing an end. Over the months of gathering information and walking through people's lives, I made several requests to interview Mr. Nagin.

12 hours before I flew back to New Orleans for a microscopic look, the deputy director of communications, Terry Davis, surprised me late in the evening with a call. His boss, the mayor, wouldn't be available, not even to comment on Rita or the hospitality shown Katrina by Texas. But he did offer me a colonel.

May 2006. Less than a month before the start of a new hurricane season, two people I'd never seen before were waiting at the Louis Armstrong International Airport when I stepped off Southwest Flight 373. Lawrence Mackie was a struggling young entrepreneur who had reshuffled his entire day to show me the real McCoy. His assistant, Latefa Marshall, stood at his side holding a website photo of me.

The owner of Mackie Construction ended our tour with the words, "New Orleans is coming back alright." Stay tuned for the rest of the story and film at 11.

Later that evening, I zapped beignets from Cafe Du Monde in the microwave and left a trail of white dust on my kitchen counter. I found a favorite CD from 1991, *Warm Your Heart,* and imagined Aaron Nelville weary of requests to hear one song in particular.

My neighbors were hit by two hurricanes. Katrina is known. Rita forgotten.

Louisiana 1927

What has happened down here is the wind have changed
Clouds rolled in from the North and it started to rain
It rained real hard and it rained for a real long time
Six feet of water in the streets of Evangeline
The river rose all day, the river rose all night
Some people got lost in the flood, some people got away alright
River had busted through, clear down to Plaquemines
Six feet of water in the streets of Evangeline
Louisiana, Louisiana, they trying to wash us away
Louisiana, Louisiana, they trying to wash us away

Joyce King

NATIONAL HURRICANE CENTER
2006 Storm Names

Alberto
Beryl
Chris
Debby
Ernesto
Florence
Gordon
Helene
Isaac
Joyce
Kirk
Leslie
Michael
Nadine
Oscar
Patty
Rafael
Sandy
Tony
Valerie
William

ACKNOWLEDGEMENTS

I thank the Creator for the journey that allowed me to talk with people who shared so much not written here. It is my wish that these handful of stories become representative of the many ordinary lives, people who showed extraordinary courage and compassion in the face of suffering and loss. I thank law enforcement and first responders who don't wait to be asked. I thank Angel San Juan who was my rock. Angel, it really is *our* book. I thank Valerie and Robert Roussell, my New Orleans neighbors just around the corner. To Coyotito Soublet, his fiancée, Jessica, and their baby, Jalen, I'll miss you when you return to New Orleans. To Jamie and Billy Rowles, I love you more, but I suspect you've guessed that by now. I thank my dear friend, Mitch Woods, for always putting up with me and being able to keep a presidential secret so long. I love you and Keesha both. Scott West, man, it's been an awesome 20 years. We've got the love most friends only dream of. And finally, to my amazing family, thank you hardly seems appropriate. To my mother, Lida, you are the same to me now as when you were 36—effervescent, sweet, and kind. The teacake queen. To Rod, thank you for staying a friend. I only want good things for your life. To our oldest son, Roderick, love and success for "my little Hershey bar." And for Brandon Xavier, I want the world for you my darling, (and a laptop) on a silver platter. Poor you, a writer too. And I promise you, Bran, Gov. Perry is already married. Don't worry, I'll find a date.

ABOUT THE AUTHOR

Joyce King is an award-winning journalist and "storyteller." Her guest columns, stories and articles have appeared in many publications, including *USA Today*. The former veteran broadcaster frequently lectures for university programs. She lives in Dallas with her son.